Merry Xmas
and a Happy New Year
1930 —

Leslie + Anne
+ Family —

OLIVER WENDELL HOLMES.

THE EARLY POEMS

OF

Oliver Wendell Holmes

WITH A BIOGRAPHICAL SKETCH

By HENRY KETCHAM

A. L. BURT COMPANY, PUBLISHERS,

BIOGRAPHICAL SKETCH.

BY

HENRY KETCHAM

THE AUTHOR TO THE PUBLISHERS.

I THANK you for the pains you have taken to bring together the poems now added to this collection; one of them having been accidentally omitted and the existence of the others forgotten. So many productions which bear the plain marks of immaturity and inexperience have been allowed to remain, because they were in the earlier editions, that a few occasional and careless stanzas may be added to their company without any apology. I have no doubt you are right in thinking that there is no harm in allowing a few crudities to keep their place among the rest; for, as you suggest, the readers of a book are of various ages and tastes, and what sounds altogether schoolboy-like to the author may be very author-like to the schoolboy. Some of the more questionable extravagances to be found in the earlier portion of the volume have, as I learn, pleased a good many young people ; let us call these, and all the others that we have outgrown, *Juvenile Poems*, but keep them, lest some of the smaller sort that were, or are, or are to be, should lament their absence. I thought of mentioning the date at which the several poems were written, which would explain some of their differences ; but the reader can judge them nearly enough, perhaps without this assistance.

To save a question that is sometimes put, it is proper to say that in naming two of the poems after two of the Muses, nothing more was intended than a suggestion of their general character and aim. In a former note of mine (which you printed as a kind of preface to the last edition), I made certain explanations which I thought might be needed ; but as nobody seems to have misinterpreted anything, we will trust our book hereafter to itself, not doubting that whatever is good in it will redeem and justify the rest.

BOSTON, January 13, 1849.

CONTENTS.

POEMS ADDED SINCE THE FIRST EDITION.

CONTENTS.

PICTURES FROM OCCASIONAL POEMS.

BIOGRAPHICAL SKETCH.

One of the most marked characteristics of Oliver Wendell Holmes was his geniality, his comradeship. While he was in college he wrote, " I am acquainted with a great many different fellows who do not speak to each other. Still I find pleasant companions and a few good friends among these jarring elements." These words are suggestive of much of his character through life. He had unusual power in drawing men to him, and therefore to one another, and in eliciting from them, or else creating in them, an abundance of good humor. That remarkable constellation of literary stars which brightened Boston and Cambridge, and indeed the United States, during many decades of this present century, can hardly be said to have been held together by any one man; and yet, if one was more influential than the others in this, that one was unquestionably Holmes. Always witty and humorous, frequently pathetic, he had the power of fascination. He readily took men into his confidence, and they naturally gave him theirs in return. This trait comes out decidedly in his writing as well as in his personal converse. Such chatty papers as the series of The Breakfast Table, leave in the reader a sense of personal acquaintance and confidential fellowship with the author. His personal influence gave an additional charm to all who were favored with his acquaintance.

The facts of his life are few. He was born in Cambridge in 1809, the year made illustrious by the birth of Lincoln, Gladstone, Darwin, and Tennyson. Except for two trips to Europe, one in early life and the other in old age—if so buoyant a spirit could ever be called old—he spent his life almost within sight of the State House in Boston.

He was graduated from Harvard College in 1829. Several famous men were in his class. Indeed it was considered a notable class. But the classmate who is to-day the best known was S. F. Smith, author of *My country 'tis of thee*. Even while in college Holmes developed poetical abilities of no mean order, but it never seems to have occurred to him that he was fitted for a literary career. He was barely twenty-one years of age when he wrote "Old Ironsides." These lines were reprinted far and wide in the newspapers of the country. In Washington city they were printed on handbills and circulated through the streets. It is not too much to say **that** they stirred the nation. They quickly accomplished their object and the frigate Constitution was saved from destruction. The youthful author became instantly famous. And yet he did not suspect that he was suited to a literary career.

After graduation he studied law, but at the end of a year gave it up and turned his attention to medicine. This proved congenial to him. It roused his enthusiasm, and soon we find him in Paris studying with zeal and cherishing the very highest ambitions for excellence in his profession. Having successfully completed his studies he returned home thoroughly equipped for the practice of his profession.

He did not, however, leap into sudden fame, nor even into that measure of success to which his preparation entitled him. Indeed, he never had more than a moderate practice. When a young doctor playfully remarks, " Small *fevers* gratefully received," men will laugh at the joke, but the average citizen prefers a more solemn doctor for his own fever. Neither were Holmes's poems a drawing advertisement for the building up of a medical practice. The general public are sceptical to believe that a poet, full of humor and fairly bubbling over with boyish exuberance, is the best person to be entrusted with a case of critical illness. He seems to have understood the situation perfectly for he wrote

> Don't you know that people won't employ
> A man that wrongs his manliness by laughing like a boy ?

In short, he seemed to be lacking on the business side of his vocation. Thus while his practice was never large it gave him a fair living.

But upon the scientific side of his profession he was brilliantly successful. From the first he took prizes for medical essays. In 1838 he was appointed lecturer on Anatomy at Dartmouth College, and nine years later he became Professor of Anatomy and Physiology in Harvard College. This position he held with great popularity for the long period of thirty-five years. President Eliot regarded his work as highly efficient, and declared that he did a great deal to make the Harvard Medical School what it has become.

During the middle period of his life Holmes was in the lecture field. At that time lecture courses before lyceums and other associations were common. Far and wide, especially in New England, there was a demand for literary men to speak from the rostrum. The lectures of that day were of a high order, those of Emerson, perhaps, being the

standard.   The compensation was small as compared
with the present day.   Still it was something, and
the proceeds of a successful lecture tour would be
welcome to a literary man in moderate circum-
stances.   But the trials and exposures of these tours
forced him out.   The conveniences of travelling
in those days were crude.   The railway cars were
uncomfortable, ill-heated, and ill-ventilated at best.
The winter rides from the railway stations, the
accommodations of the hotel, the bleakness, frequently, of the spare room of private hospitality,
made the lecture tour anything but a jolly excur-
sion.   Holmes's tendency to asthma made it a seri-
ous matter to him, as it was a discomfort to every
one.   Though he was in great demand, and was
always sure of a cordial welcome wherever he
appeared, still this business of lecturing was hard
work and poor pay.   It was therefore soon aban-
doned.   But the delivery of a course before the
Lowell Institute was in every respect different.
The hall was near his home, reached by an easy
and pleasant walk.   His subject was the British
Poets.   He spoke to crowded audiences composed of the most intelligent and cultured of
Boston people, and the lectures were received with
enthusiasm.   Such lecturing was a pleasure and an
honor.

The last incident, in a life not overcrowded with incidents, was a brief trip with his daughter, which he has recorded in " Our Hundred Days in Europe." He was at this time seventy-seven years of age, The most of the time was spent in England, and this visit was an ovation from start to finish. He was lionized by society in an almost incredible number of receptions, etc. He was sought out by men of letters. But chiefly, he was decorated by three of the four universities of Great Britain. Edinburgh and Cambridge conferred on him the degree of LL. D., and Oxford that of D. C. L.

He glided gently into the period of old age ; persisting in calling himself young,—" eighty years *young*." The delightful spirits of youth he retained through a long life. But the signs and incidents of age came in quick succession. In 1873 Agassiz died. In 1877 Motley died. In 1882 he laid down the duties of his lectureship at Harvard after having completed thirty-six annual courses. The college elected him professor *emeritus*. That same year both Longfellow and Emerson died. In 1884 his son Edward died. Three years later his wife died, after which his daughter came to live with him. But two years later, or in 1889, she died. The previous year his classmate, the Rev. James Freeman Clarke, who for more than sixty years had been his intimate—possibly his most intimate—friend, died. In 1891 Lowell died, Whittier in 1892, and Parkman in 1893. Thus was the author of "The Last Leaf" left almost alone, so far as concerned his early friends. Two years later he followed Whittier.

Just here we may quote a few sentences from a letter to the Rev. Phillips Brooks, in which, after expressing warm appreciation of his friend's sermon, he says: "My natural Sunday home is King's Chapel. In that church I have worshipped for half a century. . . . There, on the fifteenth of June, 1840, I was married, there my children were all christened, from that church the dear companion of so many blessed years was buried. In her seat I must sit, and through its door I hope to be carried to my last resting-place." This hope was realized two days after his death, which occurred October 7, 1894. Death came to him quickly and gently. He was sitting in his chair talking to his son, when he died suddenly.

His day's work was long and somewhat volumin-ous. Among his books may be noted the following: The Autocrat, Professor, and Poet, at the Break-fast Table, followed, in the evening of his life, by a series entitled Over the Teacups; various medical essays; Elsie Venner, and The Guardian Angel;

lives of Motley and of Emerson; and poems pub-lished from time to time, but now collected in one volume.

In estimating the quality of the man and his work, it must be confessed that he was provincial. His loyalty was first of all to his college class, then to his college, next to the city of Boston, after that to New England, and finally to his country. He iudeed belonged to the best of Boston—the "Brahmin Caste," to borrow his own phrase—but he was essentially Bostonese. He spent substantially all his life in Boston or Cambridge. In early life he had a summer home in Pittsfield, but that was given up and in late years his summer home was at Beverley Farms, only twenty miles from the city. He rarely got much beyond walking distance from the State House on Beacon Hill, and apparently he had no desire to do so. He was not cosmopolitan. To him Boston was always what he playfully called it, —the Hub of the solar system.

It may also be said that his work seems to lack the elements of permanency when compared with that of writers of the first grade. His work is excellent of its kind, but it is not the kind that is intended to endure. He was chiefly the philosopher, the poet, the wit of the hour; and, while unrivalled in his place, one must not claim for him a permanency which belongs to a different type of author.

His excellence was seen in three degrees,—chiefly in his conversation, next in some of his prose writings, and finally in his poetry. His title to eminence rests upon his personality. In conversation he was at his best. Wherever he sat was the head of the table. Dr. Johnson was probably more learned, Coleridge more profound, De Quincy more subtile and melodious ; but no one combined these qualities, adding the good fellowship of Holmes.

Next in brilliancy after his conversation came his prose, specifically, the Autocrat of the Breakfast Table, and for the very reason that this most nearly resembles his conversation. But as this sketch is intended to concern chiefly his poetry, we must turn, however reluctantly, from his prose to his poetry—and it is always a pleasure to turn to the poetry of this man.

One instantly observes the very large proportion of occasional poems, a larger proportion probably than can be found in any other author. For thirty-nine consecutive years he furnished the poem for the annual dinner of the class of 1829 of Harvard College. Then he had poems for various benefit dinners, for birthdays, and other occasions. It is high phrase to say that he was always equal to the occasion. He was always sure of a welcome, and his fund of wit never failed, while his felicity of adaptation and the delicacy of his treatment secured for him an audience much wider than is the usual fortune of the writers of even the best of occasional poems.

In some of his poems the prevailing trait is boyish exuberance, pure fun. An excellent example of this is The Height of the Ridiculous. Its jollity is irresistible either by old or by young. Almost equal to this is, How the Old Horse Won the Bet. Other poems combine humor and pathos so exquisitely and delicately that it is impossible to analyze them. His biographer, John T. Morse, Jr., says of the Last Leaf, that it is "a lyric in which drollery, passing nigh unto ridicule, yet stopping short of it, and sentiment becoming pathos, yet not too profound, are . . . exquisitely intermingled. [It makes] the smile and the tear dispute for mastery in a rivalry which is never quite decided." Not far from this in general effect, though widely different in form, is Bill and Joe. This has a rough-and-ready exterior, but its heart is full of fine and tender sentiment. It represents two old comrades, both crowned with honors in the world, spending an evening together, when memory brings them together as in boyhood and discloses a warmth of fellowship unknown to the world.

> To-day, old friend, remember still
> That I am Joe and you are Bill.

Another group of his poems is distinguished by intense earnestness. One of these is his youthful poem of Old Ironsides, ringing with a sentiment of patriotism which thrills the reader even to this day. Even superior to this is the Chambered Nautilus. In a preliminary note the author suggests that you find a figure of one of these shells and a section of it. The last will show you a series of enlarging compartments successively dwelt in by the animal that inhabits the shell, which is built in a widening spiral." The poem, which is comprised in forty-two lines, is a model of sentiment, fancy, and diction. The poet follows the successive building of the animal until he reaches the message which it sends to us:

> Build thee more stately mansions, O my soul,
> > As the swift seasons roll !
> > Leave thy low-vaulted past !
> Let each new temple, nobler than the last,
> Shut thee from heaven with a dome more vast,
> > Till thou at length art free,
> Leaving thine outgrown shell by life's unresting sea !

Among his longer poems may be named the Phi Beta Kappa poem on Poetry, A Rhymed Lesson

(Urania), An After-Dinner Poem (Terpsichore), and Harvard College Anniversary. However meritorious these may be, they are not equal to some of his shorter poems. The Deacon's Masterpiece, or The Wonderful " One-Hoss Shay," a Logical Story, has long been deservedly popular. It is as droll as can be, and is at the same time a good description of logic, showing that when one part of the syllogism fails the whole structure tumbles to pieces. His Angel of Peace is sung by school children throughout the land.

Holmes would not be called a religious writer. From the first he was hostile to the creed then prevailing in the orthodox churches. His real position was simple enough had it been understood. He was, in a sense, a puritan of the puritans. That is, he had the same right to criticise the creed of Jonathan Edwards as Edwards had to criticise the ecclesiasticism of the Pope. The orthodox churches were then under the influence of the theology of Edwards, and they regarded these criticisms with abhorrence. Holmes was thus a thorn in the flesh of the orthodox ministers, and his wit, wisdom, and imperturbable good humor made him a formidable antagonist. But while he showed no mercy to creeds, he was sincerely devout in his Christian faith. Most of the hymn-books now in use in the orthodox churches contain two hymns of his composition, and hymns more tender, more in accordance with the spirit of Christian sympathy and worship it would be hard to find anywhere. These are, O Love Divine, and Lord of all Being.

It is dangerous to predict what will be the most enduring of Holmes' writings, but it seems as if they will include most, if not all, of the following: Puerperal Fever as a Private Pestilence. This is strictly medical, and it stirred up much antagonism at the time, but it has long been accepted as standard authority and is such to-day. Elsie Venner, which is a popular contribution to, or presentation of, the problems involved in heredity. The Last Leaf, which was one of the favorites with the author, as it has been a favorite with many readers, including Abraham Lincoln. The Chambered Nautilus, above described. The two hymns may be added to this list.

His biographer declares that "Dr. Holmes was more ambitious to be thought a poet than anything else." During most of his lifetime his prose overshadowed his poetry, and so his ambition was not then gratified. But it is the nature of poetry to outlast prose, and it is probable that his ultimate fame will spring chiefly from his best poems.

In 1889, sixty years after graduation from college,

and when he had passed the scriptural limit of four score years, he read at the class dinner his last class poem, significantly entitled After the Curfew.   The opening and closing stanzas are well worth quoting:

> The Play is over.   While the light
> Yet lingers in the darkening hall,
> I come to say a last Good-night
> Before the final *Exeunt all.*

> .   .   .   .   .   .

> So ends "The Boys!"—a lifelong play.
> We too must hear the Prompter's call
> To fairer scenes and brighter day:
> Farewell ! I let the curtain fall.

There was but one class meeting after this, namely, in the following year.   Only three were present. This, therefore, practically closed the long series of meetings.

One fact which greatly favored Holmes was the length of his literary career.   The first poem which attracted general attention was Old Ironsides, published in 1830.   His first volume was published in 1836 and made his reputation.   Consequently he held the public attention for not less than fifty-eight years, or, if we date from Old Ironsides, for sixty-four years.   During this long period he frequently issued volumes, all of which were well received, and he never alienated the cordial welcome of the reading public.   The climax of his reputation was reached with the Autocrat papers, which not only insured for himself a wide circle of loyal admirers, but floated the young Atlantic Monthly through the first difficult and perilous period of its existence. His literary activity continued to the very end, and for many years his readers were of a later generation than his own. None the less they did him honor. His mission, in large part, was to bring sunshine into life. His humor is healthy and it has brightened many an hour.

When Holmes went to Europe in 1886, Lowell wrote for him a farewell poem. It was Holmes's wish that the lines should be used as his *envoi*. We conclude this sketch with the final stanza.

> Go, then, dear friend, by all good hopes attended ;
> To Mother England go, our carrier dove,
> Saying that this great race, from hers descended,
> Sends in its Holmes an Easter-gift of love.

HENRY KETCHAM.

To

CHARLES WENTWORTH UPHAM

THE FOLLOWING

METRICAL ESSAY

IS AFFECTIONATELY INSCRIBED

POETRY;

A METRICAL ESSAY.

Scenes of my youth![1] awake its slumbering fire!
Ye winds of Memory, sweep the silent lyre!
Ray of the past, if yet thou canst appear,
Break through the clouds of Fancy's waning year;
Chase from her breast the thin autumnal snow,
If leaf or blossom still is fresh below!

Long have I wandered; the returning tide
Brought back an exile to his cradle's side;
And as my bark her time-worn flag unrolled,
To greet the land-breeze with its faded fold,
So, in remembrance of my boyhood's time,
I lift these ensigns of neglected rhyme;—
O more than blest, that, all my wanderings through,
My anchor falls where first my pennons flew!

[1] "Scenes of my youth."

This poem was commenced a few months subsequently to the author's return to his native village, after an absence of nearly three years.

THE morning light, which rains its quivering
  beams
Wide o'er the plains, the summits, and the streams,
In one broad blaze expands its golden glow
On all that answers to its glance below;
Yet, changed on earth, each far reflected ray
Braids with fresh hues the shining brow of day;
Now, clothed in blushes by the painted flowers,
Tracks on their cheeks the rosy-fingered hours;
Now, lost in shades, whose dark entangled leaves
Drip at the noontide from their pendent eaves,
Fades into gloom, or gleams in light again
From every dew-drop on the jewelled plain.

We, like the leaf, the summit, or the wave,
Reflect the light our common nature gave,
But every sunbeam, falling from her throne,
Wears, on our hearts, some coloring of our own;
Chilled in the slave, and burning in the free,
Like the sealed cavern by the sparkling sea;
Lost, like the lightning in the sullen clod,
Or shedding radiance, like the smiles of God;
Pure, pale in Virtue, as the star above,
Or quivering roseate on the leaves of Love;
Glaring like noontide, where it glows upon
Ambition's sands,—the desert in the sun;
Or soft suffusing o'er the varied scene
Life's common coloring,—intellectual green.

Thus Heaven, repeating its material plan,
Arched over all the rainbow mind of man;
But he who, blind to universal laws,

Sees but effects, unconscious of their cause,—
Believes each image in itself is bright,
Not robed in drapery of reflected light,—
Is like the rustic who, amidst his toil,
Has found some crystal in his meagre soil,
And, lost in rapture, thinks for him alone
Earth worked her wonders on the sparkling stone,
Nor dreams that Nature, with as nice a line,
Carved countless angles through the boundless
      mine.

Thus err the many who, entranced to find
Unwonted lustre in some clearer mind,
Believe that Genius sets the laws at nought
Which chain the pinions of our wildest thought;
Untaught to measure, with the eye of art,
The wandering fancy or the wayward heart;
Who match the little only with the less,
And gaze in rapture at its slight excess,
Proud of a pebble, as the brightest gem
Whose light might crown an emperor's diadem.

And, most of all, the pure ethereal fire,
Which seems to radiate from the poet's lyre,
Is to the world a mystery and a charm,
An Ægis wielded on a mortal's arm,
While Reason turns her dazzled eye away,
And bows her sceptre to her subject's sway;
And thus the poet, clothed with godlike state,
Usurped his Maker's title—to create;
He, whose thoughts differing not in shape, but
      dress,

What others feel, more fitly can express,
Sits like the maniac on his fancied throne,
Peeps through the bars, and calls the world his
    own.

There breathes no being but has some pretence
To that fine instinct called poetic sense;
The rudest savage roaming through the wild,
The simplest rustic, bending o'er his child,
The infant listening to the warbling bird,
The mother smiling at its half-formed word;
The boy uncaged, who tracks the fields at large,
The girl, turned matron to her babe-like charge;
The freeman, casting with unpurchased hand
The vote that shakes the turrets of the land;
The slave, who, slumbering on his rusted chain,
Dreams of the palm trees on his burning plain;
The hot-cheeked reveller, tossing down the wine,
To join the chorus pealing "Auld lang syne";
The gentle maid, whose azure eye grows dim,
While Heaven is listening to her evening hymn;
The jewelled beauty, when her steps draw near
The circling dance and dazzling chandelier;
E'en trembling age, when Spring's renewing air
Waves the thin ringlets of his silvered hair;—
All, all are glowing with the inward flame,
Whose wider halo wreathes the poet's name,
While, unembalmed, the silent dreamer dies,
His memory passing with his smiles and sighs!

If glorious visions, born for all mankind,
The bright auroras of our twilight mind;

If fancies, varying as the shapes that lie
Stained on the windows of the sunset sky ;
If hopes, that beckon with delusive gleams,
Till the eye dances in the void of dreams ;
If passions, following with the winds that urge
Earth's wildest wanderer to her farthest verge;—
If these on all some transient hours bestow
Of rapture tingling with its hectic glow,
Then all are poets ; and, if earth had rolled
Her myriad centuries, and her doom were told,
Each moaning billow of her shoreless wave
Would wail its requiem o'er a poet's grave !

If to embody in a breathing word
Tones that the spirit trembled when it heard ;
To fix the image all unveiled and warm,
And carve in language its·ethereal form,
So pure, so perfect, that the lines express
No meagre shrinking, no unlaced excess ;
To feel that art, in living truth, has taught
Ourselves, reflected in the sculptured thought;—
If this alone bestow the right to claim
The deathless garland and the sacred name ;
Then none are poets, save the saints on high,
Whose harps can murmur all that words deny !

But though to none is granted to reveal,
In perfect semblance, all that each may feel,
As withered flowers recall forgotten love,
So, warmed to life, our faded passions move
In every line, where kindling fancy throws
The gleam of pleasures, or the shade of woes.

When, schooled by time, the stately queen of art
Had smoothed the pathways leading to the heart,
Assumed her measured tread, her solemn tone,
And round her courts the clouds of fable thrown,
The wreaths of heaven descended on her shrine,
And wondering earth proclaimed the Muse divine;
Yet, if her votaries had but dared profane
The mystic symbols of her sacred reign,
How had they smiled beneath the veil to find
What slender threads can chain the mighty mind!

Poets, like painters, their machinery claim,
And verse bestows the varnish and the frame;
Our grating English, whose Teutonic jar
Shakes the racked axle of Art's rattling car,
Fits like mosaic in the lines that gird
Fast in its place each many-angled word;
From Saxon lips Anacreon's numbers glide,
As once they melted on the Teian tide,
And, fresh transfused, the Iliad thrills again
From Albion's cliffs as o'er Achaia's plain!
The proud heroic, with its pulse-like beat,
Rings like the cymbals clashing as they meet;
The sweet Spenserian, gathering as it flows,
Sweeps gently onward to its dying close,
Where waves on waves in long succession pour,
Till the ninth billow melts along the shore;
The lonely spirit of the mournful lay,
Which lives immortal as the verse of Gray,
In sable plumage slowly drifts along,
On eagle pinion, through the air of song;

The glittering lyric bounds elastic by,
With flashing ringlets and exulting eye,
While every image, in her airy whirl,
Gleams like a diamond on a dancing girl![1]

[1] A few lines, perhaps deficient in dignity, were introduced at this point, in delivering the poem, and are appended in this clandestine manner for the gratification of some of my audience.

How many a stanza, blushing like the rose,
Would turn to fustian if resolved to prose!
How many an epic, like a gilded crown,
If some cold critic dared to melt it down,
Roll in his crucible a shapeless mass,
A grain of gold-leaf to a pound of brass!
Shorn of their plumes, our moonstruck sonneteers
Would seem but jackdaws croaking to the spheres;
Our gay Lotharios, with their Byron curls,
Would pine like oysters cheated of their pearls!

Wo to the spectres of Parnassus' shade,
If truth should mingle in the masquerade.
Lo, as the songster's pale creations pass,
Off come at once the "Dearest" and "Alas!"
Crack go the lines and levers used to prop
Top-heavy thoughts, and down at once they drop.
Flowers weep for *hours; Love,* shrieking for his *dove,*
Finds not the solace that he seeks—above.
Fast in the mire, through which in happier time
He ambled dryshod on the stilts of rhyme,
The prostrate poet finds at length a tongue
To curse in prose the thankless stars he sung.

And though, perchance, the haughty muse it shames,
How deep the magic of harmonious names!
How sure the story of romance to please,
Whose rounded stanza ends with Heloise!
How rich and full our intonations ride

Born with mankind, witn man's expanded range
And varying fates the poet's numbers change ;
Thus in his history may we hope to find
Some clearer epochs of the poet's mind,
As from the cradle of its birth we trace,
Slow wandering forth, the patriarchal race.

I.

When the green earth, beneath the zephyr's wing,
Wears on her breast the varnished buds of Spring ;
When the loosed current, as its folds uncoil,
Slides in the channels of the mellowed soil ;
When the young hyacinth returns to seek
The air and sunshine with her emerald beak ;

"On Torno's cliffs, or Pambamarca's side"!
But were her name some vulgar "proper noun,"
And Pambamarca changed to Belchertown,
She might be pilloried for her doubtful fame,
And no enthusiast would arise to blame ;
And he who outraged the poetic sense,
Might find a home at Belchertown's expense !

The harmless boys, scarce knowing right from wrong,
Who libel others and themselves in song,
When their first pothooks of poetic rage
Slant down the corners of an album's page,
(Where crippled couplets spread their sprawling charms,
As half taught swimmers move their legs and arms,)
Will talk of "Hesper on the brow of eve,"
And call their cousins "lovely Genevieve" ;—
While thus transformed, each dear deluded maid,
Pleased with herself in novel grace arrayed,
Smiles on the Paris who has come to crown
This new-born Helen in a gingham gown !

When the light snowdrops, starting from their
  cells,
Hang each pagoda with its silver bells ;
When the frail willow twines her trailing bow
With pallid leaves that sweep the soil below ;
When the broad elm, sole empress of the plain,
Whose circling shadow speaks a century's reign,
Wreathes in the clouds her regal diadem,—
A forest waving on a single stem ; —
Then mark the poet ; though to him unknown
The quaint-mouthed titles, such as scholars own,
See how his eye in ecstasy pursues
The steps of Nature tracked in radiant hues ;
Nay, in thyself, whate'er may be thy fate,
Pallid with toil, or surfeited with state,
Mark how thy fancies, with the vernal rose,
Awake, all sweetness, from their long repose ;
Then turn to ponder o'er the classic page,
Traced with the idyls of a greener age,
And learn the instinct which arose to warm
Art's earliest essay, and her simplest form.

To themes like these her narrow path confined
The first-born impulse moving in the mind ;
In vales unshaken by the trumpet's sound,
Where peaceful Labor tills his fertile ground,
The silent changes of the rolling years,
Marked on the soil, or dialled on the spheres,
The crested forests and the colored flowers,
The dewy grottos and the blushing bowers,
These, and their guardians, who, with liquid names,

Strephons and Chloes, melt in mutual flames,
Woo the young Muses from their mountain shade,
To make Arcadias in the lonely glade.

Nor think they visit only with their smiles
The fabled valleys and Elysian isles ;
He who is wearied of his village plain
May roam the Edens of the world in vain.
'Tis not the star-crowned cliff, the cataract's flow,
The softer foliage, or the greener glow,
The lake of sapphire, or the spar-hung cave,
The brighter sunset, or the broader wave,
Can warm his heart whom every wind has blown
To every shore, forgetful of his own.

Home of our childhood! how affection clings
And hovers round thee with her seraph wings!
Dearer thy hills, though clad in autumn brown,
Than fairest summits which the cedars crown!
Sweeter the fragrance of thy summer breeze
Than all Arabia breathes along the seas!
The stranger's gale wafts home the exile's sigh,
For the heart's temple is its own blue sky!

O happiest they, whose early love unchanged,
Hopes undissolved, and friendship unestranged,
Tired of their wanderings, still can deign to see
Love, hopes, and friendship, centring all in thee!

And thou, my village! as again I tread
Amidst thy living, and above thy dead ;
Though some fair playmates guard with chaster
    fears

Their cheeks, grown holy with the lapse of years;
Though with the dust some reverend locks may
    blend,
Where life's last mile-stone marks the journey's
    end;
On every bud the changing year recalls,
The brightening glance of morning memory falls,
Still following onward as the months unclose
The balmy lilac or the bridal rose;
And still shall follow, till they sink once more
Beneath the snow-drifts of the frozen shore,
As when my bark, long tossing in the gale,
Furled in her port her tempest-rended sail!

What shall I give thee? Can a simple lay,
Flung on thy bosom like a girl's bouquet,
Do more than deck thee for an idle hour,
Then fall unheeded, fading like the flower?
Yet, when I trod, with footsteps wild and free,
The crackling leaves beneath yon linden tree,
Panting from play, or dripping from the stream,
How bright the visions of my boyish dream!
Or, modest Charles, along thy broken edge,
Black with soft ooze and fringed with arrowy sedge,
As once I wandered in the morning sun,
With reeking sandal and superfluous gun;
How oft, as Fancy whispered in the gale,
Thou wast the Avon of her flattering tale!
Ye hills, whose foliage, fretted on the skies,
Prints shadowy arches on their evening dyes,
How should my song, with holiest charm, invest —

Each dark ravine and forest-lifting crest!
How clothe in beauty each familiar scene,
Till all was classic on my native green!

As the drained fountain, filled with autumn leaves,
The field swept naked of its garnered sheaves;
So wastes at noon the promise of our dawn,
The springs all choking, and the harvest gone.

Yet hear the lay of one whose natal star
Still seemed the brightest when it shone afar;
Whose cheek, grown pallid with ungracious toil,
Glows in the welcome of his parent soil;
And ask no garlands sought beyond the tide,
But take the leaflets gathered at your side.

Our ancient church! its lowly tower,
      Beneath the loftier spire,
Is shadowed when the sunset hour
      Clothes the tall shaft in fire;
It sinks beyond the distant eye,
      Long ere the glittering vane,
High wheeling in the western sky,
      Has faded o'er the plain.

Like Sentinel and Nun, they keep
      Their vigil on the green;
One seems to guard, and one to weep,
      The dead that lie between;
And both roll out, so full and near,
      Their music's mingling waves,

They shade the grass, whose pennoned spear
    Leans on the narrow graves.

The stranger parts the flaunting weeds,
    Whose seeds the winds have strown
So thick beneath the line he reads,
    They shade the sculptured stone;
The child unveils his clustered brow,
    And ponders for a while
The graven willow's pendent bough,
    Or rudest cherub's smile.

But what to them the dirge, the knell?
    These were the mourner's share;—
The sullen clang, whose heavy swell
    Throbbed through the beating air;—
The rattling cord,—the rolling stone,—
    The shelving sand that slid,
And, far beneath, with hollow tone,
    Rung on the coffin's lid.

The slumberer's mound grows fresh and green,
    Then slowly disappears;
The mosses creep, the gray stones lean,
    Earth hides his date and years;
But, long before the once-loved name
    Is sunk or worn away,
No lip the silent dust may claim,
    That pressed the breathing clay.

Go where the ancient pathway guides,
    See where our sires laid down

Their smiling babes, their cherished brides,
    The patriarchs of the town;
Hast thou a tear for buried love?
    A sigh for transient power?
All that a century left above,
    Go, read it in an hour!

The Indian's shaft, the Briton's ball,
    The sabre's thirsting edge,
The hot shell, shattering in its fall,
    The bayonet's rending wedge,—
Here scattered death; yet, seek the spot,
    No trace thine eye can see,
No altar,—and they need it not
    Who leave their children free!

Look where the turbid rain-drops stand
    In many a chiselled square,
The knightly crest, the shield, the brand
    Of honored names were there;—
Alas! for every tear is dried
    Those blazoned tablets knew,
Save when the icy marble's side
    Drips with the evening dew.

Or gaze upon yon pillared stone,[1]
    The empty urn of pride;

[1] "*Or gaze upon yon pillared stone.*"

The tomb of the VASSALL family is marked by a free-stone tablet, supported by five pillars, and bearing nothing but the sculptured reliefs of the Goblet and the Sun,—*Vas–Sol*—which designated a powerful family, now almost forgotten.

The exile referred to in the next stanza was a native of Honfleur in Normandy.

There stand the Goblet and the Sun,—
    What need of more beside?
Where lives the memory of the dead,
    Who made their tomb a toy?
Whose ashes press that nameless bed?
    Go, ask the village boy!

Lean o'er the slender western wall,
    Ye ever roaming girls;
The breath that bids the blossom fall
    May lift your floating curls,
To sweep the simple lines that tell
    An exile's date and doom;
And sigh, for where his daughters dwell,
    They wreathe the stranger's tomb.

And one amid these shades was born,
    Beneath this turf who lies,
Once beaming as the summer's morn,
    That closed her gentle eyes;—
If sinless angels love as we,
    Who stood thy grave beside,
Three seraph welcomes waited thee,
    The daughter, sister, bride!

I wandered to thy buried mound
    When earth was hid below
The level of the glaring ground,
    Choked to its gates with snow,
And when the summer's flowery waves
    The lake of verdure rolled,

As if a Sultan's white-robed slaves
    Had scattered pearls and gold.

Nay, the soft pinions of the air,
    That lift this trembling tone,
Its breath of love may almost bear,
    To kiss thy funeral stone;—
And, now thy smiles have passed away,
    For all the joy they gave,
May sweetest dews and warmest ray
    Lie on thine early grave!

When damps beneath, and storms above,
    Have bowed these fragile towers,
Still o'er the graves yon locust-grove
    Shall swing its Orient flowers;—
And I would ask no mouldering bust,
    If e'er this humble line,
Which breathed a sigh o'er other's dust,
    Might call a tear on mine.

<hr>

II.

But times were changed; the torch of terror came,
To light the summits with the beacon's flame;
The streams ran crimson, the tall mountain pines
Rose a new forest o'er embattled lines;
The bloodless sickle lent the warrior's steel,
The harvest bowed beneath his chariot wheel;

Where late the wood-dove sheltered her repose,
The raven waited for the conflict's close ;
The cuirassed sentry walked his sleepless round
Where Daphne smiled or Amaryllis frowned ;
Where timid minstrels sung their blushing charms,
Some wild Tyrtæus called aloud, " To arms ! "

  When Glory wakes, when fiery spirits leap,
Roused by her accents from their tranquil sleep,
The ray that flashes from the soldier's crest,
Lights, as it glances, in the poet's breast ;—
Not in pale dreamers, whose fantastic lay
Toys with smooth trifles like a child at play,
But men, who act the passions they inspire,
Who wave the sabre as they sweep the lyre !

  Ye mild enthusiasts, whose pacific frowns
Are lost like dew-drops caught in burning towns,
Pluck as ye will the radiant plumes of fame,
Break Cæsar's bust to make yourselves a name,
But, if your country bares the avenger's blade
For wrongs unpunished, or for debts unpaid,
When the roused nation bids her armies form,
And screams her eagle through the gathering
      storm ;
When from your ports the bannered frigate rides,
Her black bows scowling to the crested tides,
Your hour has past ; in vain your feeble cry,
As the babe's wailings to the thundering sky !

  Scourge of mankind ! with all the dread array,
That wraps in wrath thy desolating way,
  2

As the wild tempest wakes the slumbering sea,
Thou only teachest all that man can be.
Alike thy tocsin has the power to charm
The toil-knit sinews of the rustic's arm,
Or swell the pulses in the poet's veins,
And bid the nations tremble at his strains.

The city slept beneath the moonbeam's glance,
Her white walls gleaming through the vines of
 France,
And all was hushed, save where the footsteps fell,
On some high tower, of midnight sentinel.
But one still watched ; no self-encircled woes
Chased from his lids the angel of repose ;
He watched, he wept, for thoughts of bitter years
Bowed his dark lashes, wet with burning tears ;
His country's sufferings and her children's shame
Streamed o'er his memory like a forest's flame ;
Each treasured insult, each remembered wrong,
Rolled through his heart and kindled into song ;
His taper faded ; and the morning gales
Swept through the world the war-song of Mar-
 seilles ! [1]

Now, while around the smiles of Peace expand,
And Plenty's wreaths festoon the laughing land ;
While France ships outward her reluctant ore,
And half our navy basks upon the shore ;

[1] " *Swept through the world the war song of Marseilles.*"

The music and words of the Marseilles Hymn were composed in one night.

From ruder themes our meek-eyed Muses turn
To crown with roses their enamelled urn.

If e'er again return those awful days
Whose clouds were crimsoned with the beacon's
    blaze,
Whose grass was trampled by the soldier's heel,
Whose tides were reddened round the rushing keel,
God grant some lyre may wake a nobler strain,
To rend the silence of our tented plain !
When Gallia's flag its triple fold displays,
Her marshalled legions peal the Marseillaise ;
When round the German close the war clouds dim,
Far through their shadows floats his battle-hymn ;
When, crowned with joy, the camps of England
    ring,
A thousand voices shout, " God save the King ! "
When victory follows with our eagle's glance,
Our nation's anthem is a country dance ! [1]

Some prouder muse, when comes the hour at
    last,
May shake our hill-sides with her bugle-blast ;
Not ours the task ; but since the lyric dress
Relieves the statelier with its sprightliness,
Hear an old song, which some, perchance, have seen
In stale gazette, or cobwebbed magazine.
There was an hour when patriots dared profane

[1] " *Our nation's anthem is a country dance !* "

The popular air of " Yankee Doodle," like the dagger of
Hudibras, serves a pacific as well as a martial purpose.

The mast that Britain strove to bow in vain;[1]
And one who listened to the tale of shame,
Whose heart still answered to that sacred name,
Whose eye still followed o'er his country's tides
Thy glorious flag, our brave Old Ironsides!
From yon lone attic, on a summer's morn,
Thus mocked the spoilers with his school-boy scorn.

Ay, tear her tattered ensign down!
Long has it waved on high,
And many an eye has danced to see
That banner in the sky;
Beneath it rung the battle shout,
And burst the cannon's roar;—
The meteor of the ocean air
Shall sweep the clouds no more.

Her deck, once red with heroes' blood,
Where knelt the vanquished foe,
When winds were hurrying o'er the flood,
And waves were white below,
No more shall feel the victor's tread,
Or know the conquered knee;—
The harpies of the shore shall pluck
The eagle of the sea!

Oh, better that her shattered hulk
Should sink beneath the wave;

[1] " *The mast that Britain strove to bow in vain.*"

The lyric which follows was printed in the " Boston Daily Advertiser," at the time when it was proposed to break up the frigate Constitution as unfit for service.

Her thunders shook the mighty deep,
And there should be her grave;
Nail to the mast her holy flag,
Set every threadbare sail,
And give her to the god of storms,
The lightning and the gale!

III.

When florid Peace resumed her golden reign,
And arts revived, and valley bloomed again;
While War still panted on his broken blade,
Once more the Muse her heavenly wing essayed.
Rude was the song; some ballad, stern and wild,
Lulled the light slumbers of the soldier's child;
Or young romancer with his threatening glance
And fearful fables of his bloodless lance,
Scared the soft fancy of the clinging girls,
Whose snowy fingers smoothed his raven curls.
But when long years the stately form had bent,
And faithless memory her illusions lent,
So vast the outlines of Tradition grew,
That History wondered at the shapes she drew,
And veiled at length their too ambitious hues
Beneath the pinions of the Epic Muse.

Far swept her wing; for stormier days had brought
With darker passions deeper tides of thought.
The camp's harsh tumult and the conflict's glow,
The thrill of triumph and the gasp of woe,
The tender parting and the glad return,

The festal banquet and the funeral urn,—
And all the drama which at once uprears
Its spectral shadows through the clash of spears,
From camp and field to echoing verse transferred,
Swelled the proud song that listening nations heard.

Why floats the amaranth in eternal bloom
O'er Ilium's turrets and Achilles' tomb?
Why lingers fancy, where the sunbeams smile
On Circe's gardens and Calypso's isle?
Why follows memory to the gate of Troy
Her plumed defender and his trembling boy?
Lo, the blind dreamer, kneeling on the sand,
To trace these records with his doubtful hand;
In fabled tones his own emotion flows,
And other lips repeat his silent woes;
In Hector's infant see the babes that shun
Those deathlike eyes, unconscious of the sun,
Or in his hero hear himself implore,
" Give me to see, and Ajax asks no more!"

Thus live undying through the lapse of time
The solemn legends of the warrior's clime;
Like Egypt's pyramid, or Pæstum's fane,
They stand the heralds of the voiceless plain;
Yet not like them, for Time, by slow degrees,
Saps the gray stone, and wears the chiselled frieze,
And Isis sleeps beneath her subject Nile,
And crumbled Neptune strews his Dorian pile;
But Art's fair fabric, strengthening as it rears
Its laurelled columns through the mist of years,
As the blue arches of the bending skies

Still gird the torrent, following as it flies,
Spreads, with the surges bearing on mankind,
Its starred pavilion o'er the tides of mind !

In vain the patriot asks some lofty lay
To dress in state our wars of yesterday.
The classic days, those mothers of romance,
That roused a nation for a woman's glance;
The age of mystery with its hoarded power,
That girt the tyrant in his storied tower,
Have past and faded like a dream of youth,
And riper eras ask for history's truth.

On other shores, above their mouldering towns,
In sullen pomp the tall cathedral frowns,
Pride in its aisles, and paupers at the door,
Which feeds the beggars whom it fleeced of yore.
Simple and frail, our lowly temples throw
Their slender shadows on the paths below ;
Scarce steal the winds, that sweep his woodland
    tracks,
The larch's perfume from the settler's axe,
Ere, like a vision of the morning air,
His slight-framed steeple marks the house of prayer;
Its planks all reeking, and its paint undried,
Its rafters sprouting on the shady side,
It sheds the raindrops from its shingled eaves,
Ere its green brothers once have changed their leaves.

Yet Faith's pure hymn, beneath its shelter rude,
Breathes out as sweetly to the tangled wood,

As where the rays through blazing oriels pour
On marble shaft and tessellated floor;—
Heaven asks no surplice round the heart that feels,
And all is holy where devotion kneels.

Thus on the soil the patriot's knee should bend,
Which holds the dust once living to defend;
Where'er the hireling shrinks before the free,
Each pass becomes "a new Thermopylæ"!
Where'er the battles of the brave are won,
There every mountain "looks on Marathon"!

Our fathers live; they guard in glory still
The grass-grown bastions of the fortressed hill;
Still ring the echoes of the trampled gorge,
With *God and Freedom! England and Saint
    George!*
The royal cipher on the captured gun
Mocks the sharp night-dews and the blistering sun!
The red-cross banner shades its captor's bust,
Its folds still loaded with the conflict's dust;
The drum, suspended by its tattered marge,
Once rolled and rattled to the Hessian's charge;
The stars have floated from Britannia's mast,
The redcoat's trumpets blown the rebel's blast.

Point to the summits where the brave have bled,
Where every village claims its glorious dead;
Say, when their bosoms met the bayonet shock,
Their only corselet was the rustic frock;
Say, when they mustered to the gathering horn,
The titled chieftain curled his lip in scorn,

Yet, when their leader bade his lines advance,
No musket wavered in the lion's glance;
Say, when they fainted in the forced retreat,
They tracked the snow-drifts with their **bleeding**
  feet,
Yet still their banners, tossing in the blast,
Bore *Ever Ready*,[1] faithful to the last,
Through storm and battle, till they waved **again**
On Yorktown's hills and Saratoga's plain !

Then, if so fierce the insatiate patriot's flame,
Truth looks too pale, and history seems too **tame,**
Bid him await some new Columbiad's page,
To gild the tablets of an iron age,
And save his tears, which yet may fall upon
Some fabled field, some fancied Washington !

IV.

But once again, from their Æolian cave,
The winds of Genius wandered on the wave.
Tired of the scenes the timid pencil drew,
Sick of the notes the sounding clarion blew;
Sated with heroes who had worn so long
The shadowy plumage of historic song;
The new-born poet left the beaten course,
To track the passions to their living source.

Then rose the Drama ;—and the world **admired**
Her varied page with deeper thought inspired ;

[1] " *Bore* Ever Ready, *faithful to the last.*"
  ' *Semper peratus*,"—a motto of the revolutionary **standards.**

Bound to no clime, for Passion's throb is one
In Greenland's twilight or in India's sun ;
Born for no age,—for all the thoughts that roll
In the dark vortex of the stormy soul,
Unchained in song, no freezing years can tame ;
God gave them birth, and man is still the same.

So full on life her magic mirror shone,
Her sister Arts paid tribute to her throne ;
One reared her temple, one her canvas warmed,
And Music thrilled, while Eloquence informed.
The weary rustic left his stinted task
For smiles and tears, the dagger and the mask ;
The sage, turned scholar, half forgot his lore,
To be the woman he despised before ;
O'er sense and thought she threw her golden chain,
And Time, the anarch, spares her deathless reign.

Thus lives Medea, in our tamer age,
As when her buskin pressed the Grecian stage ;
Not in the cells where frigid learning delves
In Aldine folios mouldering on their shelves ;
But breathing, burning in the glittering throng,
Whose thousand bravos roll untired along,
Circling and spreading through the gilded halls
From London's galleries to San Carlo's walls !

Thus shall he live whose more than mortal **name**
Mocks with its ray the pallid torch of Fame ;
So proudly lifted, that it seems afar
No earthly Pharos, but a heavenly star ;

Who, unconfined to Art's diurnal bound,
Girds her whole zodiac in his flaming round,
And leads the passions, like the orb that guides,
From pole to pole, the palpitating tides!

———

V.

Though round the Muse the robe of song is
thrown,
Think not the poet lives in verse alone.
Long ere the chisel of the sculptor taught
The lifeless stone to mock the living thought;
Long ere the painter bade the canvas glow
With every line the forms of beauty know;
Long ere the Iris of the Muses threw
On every leaf its own celestial hue;
In fable's dress the breath of genius poured,
And warmed the shapes that later times adored.

Untaught by Science how to forge the keys,
That loose the gates of Nature's mysteries;
Unschooled by Faith, who, with her angel tread,
Leads through the labyrinth with a single thread,
His fancy, hovering round her guarded tower,
Rained through its bars like Danae's golden shower.

He spoke; the sea-nymph answered from her
cave:
He called; the naiad left her mountain wave:
He dreamed of beauty; lo, amidst his dream,
Narcissus mirrored in the breathless stream;
And night's chaste empress, in her bridal play,

Laughed through the foliage where Endymion lay;
And ocean dimpled, as the languid swell
Kissed the red lip of Cytherea's shell:
Of power,—Bellona swept the crimson field,
And blue-eyed Pallas shook her Gorgon shield;
O'er the hushed waves their mightier monarch drove,
And Ida trembled to the tread of Jove!

So every grace, that plastic language knows,
To nameless poets its perfection owes.
The rough-hewn words to simplest thoughts con
    fined,
Were cut and polished in their nicer mind;
Caught on their edge, imagination's ray
Splits into rainbows, shooting far away;—
From sense to soul, from soul to sense, it flies,
And through all nature links analogies;
He who reads right will rarely look upon
A better poet than his lexicon!

There is a race, which cold, ungenial skies
Breed from decay, as fungous growths arise;
Though dying fast, yet springing fast again,
Which still usurps an unsubstantial reign.
With frames too languid for the charms of sense,
And minds worn down with action too intense;
Tired of a world whose joys they never knew,
Themselves deceived, yet thinking all untrue;
Scarce men without, and less than girls within.
Sick of their life before its cares begin;—
The dull disease, which drains their feeble hearts,
To life's decay some hectic thrills imparts,

And lends a force which, like the maniac's power,
Pays with blank years the frenzy of an hour.

And this is Genius! Say, does Heaven degrade
The manly frame, for health, for action made?
Break down the sinews, rack the brow with pains,
Blanch the bright cheek, and drain the purple veins,
To clothe the mind with more extended sway,
Thus faintly struggling in degenerate clay?

No! gentle maid, too ready to admire,
Though false its notes, the pale enthusiast's lyre;
If this be genius, though its bitter springs
Glowed like the morn beneath Aurora's wings,
Seek not the source whose sullen bosom feeds
But fruitless flowers, and dark, envenomed weeds

But, if so bright the dear illusion seems,
Thou wouldst be partner of thy poet's dreams,
And hang in rapture on his bloodless charms,
Or die, like Raphael, in his angel arms;
Go, and enjoy thy blessed lot,—to share
In Cowper's gloom, or Chatterton's despair!

Not such were they whom, wandering o'er the
    waves,
I looked to meet, but only found their graves;
If friendship's smile, the better part of fame,
Should lend my song the only wreath I claim,
Whose voice would greet me with a sweeter tone,
Whose living hand more kindly press my own,
Than theirs,—could Memory, as her silent tread

Prints the pale flowers that blossom o'er the dead,
Those breathless lips, now closed in peace, restore,
Or wake those pulses hushed to beat no more?

Thou calm, chaste scholar! [1] I can see thee now,
The first young laurels on thy pallid brow,
O'er thy slight figure floating lightly down
In graceful folds the academic gown,
On thy curled lip the classic lines, that taught
How nice the mind that sculptured them with
  thought,
And triumph glistening in the clear blue eye,
Too bright to live,—but oh, too fair to die!

And thou, dear friend,[2] whom Science still de-
  plores,
And love still mourns, on ocean-severed shores,
Though the bleak forest twice has bowed with snow,
Since thou wast laid its budding leaves below,
Thine image mingles with my closing strain,
As when we wandered by the turbid Seine,
Both blest with hopes, which revelled, bright and
  free,
On all we longed, or all we dreamed to be;
To thee the amaranth and the cypress fell,—
And I was spared to breathe this last farewell!

But lived there one in unremembered days,
Or lives there still, who spurns the poet's bays?

[1] " *Thou calm, chaste scholar.*"
Charles Chauncy Emerson ; died May 9th, 1836.
[2] " *And thou, dear friend.*"
James Jackson, Jr., M. D. ; died March 29th, 1834.

Whose fingers, dewy from Castalia's springs,
Rest on the lore, yet scorn to touch the strings?
Who shakes the senate with the silver tone
The groves of Pindus might have sighed to own?
Have such e'er been?   Remember Canning's name!
Do such still live?   Let "Alaric's Dirge" proclaim!

Immortal Art! where'er the rounded sky
Bends o'er the cradle where thy children lie,
Their home is earth, their herald every tongue
Whose accents echo to the voice that sung.
One leap of Ocean scatters on the sand
The quarried bulwarks of the loosening land;
One thrill of earth dissolves a century's toil,
Strewed like the leaves that vanish in the soil;
One hill o'erflows, and cities sink below,
Their marbles splintering in the lava's glow;
But one sweet tone, scarce whispered to the air,
From shore to shore the blasts of ages bear;
One humble name, which oft, perchance, has borne
The tyrant's mockery and the courtier's scorn,
Towers o'er the dust of earth's forgotten graves,
As once. emerging through the waste of waves,
The rocky Titan, round whose shattered spear
Coiled the last whirlpool of the drowning sphere!

LYRICS

LYRICS.

THE LAST READER.

I SOMETIMES sit beneath a tree,
 And read my own sweet songs;
Though naught they may to others be,
 Each humble line prolongs
A tone that might have passed away,
But for that scarce remembered lay.

I keep them like a lock or leaf,
 That some dear girl has given;
Frail record of an hour, as brief
 As sunset clouds in heaven,
But spreading purple twilight still
High over memory's shadowed hill.

They lie upon my pathway bleak,
 Those flowers that once ran wild,
As on a father's care-worn cheek
 The ringlets of his child;
The golden mingling with the gray,
And stealing half its snows away.

What care I though the dust is spread
 Around these yellow leaves,

Or o'er them his sarcastic thread
    Oblivion's insect weaves;
Though weeds are tangled on the stream,
It still reflects my morning's beam.

And therefore love I such as smile
    On these neglected songs,
Nor deem that flattery's needless wile
    My opening bosom wrongs;
For who would trample, at my side,
A few pale buds, my garden's pride?

It may be that my scanty ore
    Long years have washed away,
And where were golden sands before,
    Is naught but common clay;
Still something sparkles in the sun
For Memory to look back upon.

And when my name no more is heard,
    My lyre no more is known,
Still let me, like a winter's bird,
    In silence and alone,
Fold over them the weary wing
Once flashing through the dews of spring.

Yes, let my fancy fondly wrap
    My youth in its decline,
And riot in the rosy lap
    Of thoughts that once were mine,
And give the worm my little store
When the last reader reads no more!

OUR YANKEE GIRLS.

Let greener lands and bluer skies,
    If such the wide earth shows,
With fairer cheeks and brighter eyes,
    Match us the star and rose;
The winds that lift the Georgian's veil,
    Or wave Circassia's curls,
Waft to their shores the sultan's sail,—
    Who buys our Yankee girls?

The gay grisette, whose fingers touch
    Love's thousand chords so well;
The dark Italian, loving much,
    But more than *one* can tell;
And England's fair-haired, blue-eyed dame,
    Who binds her brow with pearls;—
Ye who have seen them, can they shame
    Our own sweet Yankee girls?

And what if court or castle vaunt
    Its children loftier born?—
Who heeds the silken tassel's flaunt
    Beside the golden corn?
They ask not for the dainty toil
    Of ribboned knights and earls,
The daughters of the virgin soil,
    Our free-born Yankee girls!

By every hill whose stately pines
    Wave their dark arms above
The home where some fair being shines,
    To warm the wilds with love,
From barest rock to bleakest shore
    Where farthest sail unfurls,
That stars and stripes are streaming o'er,—
    God bless our Yankee girls!

LA GRISETTE.

Ah Clemence! when I saw thee last
    Trip down the Rue de Seine,
And turning, when thy form had past,
    I said, " We meet again,"—
I dreamed not in that idle glance
    Thy latest image came,
And only left to memory's trance
    A shadow and a name.

The few strange words my lips had taught
    Thy timid voice to speak,
Their gentler signs, which often brought
    Fresh roses to thy cheek,
The trailing of thy long loose hair
    Bent o'er my couch of pain,
All, all returned, more sweet, more fair;
    O had we met again!

I walked where saint and virgin keep
    The vigil lights of heaven,
I knew that thou hadst woes to weep,
    And sins to be forgiven;
I watched where Genevieve was laid,
    I knelt by Mary's shrine,
Beside me low, soft voices prayed;
    Alas! but where was thine?

And when the morning sun was bright,
    When wind and wave were calm,
And flamed, in thousand-tinted light,
    The rose of Notre Dame,
I wandered through the haunts of men,
    From Boulevard to Quai.
Till, frowning o'er Saint Etienne,
    The Pantheon's shadow lay.

In vain, in vain; we meet no more,
    Nor dream what fates befall;
And long upon the stranger's shore
    My voice on thee may call,
When years have clothed the line in moss,
    That tells thy name and days,
And withered, on thy simple cross,
    The wreaths of Père-la-Chaise!

AN EVENING THOUGHT.

WRITTEN AT SEA.

If sometimes in the dark blue eye,
    Or in the deep red wine,
Or soothed by gentlest melody,
    Still warms this heart of mine,
Yet something colder in the blood,
    And calmer in the brain,
Have whispered that my youth's bright flood
    Ebbs, not to flow again.

If by Helvetia's azure lake,
    Or Arno's yellow stream,
Each star of memory could awake,
    As in my first young dream,
I know that when mine eye shall greet
    The hill-sides bleak and bare,
That gird my home, it will not meet
    My childhood's sunsets there.

Oh, when love's first, sweet, stolen kiss
    Burned on my boyish brow,
Was that young forehead worn as this?
    Was that flushed cheek as now?
Were that wild pulse and throbbing heart
    Like these, which vainly strive,

41

In thankless strains of soulless art,
    To dream themselves alive?

Alas! the morning dew is gone,
    Gone ere the full of day;
Life's iron fetter still is on,
    Its wreaths all torn away;
Happy if still some casual hour
    Can warm the fading shrine,
Too soon to chill beyond the power
    Of love, or song, or wine!

A SOUVENIR.

Yes, lady! I can ne'er forget,
That once in other years we met;
Thy memory may perchance recall
A festal eve, a rose-wreathed hall,
Its tapers' blaze, its mirrors' glance,
Its melting song, its ringing dance;—
Why, in thy dream of virgin joy,
Shouldst thou recall a pallid boy?

Thine eye had other forms to seek,
Why rest upon his bashful cheek?
With other tones thy heart was stirred,
Why waste on him a gentle word?
We parted, lady,—all night long
Thine ear to thrill with dance and song,—
And I—to weep that I was born
A thing thou scarce wouldst deign to scorn.

And, lady! now that years have past,
My bark has reached the shore at last;
The gales that filled her ocean wing
Have chilled and shrunk thy hasty spring,
And eye to eye, and brow to brow,
I stand before thy presence now;—
Thy lip is smoothed, thy voice is sweet,
Thy warm hand offered when we meet.

43

Nay, lady! 'tis not now for me
To droop the lid or bend the knee.
I seek thee,—oh, thou dost not shun;
I speak,—thou listenest like a nun;
I ask thy smile,—thy lip uncurls,
Too liberal of its flashing pearls;
Thy tears,—thy lashes sink again,—
My Hebe turns to Magdalen!

O changing youth! that evening hour
Look down on ours,—the bud—the flower;
Thine faded in its virgin soil,
And mine was nursed in tears and toil;
Thy leaves were withering, one by one,
While mine were opening to the sun;—
Which now can meet the cold and storm,
With freshest leaf and hardiest form?

Ay, lady! that once haughty glance
Still wanders through the glittering dance,
And asks in vain from others' pride,
The charity thine own denied;
And as thy fickle lips could learn
To smile and praise,—that used to spurn,
So the last offering on thy shrine
Shall be this flattering lay of mine!

"QUI VIVE!"

"QUI VIVE!" The sentry's musket **rings,**
    The channelled bayonet gleams;
High o'er him, like a raven's wings
The broad tricolored banner flings
Its shadow, rustling as it swings
    Pale in the moonlight beams;
Pass on! while steel-clad sentries **keep**
Their vigil o'er the monarch's sleep,
    Thy bare, unguarded breast
Asks not the unbroken, bristling zone
That girds yon sceptred trembler's **throne;—**
    Pass on, and take thy rest!

"*Qui vive!*" How oft the midnight **air**
    That startling cry has borne!
How oft the evening breeze has **fanned**
The banner of this haughty land,
O'er mountain snow and desert **sand,**
    Ere yet its folds were torn!
Through Jena's carnage flying **red,**
Or tossing o'er Marengo's dead,
    Or curling on the towers
Where Austria's eagle quivers **yet,**
And suns the ruffled plumage, wet
    With battle's crimson showers!

" *Qui vive !* "   And is the sentry's cry,—
   The sleepless soldier's hand,—
Are these,—the painted folds that fly
And lift their emblems, printed high,
On morning mist and sunset sky,—
   The guardians of a land?
No! If the patriot's pulses sleep,
How vain the watch that hirelings keep,—
   The idle flag that waves,
When Conquest, with his iron heel,
Treads down the standards and the steel
   That belt the soil of slaves!

THE WASP AND THE HORNET.

THE two proud sisters of the sea,
    In glory and in doom !—
Well may the eternal waters be
    Their broad, unsculptured tomb !
The wind that rings along the wave,
    The clear, unshadowed sun,
Are torch and trumpet o'er the brave,
    Whose last green wreath is won !

No stranger-hand their banners furled,
    No victor's shout they heard ;
Unseen, above them ocean curled,
    Save by his own pale bird ;
The gnashing billows heaved and fell ;
    Wild shrieked the midnight gale ;
Far, far beneath the morning swell
    Were pennon, spar, and sail.

The land of Freedom !   Sea and shore
    Are guarded now, as when
Her ebbing waves to victory bore
    Fair barks and gallant men ;
Oh, many a ship of prouder name
    May wave her starry fold,
Nor trail, with deeper light of fame,
    The paths they swept of old !

FROM A BACHELOR'S PRIVATE JOURNAL.

Sweet Mary, I have never breathed
    The love it were in vain to name,
Though round my heart a serpent wreathed,
    I smiled, or strove to smile, the same.

Once more the pulse of Nature glows
    With faster throb and fresher fire,
While music round her pathway flows
    Like echoes from a hidden lyre.

And is there none with me to share
    The glories of the earth and sky?
The eagle through the pathless air
    Is followed by one burning eye.

Ah, no! the cradled flowers may wake,
    Again may flow the frozen sea,
From every cloud a star may break,—
    There comes no second Spring to me.

Go,—ere the painted toys of youth
    Are crushed beneath the tread of years;
Ere visions have been chilled to truth,
    And hopes are washed away in tears.

Go,—for I will not bid thee weep,—
    Too soon my sorrows will be thine,
And evening's troubled air shall sweep
    The incense from the broken shrine.

If Heaven can hear the dying tone
    Of chords that soon will cease to thrill,
The prayer that Heaven has heard alone,
    May bless thee when those chords are still!

4

STANZAS.

STRANGE! that one lightly whispered tone
  Is far, far sweeter unto me,
Than all the sounds that kiss the earth,
  Or breathe along the sea;
But, lady, when thy voice I greet,
Not heavenly music seems so sweet.

I look upon the fair blue skies,
  And naught but empty air I see;
But when I turn me to thine eyes,
  It seemeth unto me
Ten thousand angels spread their wings
Within those little azure rings.

The lily hath the softest leaf
  That ever western breeze hath fanned,
But thou shalt have the tender flower,
  So I may take thy hand;
That little hand to me doth yield
More joy than all the broidered field.

O lady! there be many things
  That seem right fair, below, above;
But sure not one among them all
  Is half so sweet as love;—
Let us not pay our vows alone,
But join two altars both in one.

THE PHILOSOPHER TO HIS LOVE.

DEAREST, a look is but a ray
Reflected in a certain way;
A word, whatever tone it wear,
Is but a trembling wave of air;
A touch, obedience to a clause
In nature's pure material laws.

The very flowers that bend and meet,
In sweetening others, grow more sweet;
The clouds by day, the stars by night,
Inweave their floating locks of light;
The rainbow, Heaven's own forehead's braid,
Is but the embrace of sun and shade.

How few that love us have we found!
How wide the world that girds them round!
Like mountain streams we meet and part,
Each living in the other's heart,
Our course unknown, our hope to be
Yet mingled in the distant sea.

But Ocean coils and heaves in vain,
Bound in the subtle moonbeam's chain;
And love and hope do but obey
Some cold, capricious planet's ray,
Which lights and leads the tide it charms,
To Death's dark caves and icy arms.

Alas! one narrow line is drawn,
That links our sunset with our dawn;
In mist and shade life's morning rose,
And clouds are round it at its close;
But ah! no twilight beam ascends
To whisper where that evening ends.

Oh! in the hour when I shall feel
Those shadows round my senses steal,
When gentle eyes are weeping o'er
The clay that feels their tears no more,
Then let thy spirit with me be,
Or some sweet angel, likest thee!

L'INCONNUE.

Is thy name Mary, maiden fair?
　　Such should, methinks, its music be;
The sweetest name that mortals bear,
　　Were best befitting thee;
And she, to whom it once was given,
Was half of earth and half of heaven.

I hear thy voice, I see thy smile,
　　I look upon thy folded hair;
Ah! while we dream not they beguile,
　　Our hearts are in the snare;
And she, who chains a wild bird's wing,
Must start not if her captive sing.

So, lady, take the leaf that falls,
　　To all but thee unseen, unknown;
When evening shades thy silent walls,
　　Then read it all alone;
In stillness read, in darkness seal,
Forget, despise, but not reveal!

THE STAR AND THE WATER-LILY.

THE sun stepped down from his golden throne,
    And lay in the silent sea,
And the Lily had folded her satin leaves,
    For a sleepy thing was she;
What is the Lily dreaming of?
    Why crisp the waters blue?
See, see, she is lifting her varnished lid!
    Her white leaves are glistening through!

The Rose is cooling his burning cheek
    In the lap of the breathless tide;—
The Lily hath sisters fresh and fair,
    That would lie by the Rose's side;
He would love her better than all the rest,
    And he would be fond and true;—
But the Lily unfolded her weary lids,
    And looked at the sky so blue.

Remember, remember, thou silly one,
    How fast will thy summer glide,
And wilt thou wither a virgin pale,
    Or flourish a blooming bride?
"Oh, the Rose is old, and thorny, and cold,
    And he lives on earth," said she;
"But the Star is fair and he lives in the air,
    And he shall my bridegroom be."

But what if the stormy cloud should come
    And ruffle the silver sea ?
Would he turn his eye from the distant sky,
    To smile on a thing like thee ?
Oh, no, fair Lily, he will not send
    One ray from his far-off throne ;
The winds shall blow and the waves shall flow,
    And thou wilt be left alone.

There is not a leaf on the mountain top,
    Nor a drop of evening dew,
Nor a golden sand on the sparkling shore,
    Nor a pearl in the waters blue,
That he has not cheered with his fickle smile,
    And warmed with his faithless beam,—
And will he be true to a pallid flower,
    That floats on the quiet stream ?

Alas for the Lily ! she would not heed,
    But turned to the skies afar,
And bared her breast to the trembling ray
    That shot from the rising star ;
The cloud came over the darkened sky,
    And over the waters wide :
She looked in vain through the beating rain,
    And sank in the stormy tide.

ILLUSTRATION OF A PICTURE.

' A SPANISH GIRL IN REVERY.'

SHE twirled the string of golden beads,
    That round her neck was hung,—
My grandsire's gift; the good old man
    Loved girls when he was young;
And, bending lightly o'er the cord,
    And turning half away,
With something like a youthful sigh,
    Thus spoke the maiden gray:

" Well, one may trail her silken robe,
    And bind her locks with pearls,
And one may wreathe the woodland rose
    Among her floating curls;
And one may tread the dewy grass,
    And one the marble floor,
Nor half-hid bosom heave the less,
    Nor broidered corset more!

" Some years ago, a dark-eyed girl
    Was sitting in the shade,—
There's something brings her to my mind
    In that young dreaming maid,—
And in her hand she held a flower,
    A flower, whose speaking hue

56

Said, in the language of the heart,
    ' Believe the giver true.'

" And, as she looked upon its leaves,
    The maiden made a vow
To wear it when the bridal wreath
    Was woven for her brow;
She watched the flower, as, day by day,
    The leaflets curled and died;
But he who gave it never came
    To claim her for his bride.

" Oh, many a summer's morning glow
    Has lent the rose its ray,
And many a winter's drifting snow
    Has swept its bloom away;
But she has kept that faithless pledge
    To this, her winter hour,
And keeps it still, herself alone,
    And wasted like the flower."

Her pale lip quivered, and the light
    Gleamed in her moistening eyes;—
I asked her how she liked the tints
    In those Castilian skies?
" She thought them misty,—'twas perhaps
    Because she stood too near;"
She turned away, and as she turned,
    I saw her wipe a tear.

THE DYING SENECA.

He died not as the martyr dies
    Wrapped in his living shroud of flame;
He fell not as the warrior falls,
    Gasping upon the field of fame;
A gentler passage to the grave,
The murderer's softened fury gave.

Rome's slaughtered sons and blazing piles
    Had tracked the purple demon's path.
And yet another victim lived
    To fill the fiery scroll of wrath;
Could not imperial vengeance spare
His furrowed brow and silver hair?

The field was sown with noble blood,
    The harvest reaped in burning tears,
When, rolling up its crimson flood,
    Broke the long-gathering tide of years;
His diadem was rent away,
And beggars trampled on his clay.

None wept,—none pitied;—they who knelt
    At morning by the despot's throne,
At evening dashed the laurelled bust,
    And spurned the wreaths themselves had
      strewn;
The shout of triumph echoed wide,
The self-stung reptile writhed and died!
58

A PORTRAIT.

A STILL, sweet, placid, moonlight face,
    And slightly nonchalant,
Which seems to claim a middle place
    Between one's love and aunt,
Where childhood's star has left a ray
    In woman's sunniest sky,
As morning dew and blushing day
    On fruit and blossom lie.

And yet,—and yet I cannot love
    Those lovely lines on steel;
They beam too much of heaven above,
    Earth's darker shades to feel;
Perchance some early weeds of care
    Around my heart have grown,
And brows unfurrowed seem not fair,
    Because they mock my own.

Alas! when Eden's gates were sealed,
    How oft some sheltered flower
Breathed o'er the wanderers of the field,
    Like their own bridal bower;
Yet, saddened by its loveliness,
    And humbled by its pride,
Earth's fairest child they could not bless,—
    It mocked them when they sighed.

A ROMAN AQUEDUCT.

THE sun-browned girl, whose limbs recline
 When noon her languid hand has laid
Hot on the green flakes of the pine,
 Beneath its narrow disk of shade;

As, through the flickering noontide glare,
 She gazes on the rainbow chain
Of arches, lifting once in air
 The rivers of the Roman's plain;—

Say, does her wandering eye recall
 The mountain-current's icy wave,—
Or for the dead one tear let fall,
 Whose founts are broken by their grave?

From stone to stone the ivy weaves
 Her braided tracery's winding veil,
And lacing stalks and tangled leaves
 Nod heavy in the drowsy gale.

And lightly floats the pendent vine,
 That swings beneath her slender bow,
Arch answering arch,—whose rounded line
 Seems mirrored in the wreath below.

How patient Nature smiles at Fame!
 The weeds, that strewed the victor's way,
Feed on his dust to shroud his name,
 Green where his proudest towers decay.

60

See, through that channel, empty now,
 The scanty rain its tribute pours,—
Which cooled the lip and laved the brow
 Of conquerors from a hundred shores.

Thus bending o'er the nation's bier,
 Whose wants the captive earth supplied,
The dew of Memory's passing tear
 Falls on the arches of her pride !

THE LAST PROPHECY OF CASSANDRA.

THE sun is fading in the skies
    And evening shades are gathering fast;
Fair city, ere that sun shall rise,
    Thy night hath come,—thy day is past!

Ye know not,—but the hour is nigh;
    Ye will not heed the warning breath;
No vision strikes your clouded eye,
    To break the sleep that wakes in death.

Go, age, and let thy withered cheek
    Be wet once more with freezing tears;
And bid thy trembling sorrow speak,
    In accents of departed years.

Go, child, and pour thy sinless prayer
    Before the everlasting throne;
And He who sits in glory there,
    May stoop to hear thy silver tone.

Go, warrior, in thy glittering steel,
    And bow thee at the altar's side;
And bid thy frowning gods reveal
    The doom their mystic counsels hide.

Go, maiden, in thy flowing veil,
 And bare thy brow, and bend thy knee;
When the last hopes of mercy fail,
 Thy God may yet remember thee.

Go, as thou didst in happier hours,
 And lay thine incense on the shrine;
And greener leaves, and fairer flowers,
 Around the sacred image twine.

I saw them rise,—the buried dead,—
 From marble tomb and grassy mound;
I heard the spirits' printless tread,
 And voices not of earthly sound.

I looked upon the quivering stream,
 And its cold wave was bright with flame;
And wild, as from a fearful dream,
 The wasted forms of battle came.

Ye will not hear—ye will not know,—
 Ye scorn the maniac's idle song;
Ye care not! but the voice of woe
 Shall thunder loud, and echo long.

Blood shall be in your marble halls,
 And spears shall glance, and fires shall glow;
Ruin shall sit upon your walls,
 But ye shall lie in death below.

Ay, none shall live to hear tho storm
 Around their blackened pillars sweep;
To shudder at the reptile's form,
 Or scare the wild bird from her sleep.

TO A CAGED LION.

Poor conquered monarch! though that haughty
    glance
    Still speaks thy courage unsubdued by time,
And in the grandeur of thy sullen tread
    Lives the proud spirit of thy burning clime;—
Fettered by things that shudder at thy roar,
Torn from thy pathless wilds to pace this narrow
    floor!

Thou wast the victor, and all nature shrunk
    Before the thunders of thine awful wrath;
The steel-armed hunter viewed thee from afar,
    Fearless and trackless in thy lonely path!
The famished tiger closed his flaming eye,
And crouched and panted as thy step went by!

Thou art the vanquished, and insulting man
    Bars thy broad bosom as a sparrow's wing;
His nerveless arms thine iron sinews bind,
    And lead in chains the desert's fallen king;
Are these the beings that have dared to twine
Their feeble threads around those limbs of thine?

So must it be; the weaker, wiser race,
    That wields the tempest and that rides the sea,
Even in the stillness of thy solitude
    Must teach the lesson of its power to thee;
And thou, the terror of the trembling wild,
Must bow thy savage strength, the mockery of a
    child!

5

TO MY COMPANIONS.

MINE ancient Chair! thy wide-embracing arms
 Have clasped around me even from a boy;
Hadst thou a voice to speak of years gone by,
 Thine were a tale of sorrow and of joy,
Of fevered hopes and ill-foreboding fears,
And smile unseen, and unrecorded tears.

And thou, my Table! though unwearied Time
 Hath set his signet on thine altered brow,
Still can I see thee in thy spotless prime,
 And in my memory thou art living now;
Soon must thou slumber with forgotten things,
The peasant's ashes and the dust of kings.

Thou melancholy Mug! thy sober brown
 Hath something pensive in its evening hue,
Not like the things that please the tasteless clown,
 With gaudy streaks of orange and of blue;
And I must love thee, for thou art mine own,
Pressed by my lip, and pressed by mine alone.

My broken Mirror! faithless, yet beloved,
 Thou who canst smile, and smile alike on all,
Oft do I leave thee, oft again return,
 I scorn the siren, but obey the call;
I hate thy falsehood, while I fear thy truth,
But most I love thee, flattering friend of youth.

66

Primeval Carpet! every well-worn thread
  Has slowly parted with its virgin dye;
I saw thee fade beneath the ceaseless tread,
  Fainter and fainter in mine anxious eye;
So flies the color from the brightest flower,
And heaven's own rainbow lives but for an hour.

I love you all! there radiates from our own
  A soul that lives in every shape we see;
There is a voice, to other ears unknown,
  Like echoed music answering to its key.
The dungeoned captive hath a tale to tell,
Of every insect in his lonely cell;
And these poor frailties have a simple tone,
That breathes in accents sweet to me alone.

THE LAST LEAF.

I saw him once before,
As he passed by the door,
 And again
The pavement stones resound,
As he totters o'er the ground
 With his cane.

They say that in his prime,
Ere the pruning-knife of Time
 Cut him down,
Not a better man was found
By the Crier on his round
 Through the town.

But now he walks the streets,
And he looks at all he meets
 Sad and wan,
And he shakes his feeble head,
That it seems as if he said,
 "They are gone."

The mossy marble rest
On the lips that he has prest
 In their bloom,
And the names he loved to hear
Have been carved for many a year
 On the tomb.

My grandmamma has said,—
Poor old lady, she is dead
   Long ago,—
That he had a Roman nose,
And his cheek was like a rose
   In the snow.

But now his nose is thin,
And it rests upon his chin
   Like a staff,
And a crook is in his back,
And a melancholy crack
   In his laugh.

I know it is a sin
For me to sit and grin
   At him here;
But the old three-cornered hat,
And the breeches, and all that,
   Are so queer!

And if I should live to be
The last leaf upon the tree
   In the spring,
Let them smile, as I do now,
At the old forsaken bough
   Where I cling.

TO A BLANK SHEET OF PAPER.

WAN-VISAGED thing ! thy virgin leaf
    To me looks more than deadly pale,
Unknowing what may stain thee yet,—
    A poem or a tale.

Who can thy unborn meaning scan ?
    Can Seer or Sibyl read thee now ?
No,—seek to trace the fate of man
    Writ on his infant brow.

Love may light on thy snowy cheek,
    And shake his Eden-breathing plumes ;
Then shalt thou tell how Lelia smiles,
    Or Angelina blooms.

Satire may lift his bearded lance,
    Forestalling Time's slow-moving scythe,
And, scattered on thy little field,
    Disjointed bards may writhe.

Perchance a vision of the night,
    Some grizzled spectre, gaunt and thin,
Or sheeted corpse, may stalk along,
    Or skeleton may grin !

70

If it should be in pensive hour
    Some sorrow-moving theme I try,
Ah, maiden, how thy tears will fall,
    For all I doom to die!

But if in merry mood I touch
    Thy leaves, then shall the sight of thee
Sow smiles as thick on rosy lips
    As ripples on the sea.

The Weekly press shall gladly stoop
    To bind thee up among its sheaves;
The Daily steal thy shining ore,
    To gild its leaden leaves.

Thou hast no tongue, yet thou canst speak,
    Till distant shores shall hear the sound;
Thou hast no life, yet thou canst breathe
    Fresh life on all around.

Thou art the arena of the wise,
    The noiseless battle-ground of fame;
The sky where halos may be wreathed
    Around the humblest name.

Take, then, this treasure to thy trust,
    To win some idle reader's smile,
Then fade and moulder in the dust,
    Or swell some bonfire's crackling pile!

TO AN INSECT.

I LOVE to hear thine earnest voice,
    Wherever thou art hid,
Thou testy little dogmatist,
    Thou pretty Katydid!
Thou mindest me of gentlefolks,—
    Old gentlefolks are they,—
Thou say'st an undisputed thing
    In such a solemn way.

Thou art a female, Katydid!
    I know it by the trill
That quivers through thy piercing notes,
    So petulant and shrill,
I think there is a knot of you
    Beneath the hollow tree,—
A knot of spinster Katydids,—
    Do Katydids drink tea?

Oh, tell me where did Katy live,
    And what did Katy do?
And was she very fair and young,
    And yet so wicked, too?
Did Katy love a naughty man,
    Or kiss more cheeks than one?
I warrant Katy did no more
    Than many a Kate has done.

Dear me! I'll tell you all about
    My fuss with little Jane,
And Ann, with whom I used to walk
    So often down the lane,
And all that tore their locks of black,
    Or wet their eyes of blue,—
Pray tell me, sweetest Katydid,
    What did poor Katy do?

Oh, no! the living oak shall crash,
    That stood for ages still,
The rock shall rend its mossy base
    And thunder down the hill,
Before the little Katydid
    Shall add one word, to tell
The mystic story of the maid
    Whose name she knows so well.

Peace to the ever murmuring race!
    And when the latest one
Shall fold in death her feeble wings
    Beneath the autumn sun,
Then shall she raise her fainting voice
    And lift her drooping lid,
And then the child of future years
    Shall hear what Katy did.

THE DILEMMA.

Now, by the blessed Paphian queen,
Who heaves the breast of sweet sixteen:
By every name I cut on bark
Before my morning star grew dark;
By Hymen's torch, by Cupid's dart,
By all that thrills the beating heart;
The bright black eye, the melting blue,—
I cannot choose between the two.

I had a vision in my dreams;—
I saw a row of twenty beams;
From every beam a rope was hung,
In every rope a lover swung;
I asked the hue of every eye,
That bade each luckless lover die;
Ten shadowy lips said, heavenly blue,
And ten accused the darker hue.

I asked a matron, which she deemed
With fairest light of beauty beamed;
She answered, some thought both were fair,—
Give her blue eyes and golden hair.
I might have liked her judgment well,
But, as she spoke, she rung the bell,
And all her girls, nor small nor few,
Came marching in,—their eyes were blue.

74

I asked a maiden; back she flung
The locks that round her forehead hung,
And turned her eye, a glorious one,
Bright as a diamond in the sun,
On me, until beneath its rays
I felt as if my hair would blaze;
She liked all eyes but eyes of green;
She looked at me; what could she mean!

Ah! many lids Love lurks between,
Nor heeds the coloring of his screen;
And when his random arrows fly,
The victim falls, but knows not why.
Gaze not upon his shield of jet,
The shaft upon the string is set;
Look not beneath his azure veil,
Though every limb were cased in mail.

Well, both might make a martyr break
The chain that bound him to the stake;
And both, with but a single ray,
Can melt our very hearts away;
And both, when balanced, hardly seem
To stir the scales, or rock the beam;
But that is dearest, all the while,
That wears for us the sweetest smile.

MY AUNT.

My aunt! my dear unmarried aunt!
    Long years have o'er her flown;
Yet still she strains the aching clasp
    That binds her virgin zone;
I know it hurts her,—though she looks
    As cheerful as she can;
Her waist is ampler than her life,
    For life is but a span.

My aunt! my poor deluded aunt!
    Her hair is almost gray;
Why will she train that winter curl
    In such a spring-like way?
How can she lay her glasses down,
    And say she reads as well,
When, through a double convex lens,
    She just makes out to spell?

Her father,—grandpapa! forgive
    This erring lip its smiles,—
Vowed she should make the finest girl
    Within a hundred miles;
He sent her to a stylish school;
    'Twas in her thirteenth June;
And with her, as the rules required,
    "Two towels and a spoon."

They braced my aunt against a board,
    To make her straight and tall;
They laced her up, they starved her down,
    To make her light and small;
They pinched her feet, they singed her hair,
    They screwed it up with pins;
Oh, never mortal suffered more
    In penance for her sins.

So, when my precious aunt was done,
    My grandsire brought her back;
(By daylight, lest some rabid youth
    Might follow on the track;)
" Ah!" said my grandsire, as he shook
    Some powder in his pan,
" What could this lovely creature do
    Against a desperate man!"

Alas! nor chariot, nor barouche,
    Nor bandit cavalcade,
Tore from the trembling father's arms
    His all-accomplished maid.
For her how happy had it been!
    And heaven had spared to me
To see one sad, ungathered rose
    On my ancestral tree.

THE TOADSTOOL.

THERE's a thing that grows by the fainting flower,
And springs in the shade of the lady's bower;
The lily shrinks, and the rose turns pale,
When they feel its breath in the summer gale,
And the tulip curls its leaves in pride,
And the blue-eyed violet starts aside;
But the lily may flaunt, and the tulip stare,
For what does the honest toadstool care?

She does not glow in a painted vest,
And she never blooms on the maiden's breast;
But she comes, as the saintly sisters do,
In a modest suit of a Quaker hue.
And, when the stars in the evening skies
Are weeping dew from their gentle eyes,
The toad comes out from his hermit cell,
The tale of his faithful love to tell.
Oh, there is light in her lover's glance,
That flies to her heart like a silver lance;
His breeches are made of spotted skin,
His jacket is tight, and his pumps are thin;
In a cloudless night you may hear his song,
As its pensive melody floats along,
And, if you will look by the moonlight fair,
The trembling form of the toad is there.

And he twines his arms round her slender stem,
In the shade of her velvet diadem;
But she turns away in her maiden shame,
And will not breathe on the kindling flame;
He sings at her feet through the livelong night,
And creeps to his cave at the break of light;
And whenever he comes to the air above,
His throat is swelling with baffled love.

THE MEETING OF THE DRYADS.[1]

It was not many centuries since,
    When, gathered on the moonlit green,
Beneath the Tree of Liberty,
    A ring of weeping sprites were seen.

The freshman's lamp had long been dim,
    The voice of busy day was mute,
And tortured melody had ceased
    Her sufferings on the evening flute.

They met not as they once had met,
    To laugh o'er many a jocund tale;
But every pulse was beating low,
    And every cheek was cold and pale.

There rose a fair but faded one,
    Who oft had cheered them with her song;
She waved a mutilated arm,
    And silence held the listening throng.

"Sweet friends," the gentle nymph began,
    "From opening bud to withering leaf,
One common lot has bound us all,
    In every change of joy and grief.

[1] Written after a general pruning of the trees around Harvard College.

" While all around has felt decay,
    We rose in ever living prime,
With broader shade and fresher green,
    Beneath the crumbling step of Time.

" When often by our feet has past
    Some biped, nature's walking whim,
Say, have we trimmed one awkward shape,
    Or lopped away one crooked limb ?

" Go on, fair Science; soon to thee
    Shall Nature yield her idle boast;
Her vulgar fingers formed a tree,
    But thou hast trained it to a post.

" Go paint the birch's silver rind,
    And quilt the peach with softer down;
Up with the willow's trailing threads,
    Off with the sunflower's radiant crown !

" Go, plant the lily on the shore,
    And set the rose among the waves,
And bid the tropic bud unbind
    Its silken zone in arctic caves;

" Bring bellows for the panting winds,
    Hang up a lantern by the moon,
And give the nightingale a fife,
    And lend the eagle a balloon !

" I cannot smile,—the tide of scorn,
    That rolled through every bleeding vein,
Comes kindling fiercer as it flows
    Back to its burning source again.

6

" Again in every quivering leaf
    That moment's agony I feel,
When limbs, that spurned the northern blast,
    Shrunk from the sacrilegious steel.

" A curse upon the wretch who dared
    To crop us with his felon saw !
May every fruit his lip shall taste.
    Lie like a bullet in his maw.

" In ever julep that he drinks,
    May gout, and bile, and headache be ;
And when he strives to calm his pain,
    May colic mingle with his tea.

" May nightshade cluster round his path,
    And thistles shoot, and brambles cling ;
May blistering ivy scorch his veins,
    And dogwood burn, and nettles sting.

" On him may never shadow fall,
    When fever racks his throbbing brow,
And his last shilling buy a rope
    To hang him on my highest bough ! "

She spoke ;—the morning's herald beam
    Sprang from the bosom of the sea,
And every mangled sprite returned
    In sadness to her wounded tree.[1]

[1] A little poem, on a similar occasion, may be found in the works of Swift, from which, perhaps, the idea was borrowed ; although I was as much surprised as amused to meet with it some time after writing the preceding lines.

THE MYSTERIOUS VISITOR.

THERE was a sound of hurrying feet,
    A tramp on echoing stairs,
There was a rush along the aisles,—
    It was the hour of prayers.

And on, like Ocean's midnight wave,
    The current rolled along,
When, suddenly, a stranger form
    Was seen amidst the throng.

He was a dark and swarthy man,
    That uninvited guest;
A faded coat of bottle green
    Was buttoned round his breast.

There was not one among them all
    Could say from whence he came;
Nor beardless boy, nor ancient man,
    Could tell that stranger's name.

All silent as the sheeted dead,
    In spite of sneer and frown,
Fast by a gray-haired senior's side
    He sat him boldly down.

There was a look of horror flashed
From out the tutor's eyes;
When all around him rose to pray,
The stranger did not rise!

A murmur broke along the crowd,
The prayer was at an end;
With ringing heels and measured tread
A hundred forms descend.

Through sounding aisles, o'er grating stair,
The long procession poured,
Till all were gathered on the seats
Around the Commons board.

That fearful stranger! down he sat,
Unasked, yet undismayed;
And on his lip a rising smile
Of scorn or pleasure played.

He took his hat and hung it up,
With slow but earnest air;
He stripped his coat from off his back,
And placed it on a chair.

Then from his nearest neighbor's side
A knife and plate he drew;
And, reaching out his hand again,
He took his teacup too.

How fled the sugar from the bowl!
How sunk the azure cream!

They vanished like the shapes that float
    Upon a summer's dream.

A long, long draught,—an outstretched hand,
    And crackers, toast, and tea,
They faded from the stranger's touch
    Like dew upon the sea.

Then clouds were dark on many a brow,
    Fear sat upon their souls,
And, in a bitter agony,
    They clasped their buttered rolls.

A whisper trembled through the crowd,—
    Who could the stranger be?
And some were silent, for they thought
    A cannibal was he.

What if the creature should arise,
    For he was stout and tall,—
And swallow down a sophomore,
    Coat, crow's foot, cap, and all!

All suddenly the stranger rose;
    They sat in mute despair;
He took his hat from off the peg,
    His coat from off the chair.

Four freshmen fainted on the seat,
    Six swooned upon the floor;
Yet on the fearful being passed,
    And shut the chapel door.

There is full many a starving man,
    That walks in bottle green,
But never more that hungry one
    In Common's-hall was seen.

Yet often at the sunset hour,
    When tolls the evening bell,
The freshman lingers on the steps,
    That frightful tale to tell.

THE SPECTRE PIG.

A BALLAD.

It was the stalwart butcher man,
    That knit his swarthy brow,
And said the gentle Pig must die,
    And sealed it with a vow.

And oh! it was the gentle Pig
    Lay stretched upon the ground,
And ah! it was the cruel knife
    His little heart that found.

They took him then, those wicked men,
    They trailed him all along;
They put a stick between his lips,
    And through his heels a thong;

And round and round an oaken beam
    A hempen cord they flung,
And, like a mighty pendulum,
    All solemnly he swung!

Now say thy prayers, thou sinful man,
    And think what thou hast done,
And read thy catechism well,
    Thou bloody minded one;

87

For if his sprite should walk by night,
    It better were for thee,
That thou wert mouldering in the ground,
    Or bleaching in the sea.

It was the savage butcher then,
    That made a mock of sin,
And swore a very wicked oath,
    He did not care a pin.

It was the butcher's youngest son,—
    His voice was broke with sighs,
And with his pocket handkerchief
    He wiped his little eyes;

All young and ignorant was he,
    But innocent and mild,
And, in his soft simplicity,
    Out spoke the tender child;—

"O father, father, list to me;
    The pig is deadly sick,
And men have hung him by his heels,
    And fed him with a stick."

It was the bloody butcher then,
    That laughed as he would die,
Yet did he soothe the sorrowing child,
    And bid him not to cry;—

"O Nathan, Nathan, what's a Pig,
    That thou shouldst weep and wail?
Come, bear thee like a butcher's child,
    And thou shalt have his tail!"

It was the butcher's daughter then,
    So slender and so fair,
That sobbed as if her heart would break,
    And tore her yellow hair;

And thus she spoke in thrilling tone,—
    Fast fell the tear-drops big;
"Ah! woe is me! Alas! Alas!
    The Pig! The Pig! The Pig!"

Then did her wicked father's lips
    Make merry with her woe,
And call her many a naughty name,
    Because she whimpered so.

Ye need not weep, ye gentle ones,
    In vain your tears are shed,
Ye cannot wash his crimson hand,
    Ye cannot soothe the dead.

The bright sun folded on his breast
    His robes of rosy flame,
And softly over all the west
    The shades of evening came.

He slept, and troops of murdered Pigs
    Were busy with his dreams;
Loud rang their wild, unearthly shrieks,
    Wide yawned their mortal seams.

The clock struck twelve; the Dead hath heard;
    He opened both his eyes,
And sullenly he shook his tail
    To lash the feeding flies.

One quiver of the hempen cord,—
　　One struggle and one bound,—
With stiffened limb and leaden eye,
　　The Pig was on the ground!

And straight towards the sleeper's house
　　His fearful way he wended;
And hooting owl, and hovering bat,
　　On midnight wing attended.

Back flew the bolt, up rose the latch,
　　And open swung the door,
And little mincing feet were heard
　　Pat, pat along the floor.

Two hoofs upon the sanded floor,
　　And two upon the bed;
And they are breathing side by side,
　　The living and the dead!

" Now wake, now wake, thou butcher man!
　　What makes thy cheek so pale?
Take hold! take hold! thou dost not fear
　　To clasp a spectre's tail?"

Untwisted every winding coil;
　　The shuddering wretch took hold,
All like an icicle it seemed,
　　So tapering and so cold.

"Thou com'st with me, thou butcher man!"—
　　He strives to loose his grasp,
But, faster than the clinging vine,
　　Those twining spirals clasp.

And open, open swung the door,
    And, fleeter than the wind,
The shadowy spectre swept before,
    The butcher trailed behind.

Fast fled the darkness of the night,
    And morn rose faint and dim ;
They called full loud, they knocked **full long,**
    They did not waken him.

Straight, straight towards that oaken **beam,**
    A trampled pathway ran ;
A ghastly shape was swinging there,—
    It was the butcher man.

LINES BY A CLERK.

Oh! I did love her dearly,
 And gave her toys and rings,
And I thought she meant sincerely,
 When she took my pretty things;
But her heart has grown as icy
 As a fountain in the fall,
And her love, that was so spicy,
 It did not last at all.

I gave her once a locket,
 It was filled with my own hair,
And she put it in her pocket
 With very special care.
But a jeweller has got it,—
 He offered it to me,
And another that is not it
 Around her neck I see.

For my cooings and my billings
 I do not now complain,
But my dollars and my shillings
 Will never come again;
They were earned with toil and sorrow,
 But I never told her that,
And now I have to borrow,
 And want another hat.

Think, think, thou cruel Emma,
    When thou shalt hear my woe,
And know my sad dilemma,
    That thou hast made it so.
See, see my beaver rusty,
    Look, look upon this hole,
This coat is dim and dusty;
    Oh, let it rend thy soul!

Before the gates of fashion
    I daily bent my knee,
But I sought the shrine of passion,
    And found my idol,—thee;
Though never love intenser
    Had bowed a soul before it,
Thine eye was on the censer,
    And not the hand that bore it.

REFLECTIONS OF A PROUD PEDESTRIAN.

I saw the curl of his waving lash,
    And the glance of his knowing eye,
And I knew that he thought he was cutting a dash,
    As his steed went thundering by.

And he may ride in the rattling gig,
    Or flourish the Stanhope gay,
And dream that he looks exceeding big
    To the people that walk in the way ;

But he shall think, when the night is still,
    On the stable-boy's gathering numbers,
And the ghost of many a veteran bill
    Shall hover around his slumbers ;

The ghastly dun shall worry his sleep,
    And constables cluster around him,
And he shall creep from the wood-hole deep
    Where their spectre eyes have found him !

Ay ! gather your reins, and crack your thong,
    And bid your steed go faster ;
He does not know, as he scrambles along,
    That he has a fool for his master ;

And hurry away on your lonely ride,
    Nor deign from the mire to save me ;
I will paddle it stoutly at your side
    With the tandem that nature gave me !

THE POET'S LOT.

WHAT is a poet's love?—
  To write a girl a sonnet.
To get a ring, or some such thing,
  And fustianize upon it.

What is a poet's fame?—
  Sad hints about his reason,
And sadder praise from garreteers,
  To be returned in season.

Where go the poet's lines?—
  Answer, ye evening tapers!
Ye auburn locks, ye golden curls,
  Speak from your folded papers!

Child of the ploughshare, smile;
  Boy of the counter, grieve not,
Though muses round thy trundle-bed
  Their broidered tissue weave not.

The poet's future holds
  No civic wreath above him;
Nor slated roof, or varnished chaise,
  Nor wife nor child to love him.

Maid of the village inn,
    Who workest woe on satin
(The grass in black, the graves in **green,**
    The epitaph in Latin),

Trust not to them who say,
    In stanzas, they adore thee;
Oh rather sleep in churchyard clay,
    With urns and cherubs o'er thee!

DAILY TRIALS.

BY A SENSITIVE MAN.

Oh there are times
When all this fret and tumult that we hear
Do seem more stale than to the sexton's ear
    His own dull chimes.

Ding dong! ding dong!
The world is in a simmer like a sea
Over a pent volcano,—woe is me
    All the day long!

From crib to shroud!
Nurse o'er our cradles screameth lullaby,
And friends in boots tramp round us as we die,
    Snuffling aloud.

At morning's call
The small-voiced pug-dog welcomes in the sun,
And flea-bit mongrels, wakening one by one,
    Give answer all.

When evening dim
Draws round us, then the lonely caterwaul
Tart solo, sour duet, and general squall,—
    These are our hymn.

Women, with tongues
Like polar needles, ever on the jar,—
Men, plugless word-spouts, whose deep fountains are
     Within their lungs.

Children, with drums
Strapped round them by the fond paternal ass,
Peripatetics with a blade of grass
     Between their thumbs.

Vagrants, whose arts
Have caged some devil in their mad machine,
Which grinding, squeaks, with husky groans between,
     Come out by starts.

Cockneys that kill
Thin horses of a Sunday,—men, with clams,
Hoarse as young bisons roaring for their dams
     From hill to hill.

Soldiers, with guns
Making a nuisance of the blessed air,
Child-crying bellmen, children in despair
     Screeching for buns.

Storms, thunders, waves!
Howl, crash, and bellow till ye get your fill;
Ye sometimes rest; men never can be still
     But in their graves.

EVENING.

BY A TAILOR.

Day hath put on his jacket, and around
His burning bosom buttoned it with stars.
Here will I lay me on the velvet grass,
That is like padding to earth's meagre ribs,
And hold communion with the things about me.
Ah me! how lovely is the golden braid,
That binds the skirt of night's descending robe!
The thin leaves, quivering on their silken threads,
Do make a music like to rustling satin,
As the light breezes smooth their downy nap.

Ha! what is this that rises to my touch,
So like a cushion? Can it be a cabbage?
It is, it is that deeply injured flower,
Which boys do flout us with;—but yet I love thee,
Thou giant rose, wrapped in a green surtout.
Doubtless in Eden thou didst blush as bright
As these, thy puny brethren; and thy breath
Sweetened the fragrance of her spicy air;
But now thou seemest like a bankrupt beau,
Stripped of his gaudy hues and essences,
And growing portly in his sober garments.

Is that a swan that rides upon the water?
Oh! no, it is that other gentle bird,

Which is the patron of our noble calling.
I well remember, in my early years,
When these young hands first closed upon a goose;
I have a scar upon my thimble finger,
Which chronicles the hour of young ambition.
My father was a tailor, and his father,
And my sire's grandsire, all of them were tailors;
They had an ancient goose,—it was an heirloom
From some remoter tailor of our race.
It happened I did see it on a time
When none was near, and I did deal with it,
And it did burn me, oh, most fearfully!

It is a joy to straighten out one's limbs,
And leap elastic from the level counter,
Leaving the petty grievances of earth,
The breaking thread, the din of clashing shears,
And all the needles that do wound the spirit,
For such a pensive hour of soothing silence.
Kind Nature, shuffling in her loose undress,
Lays bare her shady bosom;—I can feel
With all around me;—I can hail the flowers
That sprig earth's mantle,—and yon quiet bird,
That rides the stream, is to me as a brother,
The vulgar know not all the hidden pockets,
Where Nature stows away her loveliness.
But this unnatural posture of the legs
Cramps my extended calves, and I must go
Where I can coil them in their wonted fashion.

THE DORCHESTER GIANT.

THERE was a giant in time of old,
    A mighty one was he;
He had a wife, but she was a scold,
So he kept her shut in his mammoth fold;
    And he had children three.

It happened to be an election day,
    And the giants were choosing a king;
The people were not democrats then,
They did not talk of the rights of men,
    And all that sort of thing.

Then the giant took his children three
    And fastened them in the pen;
The children roared; quoth the giant, "Be still!"
And Dorchester Heights and Milton Hill
    Rolled back the sound again.

Then he brought them a pudding stuffed with plums,
    As big as the State-House dome;
Quoth he, "There's something for you to eat;
So stop your mouths with your 'lection treat,
    And wait till your dad comes home."

So the giant pulled him a chestnut stout,
    And whittled the boughs away ;
The boys and their mother set up a shout,
Said he, " You're in, and you can't get out,
    Bellow as loud as you may."

Off he went, and he growled a tune
    As he strode the fields along ;
'Tis said a buffalo fainted away,
And fell as cold as a lump of clay,
    When he heard the giant's song.

But whether the story's true or not,
    It is not for me to show ;
There's many a thing that's twice as queer
In somebody's lectures that we hear,
    And those are true, you know.

What are those lone ones doing now,
    The wife and the children sad ?
Oh! they are in a terrible rout,
Screaming, and throwing their pudding about,
    Acting as they were mad.

They flung it over to Roxbury hills,
    They flung it over the plain,
And all over Milton and Dorchester too
Great lumps of pudding the giants threw ;
    They tumbled as thick as rain.

*   *   *   *   *   *

Giant and mammoth have passed away,
    For ages have floated by ;
The suet is hard as a marrow bone,
And every plum is turned to a stone,
    But there the puddings lie.

And if, some pleasant afternoon,
    You'll ask me out to ride,
The whole of the story I will tell,
And you shall see where the puddings fell,
    And pay for the punch besides.

TO THE PORTRAIT OF "A GENTLEMAN."

IN THE ATHENÆUM GALLERY.

It may be so,—perhaps thou hast
    A warm and loving heart;
I will not blame thee for thy face,
    Poor devil as thou art.

That thing, thou fondly deem'st a nose,
    Unsightly though it be,—
In spite of all the cold world's scorn,
    It may be much to thee.

Those eyes,—among thine elder friends
    Perhaps they pass for blue;—
No matter,—if a man can see,
    What more have eyes to do?

Thy mouth,—that fissure in thy face
    By something like a chin,—
May be a very useful place
    To put thy victual in.

I know thou hast a wife at home,
    I know thou hast a child,
By that subdued, domestic smile
    Upon thy features mild.

That wife sits fearless by thy side,
    That cherub on thy knee;
They do not shudder at thy looks,
    They do not shrink from thee.

Above thy mantel is a hook,—
    A portrait once was there;
It was thine only ornament,—
    Alas! that hook is bare.

She begged thee not to let it go,
    She begged thee all in vain;
She wept,—and breathed a trembling prayer
    To meet it safe again.

It was a bitter sight to see
    That picture torn away;
It was a solemn thought to think
    What all her friends would say!

And often in her calmer hours,
    And in her happy dreams,
Upon its long-deserted hook
    The absent portrait seems.

Thy wretched infant turns his head
    In melancholy wise,
And looks to meet the placid stare
    Of those unbending eyes.

I never saw thee, lovely one,—
  Perchance I never may ;
It is not often that we cross
  Such people in our way ;

But if we meet in distant years,
  Or on some foreign shore,
Sure I can take my Bible oath,
  I've seen that face before.

TO THE PORTRAIT OF "A LADY."

IN THE ATHENÆUM GALLERY.

WELL, Miss, I wonder where you live,
　　I wonder what's your name,
I wonder how you came to be
　　In such a stylish frame;
Perhaps you were a favorite child,
　　　　Perhaps an only one;
Perhaps your friends were not aware
　　You had your portrait done!

Yet you must be a harmless soul;
　　I cannot think that Sin
Would care to throw his loaded dice,
　　With such a stake to win;
I cannot think you would provoke
　　The poet's wicked pen,
Or make young women bite their lips,
　　Or ruin fine young men.

Pray, did you ever hear, my love,
　　Of boys that go about,
Who, for a very trifling sum
　　Will snip one's picture out?

107

I'm not averse to red and white,
  But all things have their place,
I think a profile cut in black
  Would suit your style of face!

I love sweet features; I will own
  That I should like myself
To see my portrait on a wall,
  Or bust upon a shelf;

But nature sometimes makes one up
  Of such sad odds and ends,
It really might be quite as well
  Hushed up among one's friends!

THE COMET.

The Comet! He is on his way,
　　And singing as he flies;
The whizzing planets shrink before
The spectre of the skies;
Ah! well may regal orbs burn blue,
And satellites turn pale,
Ten million cubic miles of head,
　　Ten billion leagues of tail!

On, on by whistling spheres of light,
　　He flashes and he flames;
He turns not to the left nor right,
　　He asks them not their names;
One spurn from his demoniac heel,—
　　Away, away they fly,
Where darkness might be bottled up
　　And sold for "Tyrian dye."

And what would happen to the land,
　　And how would look the sea,
If in the bearded devil's path
　　Our earth should chance to be?
Full hot and high the sea would boil,
　　Full red the forests gleam;
Methought I saw and heard it all
　　In a dyspeptic dream!

I saw a tutor take his tube
    The Comet's course to spy ;
I heard a scream,—the gathered rays
    Had stewed the tutor's eye ;
I saw a fort,—the soldiers all
    Were armed with goggles green ;
Pop cracked the guns ! whiz flew the balls !
    Bang went the magazine !

I saw a poet dip a scroll
    Each moment in a tub,
I read upon the warping back,
    "The Dream of Beelzebub" ;
He could not see his verses burn,
    Although his brain was fried,
And ever and anon he bent
    To wet them as they dried.

I saw the scalding pitch roll down
    The crackling, sweating pines,
And streams of smoke, like water-spouts,
    Burst through the rumbling mines ;
I asked the firemen why they made
    Such noise about the town ;
They answered not,—but all the while
    The brakes went up and down.

I saw a roasting pullet sit
    Upon a baking egg ;
I saw a cripple scorch his hand
    Extinguishing his leg ;

I saw nine geese upon the wing
    Towards the frozen pole,
And every mother's gosling fell
    Crisped to a crackling coal.

I saw the ox that browsed the grass
    Writhe in the blistering rays,
The herbage in his shrinking jaws
    Was all a fiery blaze;
I saw huge fishes, boiled to rags,
    Bob through the bubbling brine;
And thoughts of supper crossed my soul;
    I had been rash at mine.

Strange sights! strange sounds! O fearful dream!
    Its memory haunts me still,
The steaming sea, the crimson glare,
    That wreathed each wooded hill;
Stranger! if through thy reeling brain,
    Such midnight visions sweep,
Spare, spare, oh, spare thine evening meal,
    And sweet shall be thy sleep!

A NOONTIDE LYRIC.

The dinner-bell, the dinner-bell
 Is ringing loud and clear;
Through hill and plain, through street and lane,
 It echoes far and near;
From curtained hall, and whitewashed stall,
 Wherever men can hide,
Like bursting waves from ocean caves,
 They float upon the tide.

I smell the smell of roasted meat!
 I hear the hissing fry!
The beggars know where they can go,
 But where, oh, where shall I?
At twelve o'clock men took my hand,
 At two they only stare,
And eye me with a fearful look,
 As if I were a bear!

The poet lays his laurels down
 And hastens to his greens;
The happy tailor quits his goose,
 To riot on his beans;
The weary cobbler snaps his thread,
 The printer leaves his pi;
His very devil hath a home,
 But what, oh, what have I?

Methinks I hear an angel voice,
    That softly seems to say :
" Pale stranger, all may yet be well,
    Then wipe thy tears away ;
Erect thy head, and cock thy hat,
    And follow me afar,
And thou shalt have a jolly meal
    And charge it at the bar."

I hear the voice ! I go ! I go !
    Prepare your meat and wine !
They little heed their future need,
    Who pay not when they dine.
Give me to-day the rosy bowl,
    Give me one golden dream,—
To-morrow kick away the stool,
    And dangle from the beam!

8

THE BALLAD OF THE OYSTERMAN.

It was a tall young oysterman lived by the river-
side,
His shop was just upon the bank, his boat was on
the tide;
The daughter of a fisherman, that was so straight
and slim,
Lived over on the other bank, right opposite to
him.

It was the pensive oysterman that saw a lovely
maid,
Upon a moonlight evening, a sitting in the shade;
He saw her wave her handkerchief, as much as if to
say,
"I'm wide awake, young oysterman, and all the
folks away."

Then up arose the oysterman, and to himself said
he,
"I guess I'll leave the skiff at home, for fear that
folks should see;
I read it in the story-book, that, for to kiss his dear,
Leander swam the Hellespont,—and I will swim
this here."

Tnd he has leaped into the waves, and crossed the
shining stream,

And he has clambered up the bank, all in the moonlight gleam;
Oh, there were kisses sweet as dew, and words as
  soft as rain,—
But they have heard her father's step, and in he
  leaps again!

Out spoke the ancient fisherman,—" Oh, what was
  that, my daughter?"
" 'Twas nothing but a pebble, sir, I threw into the
  water;"
" And what is that, pray tell me, love, that paddles
  off so fast?"
" It's nothing but a porpoise, sir, that's been a
  swimming past."

Out spoke the ancient fisherman,—" Now bring me
  my harpoon!
I'll get into my fishing-boat, and fix the fellow
  soon;"
Down fell that pretty innocent, as falls a snow-
  white lamb,
Her hair drooped round her pallid cheeks, like sea-
  weed on a clam.

Alas for those two loving ones! she waked not from
  her swound,
And he was taken with the cramp, and in the
  waves was drowned;
But Fate has metamorphosed them, in pity of their
  woe,
And now they keep an oyster-shop for mermaids
  down below.

THE MUSIC-GRINDERS.

THERE are three ways in which men take
    One's money from his purse,
And very hard it is to tell
    Which of the three is worse;
But all of them are bad enough
    To make a body curse.

You're riding out some pleasant day,
    And counting up your gains;
A fellow jumps from out a bush,
    And takes your horse's reins,
Another hints some words about
    A bullet in your brains.

It's hard to met such pressing friends
    In such a lonely spot;
It's very hard to lose your cash,
    But harder to be shot;
And so you take your wallet out,
    Though you would rather not.

Perhaps you're going out to dine,—
    Some filthy creature begs
You'll hear about the cannon-ball
    That carried off his pegs,
And says it is a dreadful thing
    For men to lose their legs.

I16

He tells you of his starving wife,
    His children to be fed,
Poor little, lovely innocents,
    All clamorous for bread,—
And so you kindly help to put
    A bachelor to bed.

You're sitting on your window-seat
    Beneath a cloudless moon;
You hear a sound, that seems to wear
    The semblance of a tune,
As if a broken fife should strive
    To drown a cracked bassoon.

And nearer, nearer still, the tide
    Of music seems to come,
There's something like a human voice,
    And something like a drum;
You sit in speechless agony,
    Until your ear is numb.

Poor "home, sweet home," should seem to be
    A very dismal place;
Your "auld acquaintance," all at once,
    Is altered in the face;
Their discords sting through Burns and Moore,
    Like hedgehogs dressed in lace.

You think they are crusaders, sent
    From some infernal clime,
To pluck the eyes of Sentiment,
    And dock the tail of Rhyme,

To crack the voice of Melody,
    And break the legs of Time.

But hark! the air again is still,
    The music all is ground,
And silence, like a poultice, comes
    To heal the blows of sound;
It cannot be,—it is,—it is,—
    A hat is going round!

No! Pay the dentist when he leaves
    A fracture in your jaw;
And pay the owner of the bear,
    That stunned you with his paw,
And buy the lobster, that has had
    Your knuckles in his claw;

But if you are a portly man,
    Put on your fiercest frown,
And talk about a constable
    To turn them out of town;
Then close your sentence with an oath,
    And shut the window down!

And if you are a slender man,
    Not big enough for that,
Or, if you cannot make a speech,
    Because you are a flat,
Go very quietly and drop
    A button in the hat!

THE TREADMILL SONG.

THE stars are rolling in the sky,
    The earth rolls on below,
And we can feel the rattling wheel
    Revolving as we go.
Then tread away, my gallant boys,
    And make the axle fly;
Why should not wheels go round about,
    Like planets in the sky?

Wake up, wake up, my duck-legged man,
    And stir your solid pegs!
Arouse, arouse, my gawky friend,
    And shake your spider legs;
What though you're awkward at the trade,
    There's time enough to learn,—
So lean upon the rail, my lad,
    And take another turn.

They've built us up a noble wall,
    To keep the vulgar out;
We've nothing in the world to do,
    But just to walk about;
So faster, now, you middle men,
    And try to beat the ends,—
It's pleasant work to ramble round
    Among one's honest friends.

Here, tread upon the long man's toes,
    He shan't be lazy here,—
And punch the little fellow's ribs,
    And tweak that lubber's ear,—
He's lost them both,—don't pull his hair,
    Because he wears a scratch,
But poke him in the further eye,
    That isn't in the patch.

Hark! fellows, there's the supper-bell,
    And so our work is done;
It's pretty sport,—suppose we take
    A round or two for fun!
If ever they should turn me out,
    When I have better grown,
Now hang me, but I mean to have
    A treadmill of my own!

THE SEPTEMBER GALE.

I'm not a chicken; I have seen
    Full many a chill September,
And though I was a youngster then,
    That gale I well remember;
The day before, my kite-string snapped,
    And I, my kite pursuing,
The wind whisked off my palm-leaf hat;—
    For me two storms were brewing!

It came as quarrels sometimes do,
    When married folks get clashing;
There was a heavy sigh or two,
    Before the fire was flashing,—
A little stir among the clouds,
    Before they rent asunder,—
A little rocking of the trees,
    And then came on the thunder.

Lord! how the ponds and rivers boiled,
    And how the shingles rattled!
And oaks were scattered on the ground
    As if the Titans battled;
And all above was in a howl,
    And all below a clatter,—

The earth was like a frying-pan,
  Or some such hissing matter.

It chanced to be our washing-day,
  And all our things were drying:
The storm came roaring through the lines,
  And set them all a flying;
I saw the shirts and petticoats
  Go riding off like witches;
I lost, ah! bitterly I wept,—
  I lost my Sunday breeches!

I saw them straddling through the air,
  Alas! too late to win them;
I saw them chase the clouds as if
  The devil had been in them;
They were my darlings and my pride,
  My boyhood's only riches,—
"Farewell, farewell," I faintly cried,—
  "My breeches! O my breeches!"

That night I saw them in my dreams,
  How changed from what I knew them!
The dews had steeped their faded threads,
  The winds had whistled through them;
I saw the wide and ghastly rents
  Where demon claws had torn them;
A hole was in their amplest part,
  As if an imp had worn them.

I have had many happy years,
  And tailors kind and clever,

But those young pantaloons have gone
    Forever and forever!
And not till fate has cut the last
    Of all my earthly stitches,
This aching heart shall cease to mourn
    My loved, my long-lost breeches!

THE HEIGHT OF THE RIDICULOUS.

I WROTE some lines once on a time
    In wondrous merry mood,
And thought, as usual, men would say
    They were exceeding good.

They were so queer, so very queer,
    I laughed as I would die;
Albeit, in the general way,
    A sober man am I.

I called my servant, and he came;
    How kind it was of him,
To mind a slender man like me,
    He of the mighty limb!

"These to the printer," I exclaimed,
    And, in my humorous way,
I added (as a trifling jest),
    "There'll be the devil to pay."

He took the paper, and I watched,
    And saw him peep within;
At the first line he read, his face
    Was all upon the grin.

He read the next; the grin grew broad,
    And shot from ear to ear;
He read the third; a chuckling noise
    I now began to hear.

The fourth; he broke into a roar;
    The fifth; his waistband split;
The sixth; he burst five buttons off,
    And tumbled in a fit.

Ten days and nights, with sleepless eye,
    I watched that wretched man,
And since, I never dare to write
    As funny as I can.

THE HOT SEASON.

THE folks, that on the first of May
 Wore winter-coats and hose,
Began to say, the first of June,
 "Good Lord! how hot it grows."
At last two Fahrenheits blew up,
 And killed two children small,
And one barometer shot dead
 A tutor with its ball!

Now all day long the locusts sang
 Among the leafless trees;
Three new hotels warped inside out,
 The pumps could only wheeze;
And ripe old wine, that twenty years
 Had cobwebbed o'er in vain,
Came spouting through the rotten corks,
 Like Jolys' best Champagne!

The Worcester locomotives did
 Their trip in half an hour;
The Lowell cars ran forty miles
 Before they checked the power;
Roll brimstone soon became a drug,
 And loco-focos fell;

All asked for ice, but everywhere
    Saltpetre was to sell.

Plump men of mornings ordered tights,
    But, ere the scorching noons,
Their candle-moulds had grown as loose
    As Cossack pantaloons!
The dogs ran mad,—men could not try
    If water they would choose;
A horse fell dead,—he only left
    Four red-hot, rusty shoes!

But soon the people could not bear
    The slightest hint of fire;
Allusions to caloric drew
    A flood of savage ire;
The leaves on heat were all torn out
    From every book at school,
And many blackguards kicked and caned,
    Because they said,—" Keep cool!"

The gas-light companies were mobbed,
    The bakers all were shot,
The penny press began to talk
    Of Lynching Poctor Nott;
And all about the warehouse steps
    Were angry men in droves,
Crashing and splintering through the doors
    To smash the patent stoves!

The abolition men and maids
    Were tanned to such a hue,

You scarce could tell them from their friends
    Unless their eyes were blue ;
And, when I left, society
    Had burst its ancient guards,
And Brattle Street and Temple Place
    Were interchanging cards.

POEMS

ADDED SINCE THE FIRST EDITION.

DEPARTED DAYS.

Yes, dear departed, cherished days,
  Could Memory's hand restore
Your morning light, your evening rays,
  From Time's gray urn once more,—
Then might this restless heart be still,
  This straining eye might close,
And Hope her fainting pinions fold,
  While the fair phantoms rose.

But, like a child in ocean's arms,
  We strive against the stream,
Each moment farther from the shore
  Where life's young fountains gleam;—
Each moment fainter wave the fields,
  And wider rolls the sea;
The mist grows dark,—the sun goes down,—
  Day breaks,—and where are we?

THE STEAMBOAT.

See how yon flaming herald treads
    The ridged and rolling waves,
As, crashing o'er their crested heads,
    She bows her surly slaves!
With foam before and fire behind,
    She rends the clinging sea,
That flies before the roaring wind,
    Beneath her hissing lee.

The morning spray, like sea-born flowers,
    With heaped and glistening bells
Falls round her fast, in ringing showers,
    With every wave that swells;
And, burning o'er the midnight deep,
    In lurid fringes thrown,
The living gems of ocean sweep
    Along her flashing zone.

With clashing wheel, and lifting keel,
    And smoking torch on high,
When winds are loud, and billows reel,
    She thunders foaming by;
When seas are silent and serene,
    With even beam she glides,

The sunshine glimmering through the green
    That skirts her gleaming sides.

Now, like a wild nymph, far apart
    She veils her shadowy form,
The beating of her restless heart
    Still sounding through the storm;
Now answers, like a courtly dame,
    The reddening surges o'er,
With flying scarf of spangled flame,
    The Pharos of the shore.

To-night yon pilot shall not sleep,
    Who trims his narrowed sail;
To-night yon frigate scarce shall keep
    Her broad breast to the gale;
And many a foresail, scooped and strained,
    Shall break from yard and stay,
Before this smoky wreath has stained
    The rising mist of day.

Hark! hark! I hear yon whistling shroud,
    I see yon quivering mast;
The black throat of the hunted cloud
    Is panting forth the blast!
An hour, and, whirled like winnowing chaff,
    The giant surge shall fling
His tresses o'er yon pennon staff,
    White as the sea-bird's wing!

Yet rest, ye wanderers of the deep ;
  Nor wind nor wave shall tire
Those fleshless arms, whose pulses leap
  With floods of living fire ;
Sleep on,—and, when the morning light
  Streams o'er the shining bay,
Oh, think of those for whom the night
  Shall never wake in day !

THE PARTING WORD.

I MUST leave thee, lady sweet!
Months shall waste before we meet;
Winds are fair, and sails are spread,
Anchors leave their ocean bed;
Ere this shining day grow dark,
Skies shall gird my shoreless bark;
Through thy tears, O lady mine,
Read thy lover's parting line.

When the first sad sun shall set,
Thou shalt tear thy locks of jet;
When the morning star shall rise
Thou shalt wake with weeping eyes;
When the second sun goes down,
Thou more tranquil shalt be grown,
Taught too well that wild despair
Dims thine eyes, and spoils thy hair.

All the first unquiet week
Thou shalt wear a smileless cheek;
In the first month's second half
Thou shalt once attempt to laugh;
Then in Pickwick thou shalt dip,
Slightly puckering round the lip,
Till at last, in sorrow's spite,
Samuel makes thee laugh outright.

While the first seven mornings last,
Round thy chamber bolted fast,
Many a youth shall fume and pout,
"Hang the girl, she's always out!"
While the second week goes round,
Vainly shall they ring and pound;
When the third week shall begin,
"Martha, let the creature in."

Now once more the flattering throng
Round thee flock with smile and song,
But thy lips, unweaned as yet,
Lisp, "Oh, how can I forget!"
Men and devils both contrive
Traps for catching girls alive;
Eve was duped, and Helen kissed
How, oh, how can you resist?

First be careful of your fan,
Trust it not to youth or man;
Love has filled a pirate's sail
Often with its perfumed gale.
Mind your kerchief most of all,
Fingers touch when kerchiefs fall;
Shorter ell than mercers clip,
Is the space from hand to lip.

Trust not such as talk in tropes,
Full of pistols, daggers, ropes;
All the hemp that Russia bears
Scarce would answer lovers' prayers;

Never thread was spun so fine,
Never spider stretched the line,
Would not hold the lovers true
That would really swing for you.

Fiercely some shall storm and swear,
Beating breasts in black despair;
Others murmur with a sigh,
You must melt or they will die;
Painted words on empty lies,
Grubs with wings like butterflies;
Let them die, and welcome, too;
Pray what better could they do?

Fare thee well, if years efface
From thy heart love's burning trace,
Keep, oh keep that hallowed seat
From the tread of vulgar feet;
If the blue lips of the sea
Wait with icy kiss for me,
Let not thine forget the vow,
Sealed how often, Love, as now!

SONG,

WRITTEN FOR THE DINNER GIVEN TO CHARLES DICKENS, BY THE YOUNG MEN OF BOSTON, FEBRUARY 1, 1842.

THE stars their early vigils keep,
　　The silent hours are near
When drooping eyes forget to weep,—
　　Yet still we linger here;
And what,—the passing churl may ask,—
　　Can claim such wondrous power,
That Toil forgets his wonted task,
　　And Love his promised hour?

The Irish harp no longer thrills,
　　Or breathes a fainter tone;
The clarion blast from Scotland's hills
　　Alas! no more is blown;
And Passion's burning lip bewails
　　Her Harold's wasted fire,
Still lingering o'er the dust that veils
　　The Lord of England's lyre.

But grieve not o'er its broken strings,
　　Nor think its soul hath died,
While yet the lark at heaven's gate sings
　　As once o'er Avon's side;

138

While gentle summer sheds her **bloom,**
 And dewy blossoms wave,
Alike o'er Juliet's storied **tomb**
 And Nelly's nameless **grave.**

Thou glorious island of the sea!
 Though wide the wasting **flood**
That parts our distant land from **thee,**
 We claim thy generous blood;
Nor o'er thy far horizon springs
 One hallowed star of fame,
But kindles, like an angel's **wings,**
 Our western skies in **flame !**

LINES

Come back to your mother, ye children, for shame,
Who have wandered like truants, for riches or
    fame !
With a smile on her face, and a sprig in her cap,
She calls you to feast from her bountiful lap.

Come out from your alleys, your courts, and your
    lanes,
And breathe, like young eagles, the air of our plains ;
Take a whiff from our fields, and your excellent wives
Will declare it's all nonsense insuring your lives.

Come you of the law, who can talk, if you please,
Till the man in the moon will allow it's a cheese,
And leave " the old lady, that never tells lies,"
To sleep with her handkerchief over her eyes.

Ye healers of men, for a moment decline
Your feats in the rhubarb and ipecac line ;
While you shut up your turnpike, your neighbors
    can go
The old roundabout road, to the regions below.

You clerk, on whose ears are a couple of pens,
And whose head is an ant-hill of units and tens;
Though Plato denies you, we welcome you still
As a featherless biped, in spite of your quill.

Poor drudge of the city! how happy he feels,
With the burs on his legs, and the grass at his
    heels!
No *dodger* behind, his bandannas to share,
No constable grumbling, "You mustn't walk
    there!"

In yonder green meadow, to memory dear,
He slaps a mosquito and brushes a tear;
The dewdrops hang round him on blossoms and
    shoots,
He breathes but one sigh for his youth and his
    boots.

There stands the old schoolhouse, hard by the old
    church;
That tree at its side had the flavor of birch;
Oh, sweet were the days of his juvenile tricks,
Though the prarie of youth had so many "big
    licks."

By the side of yon river he weeps and he slumps,
The boots fill with water, as if they were pumps;
Till, sated with rapture, he steals to his bed,
With a glow in his heart and a cold in his head.

'Tis past,—he is dreaming,—I see him again;
The ledger returns as by legerdemain;
His neckcloth is damp with an easterly flaw,
And he holds in his fingers an omnibus straw.

He dreams the chill gust is a blossomy gale,
That the straw is a rose from his dear native **vale**;
And murmurs, unconscious of space and of time,
" A I. Extra-super. Ah, isn't it PRIME!"

Oh, what are the prizes we perish to win
To the first little "shiner" we caught with **a pin!**
No soil upon earth is so dear to our eyes
As the soil we first stirred in terrestrial pies!

Then come from all parties, and parts, to our **feast;**
Though not at the "Astor," we'll give you **at least**
A bite at an apple, a seat on the grass,
And the best of old—water—at nothing a glass.

VERSES FOR AFTER-DINNER.

Φ. B. K. SOCIETY, 1844.

I was thinking last night, as I sat in the cars,
With the charmingest prospect of cinders and stars,
Next Thursday is—bless me!—how hard it will
    be,
If that cannibal president calls upon me!

There is nothing on earth that he will not devour,
From a tutor in seed to a freshman in flower;
No sage is too gray, and no youth is too green,
And you can't be too plump, though you're never
    too lean.

While others enlarge on the boiled and the roast,
He serves a raw clergyman up with a toast,
Or catches some doctor, quite tender and young,
And basely insists on a bit of his tongue.

Poor victim, prepared for his classical spit,
With a stuffing of praise, and a basting of wit,
You may twitch at your collar, and wrinkle your
    brow,
But you're up on your legs, and you're in for it
    now.

Oh, think of your friends,—they are waiting to
　　hear
Those jokes that are thought so remarkably queer;
And all the Jack Horners of metrical buns
Are prying and fingering to pick out the puns.

Those thoughts which, like chickens, will always
　　thrive best
When reared by the heat of the natural nest,
Will perish if hatched from their embryo dream
In the mist and the glow of convivial steam.

Oh pardon me, then, if I meekly retire,
With a very small flash of ethereal fire;
No rubbing will kindle your Lucifer match,
If the *fiz* does not follow the primitive scratch.

Dear friends, who are listening so sweetly the while,
With your lips double reefed in a snug little
　　smile,—
I leave you two fables, both drawn from the
　　deep,—
The shells you can drop, but the pearls you may
　　keep.

*　　*　　*　　*　　*　　*

The fish called the FLOUNDER, perhaps you may know,
Has one side for use and another for show;
One side for the public, a delicate brown,
And one that is white, which he always keeps
　　down.

A very young flounder, the flattest of flats
(And they're none of them thicker than opera hats),
Was speaking more freely than charity taught
Of a friend and relation that just had been caught.

" My ! what an exposure ! just see what a sight !
I blush for my race,—he is showing his white !
Such spinning and wriggling,—why, what does he
    wish ?
How painfully small to respectable fish ! "

Then said an old SCULPIN,—" My freedom excuse,
But you're playing the cobbler with holes in your
    shoes ;
Your brown side is up,—but just wait till you're
    tried,
And you'll find that all flounders are white on one
    side."

* * * * * *

There's a slice near the PICKEREL's pectoral fins,
Where the *thorax* leaves off and the *venter* begins ;
Which his brother, survivor of fish-hooks and lines
Though fond of his family, never declines.

He loves his relations ; he feels they'll be missed ;
But that one little tit-bit he cannot resist ;
So your bait may be swallowed, no matter how
    fast,
For you catch your next fish with a piece of the
    last.

10

And thus, O survivor, whose merciless fate
Is to take the next hook with the president's bait,
You are lost while you snatch from the end of **his**
   line
The morsel he rent from this bosom of mine!

SONG.

FOR A TEMPERANCE DINNER TO WHICH LADIES WERE INVITED. (NEW YORK MERCANTILE LIBRARY ASSOCIATION, NOVEMBER, 1842.)

A HEALTH to dear woman! She bids us untwine,
From the cup it encircles, the fast-clinging vine;
But her cheek in its crystal with pleasure will glow,
And mirror its bloom in the bright wave below.

A health to sweet woman! Ahe days are no more
When she watched for her lord till the revel was o'er,
And smoothed the white pillow, and blushed when
　　he came,
As she pressed her cold lips on his forehead of
　　flame.
Alas for the loved one! too spotless and fair
The joys of his banquet to chasten and share;
Her eye lost its light that his goblet might shine,
And the rose of her cheek was dissolved in his
　　wine.

Joy smiles in the fountain, health flows in the rills,
As their ribands of silver unwind from the hills;
They breathe not the mist of the bacchanal's
　　dream,
But the lilies of innocence float on their stream.

147

Then a health and a welcome to woman once
    more!
She brings up a passport that laughs at our door;
It is written on crimson,—its letters are pearls,—
It is countersigned *Nature.*——So, room for the
    Girls!

THE ONLY DAUGHTER.

(ILLUSTRATION OF A PICTURE.)

THEY bid me strike the idle strings,
   As if my summer days
Had shaken sunbeams from their wings,
   To warm my autumn lays;
They bring to me their painted urn,
   As if it were not time
To lift my gauntlet and to spurn
   The lists of boyish rhyme;
And, were it not that I have still
   Some weakness in my heart
That clings around my stronger will
   And pleads for gentler art,
Perchance I had not turned away
   The thoughts grown tame with toil,
To cheat this lone and pallid ray,
   That wastes the midnight oil.

Alas! with every year I feel
   Some roses leave my brow;
Too young for wisdom's tardy seal,
   Too old for garlands now;
Yet, while the dewy breath of spring
   Steals o'er the tingling air,

And spreads and fans each emerald wing
    The forest soon shall wear,
How bright the opening year would seem,
    Had I one look like thine,
To meet me when the morning beam
    Unseals these lids of mine :
Too long I bear this lonely lot,
    That bids my heart run wild
To press the lips that love me not,
    To clasp the stranger's child.

How oft beyond the dashing seas,
    Amidst those royal bowers,
Where danced the lilacs in the breeze,
    And swung the chestnut flowers,
I wandered like a wearied slave
    Whose morning task is done,
To watch the little hands that gave
    Their whiteness to the sun;
To revel in the bright young eyes,
    Whose lustre sparkled through
The sable fringe of southern skies,
    Or gleamed in Saxon blue!
How oft I heard another's name
    Called in some truant's tone;
Sweet accents! which I longed to claim,
    To learn and lisp my own!

Too soon the gentle hands, that pressed
    The ringlets of the child,
Are folded on the faithful breast
    Where first he breathed and smiled;

Too oft the clinging arms untwine,
  The melting lips forget,
And darkness veils the bridal shrine
  Where wreaths and torches met;
If Heaven but leaves a single thread
  Of Hope's dissolving chain,
Even when her parting plumes are spread,
  It bids them fold again;
The cradle rocks beside the tomb;
  The cheek now changed and chill,
Smiles on us in the morning bloom
  Of one that loves us still.

Sweet image! I have done thee wrong
  To claim this destined lay;
The leaf that asked an idle song
  Must bear my tears away.
Yet, in thy memory shouldst thou keep
  This else forgotten strain,
Till years have taught thine eyes to weep
  And flattery's voice is vain;
Oh, then, thou fledgling of the nest,
  Like the long-wandering dove,
Thy weary heart may faint for rest,
  As mine, on changeless love;
And, while these sculptured lines retrace
  The hours now dancing by,
This vision of thy girlish grace
  May cost thee, too, a sigh.

LEXINGTON.

Slowly the mist o'er the meadow was creeping,
  Bright on the dewy buds glistened the sun,
When from his couch, while his children were
    sleeping,
  Rose the bold rebel and shouldered his gun.
        Waving her golden veil
        Over the silent dale
Blithe looked the morning on cottage and spire;
        Hushed was his parting sigh,
        While from his noble eye
Flashed the last sparkle of liberty's fire.

On the smooth green where the fresh leaf is spring-
    ing
  Calmly the first-born of glory have met;
Hark! the death-volley around them is ringing!
  Look! with their life-blood the young grass is
    wet!
        Faint is the feeble breath,
        Murmuring low in death,
"Tell to our sons how their fathers have died;"
        Nerveless the iron hand,
        Raised for its native land,
Lies by the weapon that gleams at its side.

Over the hillsides the wild knell is tolling,
  From their far hamlets the yeomanry come;
152

As through the storm-clouds the thunder-burst roll-
    ing
  Circles the beat of the mustering drum.
      Fast on the soldier's path
      Darken the waves of wrath,
Long have they gathered and loud shall they fall;
      Red glares the musket's flash,
      Sharp rings the rifle's crash,
Blazing and clanging from thicket and wall.

Gayly the plume of the horseman was dancirg,
  Never to shadow his cold brow again;
Proudly at morning the war-steed was prancing,
  Reeking and panting he droops on the rein;
      Pale is the lip of scorn,
      Voiceless the trumpet horn,
Torn is the silken-fringed red cross on high;
      Many a belted breast
      Low on the turf shall rest,
Ere the dark hunters the herd have past by.

Snow-girdled crags where the hoarse wind is raving,
  Rocks where the weary floods murmur and wail,
Wilds where the fern by the furrow is waving,
  Reeled with the echoes that rode on the gale;
      Far as the tempest thrills
      Over the darkened hills,
Far as the sunshine streams over the plain,
      Roused by the tyrant band,
      Woke all the mighty land,
Girded for battle, from mountain to main.

Green be the graves where her martyrs are lying!
  Shroudless and tombless they sunk to their rest,—
While o'er their ashes the starry fold flying
  Wraps the proud eagle they roused from his
      nest.
          Borne on her northern pine,
          Long o'er the foaming brine
Spread her broad banner to storm and to sun;
          Heaven keep her ever free,
          Wide as o'er land and sea
Floats the fair emblem her heroes have won.

THE ISLAND HUNTING SONG.

No more the summer floweret charms,
    The leaves will soon be sere,
And Autumn folds his jewelled arms
    Around the dying year;
So, ere the waning seasons claim
    Our leafless groves awhile,
With golden wine and glowing flame
    We'll crown our lonely isle.

Once more the merry voices sound
    Within the antlered hall,
And long and loud the baying hounds
    Return the hunter's call;
And through the woods, and o'er the hill,
    And far along the bay,
The driver's horn is sounding shrill,—
    Up, sportsmen, and away!

No bars of steel, or walls of stone,
    Our little empire bound,
But, circling with his azure zone,
    The sea runs foaming round;
The whitening wave, the purpled skies,
    The blue and lifted shore,
Braid with their dim and blending dyes
    Our wide horizon o'er.

And who will leave the grave debate
    That shakes the smoky town,
To rule amid our island-state,
    And wear our oak-leaf crown?
And who will be awhile content
    To hunt our woodland game,
And leave the vulgar pack that scent
    The reeking track of fame?

Ah, who that shares in toils like these
    Will sigh not to prolong
Our days beneath the broad-leaved trees,
    Our nights of mirth and song?
Then leave the dust of noisy streets,
    Ye outlaws of the wood,
And follow through his green retreats
    Your noble Robin Hood.

QUESTIONS AND ANSWERS.

WHERE, oh where are the visions of morning,
　　Fresh as the dews of our prime?
Gone, like tenants that quit without warning,
　　Down the back entry of time.

Where, oh where are life's lilies and roses,
　　Nursed in the golden dawn's smile?
Dead as the bulrushes round little Moses,
　　On the old banks of the Nile.

Where are the Marys, and Anns, and Elizas,
　　Loving and lovely of yore?
Look in the columns of old *Advertisers,*—
　　Married and dead by the score.

Where the gray colts and the ten-year-old fillies,
　　Saturday's triumph and joy?
Gone like our friend πόδας ὠκυς Achilles,
　　Homer's ferocious old boy.

Die-away dreams of ecstatic emotion,
　　Hopes like young eagles at play,
Vows of unheard-of and endless devotion,
　　How ye have faded away!

Yet, though the ebbing of Time's mighty river
　　Leave our young blossoms to die,
Let him roll smooth in his current forever,
　　Till the last pebble is dry.

A SONG,

FOR THE CENTENNIAL CELEBRATION OF HARVARD COLLEGE, 1836.

WHEN the Puritans came over,
    Our hills and swamps to clear,
The woods were full of catamounts,
    And Indians red as deer,
With tomahawks and scalping-knives,
    That make folks' heads look queer;—
Oh, the ship from England used to bring
    A hundred wigs a year!

The crows came cawing through the air
    To pluck the pilgrims' corn,
The bears came snuffing round the door
    Whene'er a babe was born,
The rattlesnakes were bigger round
    Than the butt of the old ram's horn
The deacon blew at meeting time
    On every " Sabbath " morn.

But soon they knocked the wigwams down,
    And pine-tree trunk and limb
Began to sprout among the leaves
    In shape of steeples slim;

158

And out the little wharves were stretched
　　Along the ocean's rim,
And up the little schoolhouse shot
　　To keep the boys in trim.

And when, at length, the College rose,
　　The sachem cocked his eye
At every tutor's meagre ribs
　　Whose coat-tails whistled by ;
But, when the Greek and Hebrew words
　　Came tumbling from their jaws,
The copper-colored children all
　　Ran screaming to the squaws.

And who was on the Catalogue
　　When college was begun ?
Two nephews of the President,
　　And *the* Professor's son,
(They turned a little Indian by,
　　As brown as any bun) ;
Lord ! how the seniors knocked about
　　The freshman class of one !

They had not then the dainty things
　　That commons now afford,
But *succotash* and *hominy*
　　Were smoking on the board ;
They did not rattle round in gigs,
　　Or dash in long-tail blues,
But always on Commencement Days
　　The tutors blacked their shoes.

God bless the ancient Puritans!
　　Their lot was hard enough;
But honest hearts make iron arms,
　　And tender maids are tough;
So love and faith have formed and fed
　　Our true-born Yankee stuff,
And keep the kernel in the shell
　　The British found so rough!

TERPSICHORE.[1]

In narrowest girdle, O reluctant Muse,
In closest frock and Cinderella shoes,
Bound to the foot-lights for thy brief display,
One zephyr step, and then dissolve away !

Short is the space that gods and men can spare
To Song's twin brother when she is not there.
Let others water every lusty line,
As Homer's heroes did their purple wine ;
Pierian revellers !   Known in strains like these
The native juice, the real honest squeeze,—
Strains that, diluted to the twentieth power,
In yon grave temple [2] might have filled an hour.

Small room for Fancy's many-chorded lyre,
For Wit's bright rockets with their trains of fire,
For Pathos, struggling vainly to surprise
The iron tutor's tear denying eyes,
For Mirth, whose finger with delusive wile

[1] Read at the Annual Dinner of the Φ. B. K. Society, at Cambridge, August 24, 1843.

[2] The Annual Poem is always delivered in the neighboring church.

11

Turns the grim key of many a rusty smile,
For Satire, emptying his corrosive flood
On hissing Folly's gas-exhaling brood,
The pun, the fun, the moral and the joke,
The hit, the thrust, the pugilistic poke,—
Small space for these, so pressed by niggard Time,
Like that false matron, known to nursery rhyme,—
Insidious Morey,—scarce her tale begun,
Ere listening infants weep the story done.

O had we room to rip the mighty bags
That Time, the harlequin, has stuffed with rags!
Grant us one moment to unloose the strings,
While the old gray-beard shuts his leather wings.
But what a heap of motley trash appears
Crammed in the bundles of successive years!
As the lost rustic on some festal day
Stares through the concourse in its vast array,—
Where in one cake a throng of faces runs,
All stuck together like a sheet of buns,—
And throws the bait of some unheeded name,
Or shoots a wink with most uncertain aim,
So roams my vision, wandering over all,
And strives to choose, but knows not where to fall.

Skins of flayed authors,—husks of dead reviews,—
The turn-coat's clothes,—the office-seeker's shoes,—
Scraps from cold feasts, where conversation runs
Through mouldy toasts to oxidated puns,
And grating songs a listening crowd endures,
Rasped from the throats of bellowing amateurs ;—

Sermons, whose writers played such dangerous tricks
Their own heresiarchs called them heretics
(Strange that one term such distant poles should
    link,
The Priestleyan's copper and the Puseyan's zinc);—
Poems that shuffle with superfluous legs
A blindfold minuet over addled eggs,
Where all the syllables that end in êd,
Like old dragoons, have cuts across the head;—
Essays so dark Champollion might despair
To guess what mummy of a thought was there,
Where our poor English, striped with foreign phrase,
Looks like a Zebra in a parson's chaise;—
Lectures that cut our dinners down to roots,
Or prove (by monkeys) men should stick to fruits;
Delusive error,—as at trifling charge
Professor Gripes will certify at large;—
Mesmeric pamphlets, which to facts appeal,
Each fact as slippery as a fresh-caught eel;—
And figured heads, whose hieroglyphs invite
To wandering knaves that discount fools at sight;—
Such things as these, with heaps of unpaid bills,
And candy puffs and homœopathic pills,
And ancient bell-crowns with contracted rim,
And bonnets hideous with expanded brim,
And coats whose memory turns the sartor pale,
Their sequels tapering like a lizard's tail;—
How might we spread them to the smiling day,
And toss them, fluttering like the new-mown hay,
To laughter's light or sorrow's pitying shower,
Were these brief minutes lengthened to an hour.

The narrow moments fit like Sunday shoes,
How vast the heap, how quickly must we choose;
A few small scraps from out his mountain mass
We snatch in haste, and let the vagrant pass.

This shrunken CRUST that Cerberus could not bite,
Stamped (in one corner) " Pickwick copyright,"
Kneaded by youngsters, raised by flattery's yeast,
Was once a loaf, and helped to make a feast.
He for whose sake the glittering show appears
Has sown the world with laughter and with tears,
And they whose welcome wets the bumper's brim
Have wit and wisdom,—for they all quote him.
So, many a tongue the evening hour prolongs
With spangled speeches,—let alone the songs,—
Statesmen grow merry, lean attorneys laugh,
And weak teetotals warm to half and half,
And beardless Tullys, new to festive scenes,
Cut their first crop of youth's precocious greens,
And wits stand ready for impromptu claps,
With loaded barrels and percussion caps,
And Pathos, cantering through the minor keys,
Waves all her onions to the trembling breeze;
While the great yeasted views with silent glee
His scattered limbs in Yankee fricassee.

Sweet is the scene where genial friendship plays
The pleasing game of interchanging praise;
Self-love, grimalkin of the human heart,
Is ever pliant to the master's art;
Soothed with a word, she peacefully withdraws
And sheathes in velvet her obnoxious claws,

And thrills the hand that smooths her glossy fur
With the light tremor of her grateful purr.

But what sad music fills the quiet hall,
If on her back a feline rival fall;
And oh, what noises shake the tranquil house,
If old Self-interest cheats her of a mouse!

Thou, O my country, hast thy foolish ways,
Too apt to purr at every stranger's praise;
But, if the stranger touch thy modes or laws,
Off goes the velvet and out come the claws!
And thou, Illustrious! but too poorly paid
In toasts from Pickwick for thy great crusade,
Though, while the echoes labored with thy name,
The public trap denied thy little game,
Let other lips our jealous laws revile,—
The marble Talfourd or the rude Carlyle,—
But on thy lids, that Heaven forbids to close
Where'er the light of kindly nature glows,
Let not the dollars that a churl denies
Weigh like the shillings on a dead man's eyes!
Or, if thou wilt, be more discreetly blind,
Nor ask to see all wide extremes combined.

Not in our wastes the dainty blossoms smile,
That crowd the gardens of thy scanty isle.
There white-cheeked Luxury weaves a thousand
        charms;—
Here sun-browned Labor swings his naked arms.
Long are the furrows he must trace between
The ocean's azure and the prairie's green;

Full many a blank his destined realm displays,
Yet see the promise of his riper days:
Far through yon depths the panting engine moves,
His chariots ringing in their steel-shod grooves;
And Erie's naiad flings her diamond wave
O'er the wild sea-nymph in her distant cave!
While tasks like these employ his anxious hours,
What if his corn-fields are not edged with flowers?
Though bright as silver the meridian beams
Shine through the crystal of thine English streams,
Turbid and dark the mighty wave is whirled
That drains our Andes and divides a world!

But lo! a PARCHMENT!   Surely it would seem
The sculptured impress speaks of power supreme;
Some grave design the solemn page must claim
That shows so broadly an emblazoned name;
A sovereign's promise!   Look, the lines afford
All Honor gives when Caution asks his word;
There sacred Faith has laid her snow-white hands,
And awful Justice knit her iron bands;
Yet every leaf is stained with treachery's dye,
And every letter crusted with a lie.
Alas! no treason has degraded yet
The Arab's salt, the Indian's calumet;
A simple rite, that bears the wanderer's pledge,
Blunts the keen shaft and turns the dagger's edge;—
While jockeying senates stop to sign and seal,
And freeborn statesmen legislate to steal.
Rise, Europe, tottering with thine Atlas load,
Turn thy proud eye to Freedom's blest abode,

And round her forehead, wreathed with heavenly
    flame,
Bind the dark garland of her daughter's shame!
Ye ocean clouds, that wrap the angry blast,
Coil her stained ensign round its haughty mast,
Or tear the fold that wears so foul a scar,
And drive a bolt through every blackened star!
Once more,—once only,—we must stop so soon,—
What have we here?   A GERMAN-SILVER SPOON;
A cheap utensil, which we often see
Used by the dabblers in æsthetic tea;
Of slender fabric, somewhat light and thin,
Made of mixed metal, chiefly lead and tin;
The bowl is shallow, and the handle small
Marked in large letters with the name JEAN PAUL.
Small as it is, its powers are passing strange,
For all who use it show a wondrous change;
And first, a fact to make the barbers stare,
It beats Macassar for the growth of hair;
See those small youngsters whose expansive ears
Maternal kindness grazed with frequent shears;
Each bristling crop a dangling mass becomes,
And all the spoonies turn to Absaloms!

Nor this alone its magic power displays,
It alters strangely all their works and ways;
With uncouth words they tire their tender lungs,
The same bald phrases on their hundred tongues;
"Ever" "The Ages" in their page appear,
"Alway" the bedlamite is called a "Seer":

On every leaf the " earnest " sage may scan,
Portentous bore! their " many-sided " man,—
A weak eclectic, groping vague and dim,
Whose every angle is a half-starved whim,
Blind as a mole and curious as a lynx,
Who rides a beetle, which he calls a " Sphinx."
And oh what questions asked in club-foot rhyme
Of Earth the tongueless and the deaf-mute Time!
Here babbling " Insight " shouts in Nature's ears
His last conundrum on the orbs and spheres;
There Self-inspection sucks its little thumb,
With " Whence am I?" and " Wherefore did I
      come?"
Deluded infants! will they ever know
Some doubts must darken o'er the world below,
Though all the Platos of the nursery trail
Their "clouds of glory" at the go-cart's tail?
O might these couplets their attention claim,
That gain their author the Philistine's name;
(A stubborn race, that, spurning foreign law,
Was much belabored with an ass's jaw!)

Melodious Laura! From the sad retreats
That hold thee, smothered with excess of sweets,
Shade of a shadow, spectre of a dream,
Glance thy wan eye across the Stygian stream!
The slip-shod dreamer treads thy fragrant halls,
The sophist's cobwebs hang thy roseate walls,
And o'er the crotchets of thy jingling tunes
The bard of mystery scrawls his crooked " runes."

Yes, thou art gone, with all the tuneful hordes
That candied thoughts in amber-colored words,
And in the precincts of thy late abodes
The clattering verse-wright hammers Orphic odes.
Thou, soft as zephyr, wast content to fly
On the gilt pinions of a balmy sigh;
He, vast as Phœbus on his burning wheels,
Would stride through ether at Orion's heels;
Thy emblem, Laura, was a perfume-jar,
And thine, young Orpheus, is a pewter star;
The balance trembles,—be its verdict told
When the new jargon slumbers with the old!

Cease, playful goddess! From thine airy bound
Drop like a feather softly to the ground;
This light bolero grows a ticklish dance,
And there is mischief in thy kindling glance.
To-morrow bids thee, with rebuking frown,
Change thy gauze tunic for a home-made gown,
Too blest by fortune, if the passing day
Adorn thy bosom with its frail bouquet,
But oh still happier if the next forgets
Thy daring steps and dangerous pirouettes!

URANIA:

A RHYMED LESSON.[1]

YES, dear Enchantress,—wandering far and long,
In realms unperfumed by the breath of song,
Where flowers ill-flavored shed their sweets around,
And bitterest roots invade the ungenial ground,
Whose gems are crystals from the Epsom mine,
Whose vineyards flow with antimonial wine,
Whose gates admit no mirthful feature in,
Save one gaunt mocker, the Sardonic grin,
Whose pangs are real, not the woes of rhyme
That blue-eyed misses warble out of time;—
Truant, not recreant to thy sacred claim,
Older by reckoning, but in heart the same,
Freed for a moment from the chains of toil,
I tread once more thy consecrated soil;
Here at thy feet my old allegiance own,
Thy subject still, and loyal to thy throne!

My dazzled glance explores the crowded hall;
Alas, how vain to hope the smiles of all!
I know my audience. All the gay and young
Love the light antics of a playful tongue;

---

[1] This poem was delivered before the Boston Mercantile
Library Association, October 14, 1846.

And these, remembering some expansive line
My lips let loose among the nuts and wine,
Are all impatience till the opening pun
Proclaim the witty shamfight is begun.
Two fifths at least, if not the total half,
Have come infuriate for an earthquake laugh;
I know full well what alderman has tied
His red bandanna tight about his side ;
I see the mother, who, aware that boys
Perform their laughter with superfluous noise,
Besides her kerchief, brought an extra one
To stop the explosions of her bursting son ;
I know a tailor, once a friend of mine,
Expects great doings in the button line ;—
For mirth's concussions rip the outward case,
And plant the stitches in a tenderer place.
I know my audience ;—these shall have their due;
A smile awaits them ere my song is through !

I know myself.   Not servile for applause,
My Muse permits no deprecating clause ;
Modest or vain, she will not be denied
One bold confession, due to honest pride ;
And well she knows, the drooping veil of song
Shall save her boldness from the caviller's wrong.
Her sweeter voice the Heavenly Maid imparts
To tell the secrets of our aching hearts ;
For this, a suppliant, captive, prostrate, bound,
She kneels imploring at the feet of sound ;
For this, convulsed in thought's maternal pains,
She loads her arms with rhyme's resounding chains ;

Faint though the music of her fetters be,
It lends one charm ;—her lips are ever free!

Think not I come, in manhood's fiery noon,
To steal his laurels from the stage buffoon;
His sword of lath the harlequin may wield;
Behold the star upon my lifted shield!
Though the just critic pass my humble name,
And sweeter lips have drained the cup of fame,
While my gay stanza pleased the banquet's lords,
The soul within was tuned to deeper chords!
Say, shall my arms, in other conflicts taught
To swing aloft the ponderous mace of thought,
Lift, in obedience to a school-girl's law,
Mirth's tinsel wand or laughter's tickling straw?
Say, shall I wound with satire's rankling spear
The pure, warm hearts that bid me welcome here?
No! while I wander through the land of dreams
To strive with great and play with trifling themes,
Let some kind meaning fill the varied line ;
You have your judgment ; will you trust to mine?

———

Between two breaths what crowded mysteries
    lie,—
The first short gasp, the last and long-drawn sigh!
Like phantoms painted on the magic slide,
Forth from the darkness of the past we glide,

As living shadows for a moment seen
In airy pageant on the eternal screen,

Traced by a ray from one unchanging flame,
Then seek the dust and stillness whence we came.

But whence and why, our trembling souls in-
quire,
Caught these dim visions their awakening fire?
Oh, who forgets when first the piercing thought
Through childhood's musings found its way un-
sought.
I AM;—I LIVE.   The mystery and the fear
When the dread question—WHAT HAS BROUGHT ME
HERE?
Burst through life's twilight, as before the sun
Roll the deep thunders of the morning gun!

Are angel faces, silent and serene,
Bent on the conflicts of this little scene,
Whose dreamlike efforts, whose unreal strife,
Are but the preludes to a larger life?

Or does life's summer see the end of all,
These leaves of being mouldering as they fall,
As the old poet vaguely used to deem,
As WESLEY questioned in his youthful dream?[1]
O could such mockery reach our souls indeed,
Give back the Pharaohs' or the Athenian's creed;
Better than this a heaven of man's device,—
The Indian's sports, the Moslem's paradise!

[1] Ογη περ φύλλων γενεή, τοιήδε καὶ ἀνδρῶν.
Iliad VI., 146.

Wesley quotes this line in his account of his early doubts
and perplexities.   See Southey's *Life of Wesley*, vol. ii., p. 185.

Or is our being's only end and aim
To add new glories to our Maker's name,
As the poor insect, shrivelling in the blaze,
Lends a faint sparkle to its streaming rays?
Does earth send upwards to the Eternal's ear
The mingled discords of her jarring sphere
To swell his anthem, while Creation rings
With notes of anguish from its shattered strings?
Is it for this the immortal Artist means
These conscious, throbbing, agonized machines?

Dark is the soul whose sullen creed can bind
In chains like these the all-embracing Mind;
No! two-faced bigot, thou dost ill reprove
The sensual, selfish, yet benignant Jove,
And praise a tyrant throned in lonely pride,
Who loves himself, and cares for naught beside;
Who gave thee, summoned from primeval night,
A thousand laws, and not a single right,
A heart to feel and quivering nerves to thrill,
The sense of wrong, the death-defying will;
Who girt thy senses with this goodly frame,
Its earthly glories and its orbs of flame,
Not for thyself, unworthy of a thought,
Poor helpless victim of a life unsought,
But all for him, unchanging and supreme,
The heartless centre of thy frozen scheme!

Trust not the teacher with his lying scroll,
Who tears the charter of thy shuddering soul;
The God of love, who gave the breath that warms
All living dust in all its varied forms,

Asks not the tribute of a world like this
To fill the measure of his perfect bliss.
Though winged with life through all its radiant
        shores,
Creation flowed with unexhausted stores
Cherub and seraph had not yet enjoyed;
For this he called thee from the quickening void!
Nor this alone; a larger gift was thine,
A mightier purpose swelled his vast design;
Thought,—conscience,—will,—to make them all
        thine own,
He rent a pillar from the eternal throne!

    Made in his image, thou must nobly dare
The thorny crown of sovereignty to share.
With eye uplifted it is thine to view,
From thine own centre, heaven's o'er-arching blue;
So round thy heart a beaming circle lies
No fiend can blot, no hypocrite disguise;
From all its orbs one cheering voice is heard,
Full to thine ear it bears the Father's word,
Now, as in Eden where his first-born trod:
"Seek thine own welfare, true to man and God!"
    Think not too meanly of thy low estate;
Thou hast a choice; to choose is to create!
Remember whose the sacred lips that tell,
Angels approve thee when thy choice is well;
Remember, One, a judge of righteous men,
Swore to spare Sodom if she held but ten!
Use well the freedom which thy Master gave,
(Think'st thou that Heaven can tolerate a slave?)

And He who made thee to be just and true
Will bless thee, love thee,—ay, respect thee too!

Nature has placed thee on a changeful tide,
To breast its waves, but not without a guide;
Yet, as the needle will forget its aim,
Jarred by the fury of the electric flame,
As the true current it will falsely feel,
Warped from its axis by a freight of steel;
So will thy CONSCIENCE lose its balanced truth,
If passion's lightning fall upon thy youth;
So the pure effluence quit its sacred hold,
Girt round too deeply with magnetic gold.

Go to yon tower, where busy science plies
Her vast antennæ, feeling through the skies;
That little vernier on whose slender lines
The midnight taper trembles as it shines,
A silent index, tracks the planets' march
In all their wanderings through the ethereal arch,
Tells through the mist where dazzled Mercury burns
And marks the spot where Uranus returns.
So, till by wrong or negligence effaced,
The living index which thy Maker traced
Repeats the line each starry Virtue draws
Through the wide circuit of creation's laws;
Still tracks unchanged the everlasting ray
Where the dark shadows of temptation stray;
But, once defaced, forgets the orbs of light,
And leaves thee wandering o'er the expanse of night!

" What is thy creed ? " a hundred lips inquire ;
" Thou seekest God beneath what Christian spire ? "
Nor ask they idly, for uncounted lies
Float upward on the smoke of sacrifice ;
When man's first incense rose above the plain,
Of earth's two altars one was built by Cain !

Uncursed by doubt, our earliest creed we take ;
We love the precepts for the teacher's sake ;
The simple lessons which the nursery taught
Fell soft and stainless on the buds of thought,
And the full blossom owes its fairest hue
To those sweet tear-drops of affection's dew.

Too oft the light that led our earlier hours
Fades with the perfume of our cradle flowers ;
The clear, cold question chills to frozen doubt ;
Tired of beliefs, we dread to live without ;
Oh, then, if reason waver at thy side,
Let humbler Memory be thy gentle guide ;
Go to thy birth-place, and, if faith was there,
Repeat thy father's creed, thy mother's prayer !

Faith loves to lean on Time's destroying arm,
And age, like distance, lends a double charm ;
In dim cathedrals, dark with vaulted gloom,
What holy awe invests the saintly tomb !
There pride will bow, and anxious care expand,
And creeping avarice come with open hand ;
The gay can weep, the impious can adore,
From morn's first glimmerings on the chancel floor
Till dying sunset sheds his crimson stains
Through the faint halos of the irised panes.

12

Yet there are graves, whose rudely shapen sod
Bears the fresh footprints where the sexton trod ;
Graves where the verdure has not dared to shoot,
Where the chance wild-flower has not fixed its root,
Whose slumbering tenants, dead without a name,
The eternal record shall at length proclaim
Pure as the holiest in the long array
Of hooded, mitred, or tiaraed clay !

Come, seek the air ; some pictures we may gain
Whose passing shadows shall not be in vain ;
Not from the scenes that crowd the stranger's soil,
Not from our own amidst the stir of toil,
But when the Sabbath brings its kind release,
And Care lies slumbering on the lap of Peace.

The air is hushed ; the street is holy ground ;
Hark! The sweet bells renew their welcome sound;
As one by one awakes each silent tongue,
It tells the turret whence its voice is flung.[1]

The Chapel, last of sublunary things
That shocks our echoes with the name of Kings,

[1] The churches referred to in the lines which follow
are—

1. "King's Chapel," the foundation of which was laid by
Governor Shirley in 1749.

2. The church in Brattle Square, consecrated in 1773. The
completion of this edifice, the design of which included a
spire, was prevented by the troubles of the Revolution, and
its plain square tower presents nothing more attractive than
its massive simplicity. In the front of this tower is still seen,
half embedded in the brick-work, a cannon-ball, which was
thrown from the American fortification at Cambridge, during

Whose bell, just glistening from the font and forge,
Rolled its proud requiem for the second George,
Solemn and swelling, as of old it rang,
Flings to the wind its deep, sonorous clang ;—
The simpler pile, that, mindful of the hour
When Howe's artillery shook its half-built tower,
Wears on its bosom, as a bride might do,
The iron breastpin which the " Rebels " threw,
Wakes the sharp echoes with the quivering thrill
Of keen vibrations, tremulous and shrill ;—
Aloft, suspended in the morning's fire,
Crash the vast cymbals from the Southern spire ;—
The Giant, standing by the elm-clad green,
His white lance lifted o'er the silent scene,
Whirling in air his brazen goblet round,
Swings from its brim the swollen floods of sound ;—
While, sad with memories of the olden time,
The Northern Minstrel pours her tender chime,
Faint, single tones, that spell their ancient song,
But tears still follow as they breathe along.

Child of the soil, whom fortune sends to range
Where man and nature, faith and customs change,
Borne in thy memory, each familiar tone
Mourns on the winds that sigh in every zone.

the bombardment of the city, then occupied by the British
troops.

3. The " Old South," first occupied for public worship in
1730.

4. Park Street Church, built in 1809, the tall, white steeple
of which is the most conspicuous of all the Boston spires.

5. Christ Church, opened for public worship in 1723, and
containing a set of eight bells, the only chime in Boston.

When Ceylon sweeps thee with her perfumed breeze
Through the warm billows of the Indian seas ;
When,—ship and shadow blended both in one,—
Flames o'er thy mast the equatorial sun,
From sparkling midnight to refulgent noon
Thy canvas swelling with the still monsoon ;
When through thy shrouds the wild tornado sings,
And thy poor seabird folds her tattered wings,
Oft will delusion o'er thy senses steal,
And airy echoes ring the Sabbath peal!
Then, dim with grateful tears, in long array
Rise the fair town, the island-studded bay,
Home, with its smiling board, its cheering fire,
The half-choked welcome of the expecting sire,
The mother's kiss, and, still if aught remain,
Our whispering hearts shall aid the silent strain.—
    Ah, let the dreamer o'er the taffrail lean
To muse unheeded, and to weep unseen ;
Fear not the tropic's dews, the evening's chills,
His heart lies warm among his triple hills !

    Turned from her path by this deceitful gleam,
My wayward fancy half forgets her theme ;
See through the streets that slumbered in repose
The living current of devotion flows ;
Its varied forms in one harmonious band,
Age leading childhood by its dimpled hand,
Want, in the robe whose faded edges fall
To tell of rags beneath the tartan shawl,
And wealth, in silks that, fluttering to appear,
Lift the deep borders of the proud cashmere.

See, but glance briefly, sorrow-worn and pale,
Those sunken cheeks beneath the widow's veil;
Alone she wanders where with *him* she trod,
No arm to stay her, but she leans on God.

While other doublets deviate here and there,
What secret handcuff binds that pretty pair?
Compactest couple! pressing side to side,—
Ah, the white bonnet that reveals the bride!
By the white neckcloth, with its straitened tie,
The sober hat, the Sabbath-speaking eye,
Severe and smileless, he that runs may read
The stern disciple of Geneva's creed;
Decent and slow, behold his solemn march;
Silent he enters through yon crowded arch.
A livelier bearing of the outward man,
The light-hued gloves, the undevout rattan,
Now smartly raised or half-profanely twirled,—
A bright, fresh twinkle from the week-day world,—
Tell their plain story;—yes, thine eyes behold
A cheerful Christian from the liberal fold.

Down the chill street that curves in gloomiest
shade,
What marks betray yon solitary maid?
The cheek's red rose, that speaks of balmier air;
The Celtic blackness of her braided hair;[1]

[1] For the propriety of the term "*Celtic* blackness," see Laurence's *Lectures* (Salem, 1828), pp. 452, 453. But the ancient Celts appear to have been a xanthous, or fair-haired race. See Pritchard's *Nat. Hist. of Man* (London, 1843), pp. 183, 193, 196.

The gilded missal in her kerchief tied;
Poor Nora, exile from Killarney's side!
   Sister in toil, though blanched by colder skies,
That left their azure in her downcast eyes,
See pallid Margaret, Labor's patient child,
Scarce weaned from home, the nursling of the wild
Where white Katahdin o'er the horizon shines,
And broad Penobscot dashes through the pines;
Still, as she hastes, her careful fingers hold
The unfailing hymn-book in its cambric fold.
Six days at drudgery's heavy wheel she stands,
The seventh sweet morning folds her weary hands;
Yes, child of suffering, thou may'st well be sure
He who ordained the Sabbath loves the poor!

   This weekly picture faithful memory draws,
Nor claims the noisy tribute of applause;
Faint is the glow such barren hopes can lend,
And frail the line that asks no loftier end.
   Trust me, kind listener, I will yet beguile
Thy saddened features of the promised smile
This magic mantle thou must well divide,
It has its sable and its ermine side;
Yet, ere the lining of the robe appears,
Take thou in silence, what I give in tears.

   Dear listening soul, this transitory scene
Of murmuring stillness, busily serene;
This solemn pause, the breathing-space of man,
The halt of toil's exhausted caravan,
Comes sweet with music to thy wearied ear;
Rise with its anthems to a holier sphere!

Deal meekly, gently, with the hopes that guide
The lowliest brother straying from thy side;
If right, they bid thee tremble for thine own,
If wrong, the verdict is for God alone!

What though the champions of thy faith esteem
The sprinkled fountain or baptismal stream;
Shall jealous passions in unseemly strife
Cross their dark weapons o'er the waves of life?

Let my free soul, expanding as it can,
Leave to his scheme the thoughtful Puritan;
But Calvin's dogma shall my lips deride?
In that stern faith my angel Mary died;—
Or ask if mercy's milder creed can save,
Sweet sister, risen from thy new-made grave?

True, the harsh founders of thy church reviled
That ancient faith, the trust of Erin's child;
Must thou be raking in the crumbled past
For racks and fagots in her teeth to cast?
See from the ashes of Helvetia's pile
The whitened skull of old Servetus smile!
Round her young heart thy " Romish Upas " threw
Its firm, deep fibres, strengthening as she grew;
Thy sneering voice may call them " Popish
        tricks,"—
Her Latin prayers, her dangling crucifix,—
But *De Profundis* blessed her father's grave;
That " idol " cross her dying mother gave!
    What if some angel looks with equal eyes
On her and thee, the simple and the wise,

Writes each dark fault against thy brighter creed,
And drops a tear with every foolish bead !

Grieve, as thou must, o'er history's reeking page ;
Blush for the wrongs that stain thy happier age ;
Strive with the wanderer from the better path,
Bearing thy message meekly, not in wrath ;
Weep for the frail that err, the weak that fall,
Have thine own faith,--but hope and pray for all !

Faith ; Conscience ; Love. A meaner task re-
mains,
And humbler thoughts must creep in lowlier strains ;
Shalt thou be honest ?　Ask the wordly schools,
And all will tell thee knaves are busier fools ;
Prudent ?　Industrious ?　Let not modern pens
Instruct " Poor Richard's " fellow-citizens.
Be firm ! one constant element in luck
Is genuine, solid, old Teutonic pluck ;
See yon tall shaft ; it felt the earthquake's thrill,
Clung to its base, and greets the sunrise still.

Stick to your aim ; the mongrel's hold will slip,
But only crowbars loose the bulldog's grip ;
Small as he looks, the jaw that never yields
Drags down the bellowing monarch of the fields !

Yet in opinions look not always back ;
Your wake is nothing, mind the coming track ;
Leave what you've done for what you have to do ;
Don't be " consistent," but be simply true.

Don't catch the fidgets; you have found your
    place
Just in the focus of a nervous race,
Fretful to change, and rabid to discuss,
Full of excitements, always in a fuss ;—
Think of the patriarchs ; then compare as men
These lean-cheeked maniacs of the tongue and pen !
Run, if you like, but try to keep your breath ;
Work like a man, but don't be worked to death ;
And with new notions,—let me change the rule,—
Don't strike the iron till it's slightly cool.

Choose well your *set ;* our feeble nature seeks
The aid of clubs, the countenance of cliques ;
And with this object settle first of all
Your weight of metal and your size of ball.
Track not the steps of such as hold you cheap,
Too mean to prize, though good enough to keep ;
The " real, genuine, no-mistake Tom Thumbs "
Are little people fed on great men's crumbs.
Yet keep no followers of that hateful brood
That basely mingles with its wholesome food
The tumid reptile, which, the poet said,
Doth wear a precious jewel in his head.

If the wild filly, " Progress," thou would'st ride,
Have young companions ever at thy side ;
But, would'st thou stride the stanch old mare,
    " Success,"
Go with thine elders, though they please thee less.

Shun such as lounge through afternoons and eves,
And on thy dial write " Beware of thieves ! "
Felon of minutes, never taught to feel
The worth of treasures which thy fingers steal,
Pick my left pocket of its silver dime,
But spare the right,—it holds my golden time !

Does praise delight thee ? Choose some *ultra*
      side ;
A sure old recipe, and often tried ;
Be its apostle, congressman, or bard,
Spokesman, or jokesman, only drive it hard ;
But know the forfeit which thy choice abides,
For on two wheels the poor reformer rides,
One black with epithets the *anti* throws,
One white with flattery, painted by the *pros.*

Though books on MANNERS are not out of print,
An honest tongue may drop a harmless hint.
Stop not, unthinking, every friend you meet,
To spin your wordy fabric in the street ;
While you are emptying your colloquial pack,
The fiend *Lumbago* jumps upon his back.
Nor cloud his features with the unwelcome tale
Of how he looks, if haply thin and pale ;
Health is a subject for his child, his wife,
And the rude office that insures his life.
Look in his face, to meet thy neighbor's soul,
Not on his garments, to detect a hole ;
" How to observe," is what thy pages show,
Pride of thy sex, Miss Harriet Martineau !

Oh, what a precious book the one would be
That taught observers what they're *not* to see!

I tell in verse,—'twere better done in prose,—
One curious trick that everybody knows;
Once form this habit, and it's very strange
How long it sticks, how hard it is to change.
Two friendly people, both disposed to smile,
Who meet, like others, every little while,
Instead of passing with a pleasant bow,
And " How d'ye do? " or " How's your uncle now? "
Impelled by feelings in their nature kind,
But slightly weak, and somewhat undefined,
Rush at each other, make a sudden stand,
Begin to talk, expatiate, and expand;
Each looks quite radiant, seems extremely struck,
Their meeting so was such a piece of luck;
Each thinks the other thinks he's greatly pleased
To screw the vice in which they both are squeezed;
So there they talk, in dust, or mud, or snow,
Both bored to death, and both afraid to go!

Your hat once lifted, do not hang your fire,
Nor, like slow Ajax, fighting still, retire;
When your old castor on your crown you clap,
Go off; you've mounted your percussion cap!

Some words on LANGUAGE may be well applied,
And take them kindly, though they touch your
    pride;
Words leads to things; a scale is more precise,—
Coarse speech, bad grammar, swearing, drinking,
    vice.

Our cold Northeaster's icy fetter clips
The native freedom of the Saxon lips ;
See the brown peasant of the plastic South,
How all his passions play about his mouth !
With us, the feature that transmits the soul,
A frozen, passive, palsied breathing-hole.
The crampy shackles of the ploughboy's walk
Tie the small muscles when he strives to talk ;
Not all the pumice of the polished town
Can smooth this roughness of the barnyard down ;
Rich, honored, titled, he betrays his race
By this one mark,—he's awkward in the face ;—
Nature's rude impress, long before he knew
The sunny street that holds the sifted few.

It can't be helped, though, if we're taken young,
We gain some freedom of the lips and tongue ;
But school and college often try in vain
To break the padlock of our boyhood's chain ;
One stubborn word will prove this axiom true ;—
No quondam rustic can enunciate *view*.

A few brief stanzas may be well employed
To speak of errors we can all avoid.

Learning condemns beyond the reach of hope
The careless lips that speak of sŏap for sōap ;
Her edict exiles from her fair abode
The clownish voice that utters rŏad for rōad ;
Less stern to him who calls his cōat a cŏat.
And steers his bōat, believing it a bŏat,
She pardoned one, our classic city's boast,
Who said at Cambridge, mŏst instead of mōst,

But knit her brows and stamped her angry foot
To hear a teacher call a rōot a rŏot.

Once more; speak clearly, if you speak at all;
Carve every word before you let it fall;
Don't, like a lecturer or dramatic star,
Try over hard to roll the British R;
Do put your accents in the proper spot;
Don't,—let me beg you,—don't say " How ? " for
     " What ? "
And, when you stick on conversation's burs,
Don't strew your pathway with those dreadful *urs*.

From little matters let us pass to less,
And lightly touch the mysteries of DRESS;
The outward forms the inner man reveal,—
We guess the pulp before we cut the peel.

I leave the broadcloth,—coats and all the rest,—
The dangerous waistcoat, called by cockneys " vest,"
The things named " pants " in certain documents,
A word not made for gentlemen, but " gents ";
One single precept might the whole condense:
Be sure your tailor is a man of sense;
But add a little care, a decent pride,
And always err upon the sober side.

Three pairs of boots one pair of feet demands,
If polished daily by the owner's hands;
If the dark menial's visit save from this,
Have twice the number, for he'll sometimes miss.
One pair for critics of the nicer sex,
Close in the instep's clinging circumflex,

Long, narrow, light ; the Gallic boot of love,
A kind of cross between a boot and glove.
But, not to tread on everlasting thorns,
And sow in suffering what is reaped in corns,
Compact, but easy, strong, substantial, square,
Let native art compile the medium pair.
The third remains, and let your tasteful skill
Here show some relics of affection still ;
Let no stiff cowhide, reeking from the tan,
No rough caoutchouc, no deformed brogan,
Disgrace the tapering outline of your feet,
Though yellow torrents gurgle through the street ;
But the *patched* calfskin arm against the flood
In neat, light shoes, impervious to the mud.

Wear seemly gloves ; not black, nor yet too
　　　　light,
And least of all the pair that once was white ;
Let the dead party where you told your loves
Bury in peace its dead bouquets and gloves ;
Shave like the goat, if so your fancy bids,
But be a parent,—don't neglect your kids.

Have a good hat ; the secret of your looks
Lives with the beaver in Canadian brooks ;
Virtue may flourish in an old cravat,
But man and nature scorn the shocking hat.
Does beauty slight you from her gay abodes ?
Like bright Apollo, you must take to *Rhoades*,
Mount the new castor,—ice itself will melt ;
Boots, gloves may fail ; the hat is always felt !

Be shy of breast-pins ; plain, well-ironed white,
With small pearl buttons,—two of them in sight,—
Is always genuine, while your gems may pass,
Though real diamonds, for ignoble glass ;
But spurn those paltry cis-Atlantic lies,
That round his breast the shabby rustic ties ;
Breathe not the name, profaned to hallow things
The indignant laundress blushes when she brings !

Our freeborn race, averse to every check,
Has tossed the yoke of Europe from its *neck ;*
From the green prairie to the sea-girt town,
The whole wide nation turns its collars down.

The stately neck is manhood's manliest part ;
It takes the life-blood freshest from the heart ;
With short, curled ringlets close around it spread,
How light and strong it lifts the Grecian head !
Thine, fair Erectheus of Minerva's wall ;—
Or thine, young athlete of the Louver's hall,
Smooth as the pillar flashing in the sun
That filled the arena where thy wreaths were
        won,—
Firm as the band that clasps the antlered spoil
Strained in the winding anaconda's coil !

I spare the contrast ; it were only kind
To be a little, nay, intensely blind :
Choose for yourself : I know it cuts your ear ;
I know the points will sometimes interfere ;
I know that often, like the filial John,
Whom sleep surprised with half his drapery on,

You show your features to the astonished town
With one side standing and the other down ;—
But, O my friend ! my favorite fellow-man !
If Nature made you on her modern plan,
Sooner than wander with your windpipe bare,—
The fruit of Eden ripening in the air,—
With that lean head-stalk, that protruding chin,
Wear standing collars, were they made of tin !
And have a neck-cloth,—by the throat of Jove !
Cut from the funnel of a rusty stove !

The long-drawn lesson narrows to its close,
Chill, slender, slow, the dwindled current flows ;
Tired of the ripples on its feeble springs,
Once more the Muse unfolds her upward wings.

Land of my birth, with this unhallowed tongue,
Thy hopes, thy dangers, I perchance had sung ;
But who shall sing, in brutal disregard
Of all the essentials of the "native bard ? "
Lake, sea, shore, prairie, forest, mountain, fall,
His eye omnivorous must devour them all ;
The tallest summits and the broadest tides
His foot must compass with its giant strides,
Where Ocean thunders, where Missouri rolls,
And tread at once the tropics and the poles ;
His food all forms of earth, fire, water, air,
His home all space, his birth-place everywhere.

Some grave compatriot, having seen perhaps
The pictured page that goes in Worcester's Maps,

And read in earnest what was said in jest,
" Who drives fat oxen "—please to add the rest,—
Sprung the odd notion that the poet's dreams
Grow in the ratio of his hills and streams;
And hence insisted that the aforesaid " bard "
Pink of the future—fancy's pattern-card,—
The babe of Nature in the " giant West,"
Must be of course her biggest and her best.

But, were it true that Nature's fostering sun
Saves all its daylight for that favorite one,
If for his forehead every wreath she means,
And we, poor children, must not touch the greens;
Since rocks and rivers cannot take the road
To seek the elected in his own abode,
Some voice must answer, for her precious heir,
One solemn question :—Who shall pay his fare?
  Oh, when at length the expected bard shall
    come,
Land of our pride, to strike thine echoes dumb
(And many a voice exclaims in prose and rhyme
It's getting late, and he's behind his time),
When all thy mountains clap their hands in joy,
And all thy cataracts thunder " That's the boy,"—
Say if with him the reign of song shall end,
And Heaven declare its final dividend ?

Be calm, dear brother! whose impassioned strain
Comes from an alley watered by a drain:
The little Mincio, dribbling to the Po,
Beats all the epics of the Hoang Ho;
If loved in earnest by the tuneful maid,

13

Don't mind their nonsense,—never be afraid!
  The nurse of poets feeds her winged brood
By common firesides, on familiar food;
In a low hamlet, by a narrow stream,
Where bovine rustics used to doze and dream,
She filled young William's fiery fancy full,
While old John Shakespeare talked of beeves and
     wool!

  No Alpine needle, with its climbing spire,
Brings down for mortals the Promethean fire,
If careless Nature have forgot to frame
An altar worthy of the sacred flame.

  Unblest by any save the goat-herd's lines,
Mont Blanc rose soaring through his "sea of pines";
In vain the Arve and Arveiron dash,
No hymn salutes them but the Ranz des Vaches,
Till lazy Coleridge, by the morning's light,
Gazed for a moment on the fields of white,
And lo, the glaciers found at length a tongue,
Mont Blanc was vocal, and Chamouni sung!

  Children of wealth or want, to each is given
One spot of green, and all the blue of heaven!
Enough, if these their outward shows impart;
The rest is thine,—the scenery of the heart.
  If passion's hectic in thy stanzas glow
Thy heart's best life-blood ebbing as they flow,
If with thy verse thy strength and bloom distil,
Drained by the pulses of the fevered thrill;
If sound's sweet effluence polarize thy brain,

And thoughts turn crystals in thy fluid strain,—
Nor rolling ocean, nor the prairie's bloom,
Nor streaming cliffs, nor rayless cavern's gloom,
Need'st thou, young poet, to inform thy line;
Thy own broad signet stamps thy song divine!
   Let others gaze where silvery streams are rolled,
And chase the rainbow for its cup of gold;
To thee all landscapes were a heavenly dye,
Changed in the glance of thy prismatic eye;
Nature evoked thee in sublimer throes,
For thee her inmost Arethusa flows,—
The mighty mother's living depths are stirred,—
Thou art the starred Osiris of the herd!

   A few brief lines; they touch on solemn chords,
And hearts may leap to hear their honest words;
Yet, ere the jarring bugle-blast is blown,
The softer lyre shall breathe its soothing tone.
   New England! proudly may thy children claim
Their honored birthright by its humblest name!
Cold are thy skies, but, ever fresh and clear,
No rank malaria stains thine atmosphere;
No fungous weeds invade thy scanty soil,
Scarred by the ploughshares of unslumbering toil.
Long may the doctrines by thy sages taught,
Raised from the quarries where their sires have
     wrought,
Be like the granite of thy rock-ribbed land,—
As slow to rear, as obdurate to stand;
And as the ice, that leaves thy crystal mine,
Chills the fierce alcohol in the Creole's wine.

So may the doctrines of thy sober school
Keep the hot theories of thy neighbors cool!

If ever, trampling on her ancient path,
Cankered by treachery, or inflamed by wrath,
With smooth " Resolves," or with discordant cries,
The mad Briareus of disunion rise,
Chiefs of New England ! by your sires' renown,
Dash the red torches of the rebel down !
Flood his black hearth-stone till its flames expire,
Though your old Sachem fanned his council-fire !

But if at last,—her fading cycle run,—
The tongue must forfeit what the arm has won,
Then rise, wild Ocean ! roll thy surging shock
Full on old Plymouth's desecrated rock !
Scale the proud shaft degenerate hands have hewn,
Where bleeding Valor stained the flowers of June !
Sweep in one tide her spires and turrets down,
And howl her dirge above Monadnoc's crown !

List not the tale ; the Pilgrim's hallowed shore,
Though strewn with weeds, is granite at the core ;
Oh, rather trust that He who made her free
Will keep her true, as long as faith shall be !

Farewell ! yet lingering through the destined
    hour,
Leave, sweet Enchantress, one memorial flower !

An Angel, floating o'er the waste of snow
That clad our western desert, long ago

(The same fair spirit who, unseen by day,
Shone as a star along the Mayflower's way),
Sent, the first herald of the Heavenly plan,
To choose on earth a resting-place for man,—
Tired with his flight along the unvaried field,
Turned to soar upwards, when his glance revealed
A calm, bright bay, enclosed in rocky bounds,
And at its entrance stood three sister mounds.

The Angel spake: "This threefold hill shall be [1]
The home of Arts, the nurse of Liberty !
One stately summit from its shaft shall pour
Its deep-red blaze, along the darkened shore;
Emblem of thoughts that, kindling far and wide,
In danger's night shall be a nation's guide.
One swelling crest the citadel shall crown,
Its slanted bastions black with battle's frown,
And bid the sons that tread its scowling heights
Bare their strong arms for man and all his rights !

[1] The name first given by the English to Boston was TRI-
MOUNTAIN. The three hills upon and around which the city
is built are Beacon Hill, Fort Hill, and Copp's Hill.

In the early records of the colony, it is mentioned, under
date of May 6, 1635, that " A BEACON is to be set on the Sentry hill, at Boston, to give notice to the country of any danger ; to be guarded by one man stationed near, and fired as
occasion may be." The last beacon was blown down in 1789.

The eastern side of Fort Hill was formerly " a ragged cliff,
that seemed placed by nature in front of the entrance to the
harbor for the purposes of defence, to which it was very soon
applied, and from which it obtained its present name." Its
summit is now a beautiful green enclosure.

Copp's Hill was used as a burial-ground from a very early

One silent steep along the northern wave
Shall hold the patriarch's and the hero's grave ;
When fades the torch, when o'er the peaceful scene
The embattled fortress smiles in living green,
The cross of Faith, the anchor staff of Hope,
Shall stand eternal on its grassy slope ;
There through all time shall faithful Memory tell :
" Here Virtue toiled, and Patriot Valor fell ;
Thy free, proud fathers slumber at thy side,
Live as they lived, or perish as they died ! "

period. The part of it employed for this purpose slopes toward
the water upon the northern side. From its many interest-
ing records of the dead, I select the following, which may
serve to show what kind of dust it holds :—

"Here lies buried in a
Stone Grave 10 feet deep,
Capt DANIEL MALCOLM Mercht
who departed this Life
October 23d, 1769,
Aged 44 years,
a true son of Liberty,
a Friend to the Publick,
an Enemy to oppression,
and one of the foremost
in opposing the Revenue Acts
on America."

The gravestone from which I copied this inscription is
bruised and splintered by the bullets of the British soldiers.

THE PILGRIM'S VISION.

In the hour of twilight shadows
    The Puritan looked out;
He thought of the " bloudy Salvages"
    That lurked all round about,
Of Wituwamet's pictured knife
    And Pecksuot's whooping shout;
For the baby's limbs were feeble,
    Though his father's arms were stout.

His home was a freezing cabin
    Too bare for the hungry rat,
Its roof was thatched with ragged grass
    And bald enough of that;
The hole that served for casement
    Was glazed with an ancient hat;
And the ice was gently thawing
    From the log whereon he sat.

Along the dreary landscape
    His eyes went to and fro,
The trees all clad in icicles,
    The streams that did not flow;
A sudden thought flashed o'er him,—
    A dream of long ago,—
He smote his leathern jerkin
    And murmured " Even so!"

199

" Come hither, God-be-Glorified,
    And sit upon my knee,
Behold the dream unfolding,
    Whereof I spake to thee
By the winter's hearth in Leyden
    And on the stormy sea;
True is the dream's beginning,—
    So may its ending be !

" I saw in the naked forest
    Our scattered remnant cast,
A screen of shivering branches
    Between them and the blast;
The snow was falling round them,
    The dying fell as fast
I looked to see them perish,
    When lo, the vision passed.

" Again mine eyes were opened ;—
    The feeble had waxed strong,
The babes had grown to sturdy men,
    The remnant was a throng ;
By shadowed lake and winding stream
    And all the shores along,
The howling demons quaked to hear
    The Christian's godly song.

" They slept,—the village fathers,—
    By river, lake, and shore,
When far adown the steep of Time
    The vision rose once more ;

I saw along the winter snow
 A spectral column pour,
And high above their broken ranks
 A tattered flag they bore.

" Their Leader rode before them,
 Of bearing calm and high,
The light of Heaven's own kindling
 Throned in his awful eye ;
These were a Nation's champions
 Her dread appeal to try ;
God for the right ! I faltered,
 And lo, the train passed by.

" Once more ;—the strife is ended,
 The solemn issue tried,
The Lord of Hosts, His mighty arm
 Has helped our Israel's side ;
Gray stone and grassy hillock
 Tell where our martyrs died,
But peaceful smiles the harvest,
 And stainless flows the tide.

" A crash,—as when some swollen cloud
 Cracks o'er the tangled trees !
With side to side, and spar to spar,
 Whose smoking decks are these ?
I know Saint George's blood-red cross,
 Thou Mistress of the Seas,—
But what is she, whose streaming bars
 Roll out before the breeze ?

" Ah, well her iron ribs are knit,
    Whose thunders strive to quell
The bellowing throats, the blazing lips,
    That pealed the Armada's knell!
The mist was cleared,—a wreath of stars
    Rose o'er the crimsoned swell,
And, wavering from its haughty peak,
    The cross of England fell!

"O trembling Faith! though dark the morn,
    A heavenly torch is thine;
While feebler races melt away,
    And paler orbs decline,
Still shall the fiery pillar's ray
    Along thy pathway shine,
To light the chosen tribe that sought
    This Western Palestine!

" I see the living tide roll on;
    It crowns with flaming towers
The icy capes of Labrador,
    The Spaniard's 'land of flowers'!
It streams beyond the splintered ridge
    That parts the Northern showers;
From eastern rock to sunset wave
    The Continent is ours!"

He ceased,—the grim old Puritan,—
    Then softly bent to cheer
The pilgrim-child, whose wasting face
    Was meekly turned to hear;

And drew his toil-worn sleeve across,
    To brush the manly tear
From cheeks that never changed in woe,
    And never blanched in fear.

The weary pilgrim slumbers,
    His resting-place unknown ;
His hands were crossed, his lids were closed,
    The dust was o'er him strown ;
The drifting soil, the mouldering leaf,
    Along the sod were blown ;
His mound has melted into earth,
    His memory lives alone.

So let it live unfading,
    The memory of the dead,
Long as the pale anemone
    Springs where their tears were shed,
Or, raining in the summer's wind
    In flakes of burning red,
The wild rose sprinkles with its leaves
    The turf where once they bled !

Yea, when the frowning bulwarks
    That guard this holy strand
Have sunk beneath the trampling surge
    In beds of sparkling sand,
While in the waste of ocean
    One hoary rock shall stand
Be this its latest legend,—
    HERE WAS THE PILGRIM'S LAND !

A MODEST REQUEST.

COMPLIED WITH AFTER THE DINNER AT PRESIDENT
EVERETT'S INAUGURATION.

SCENE,—a back parlor in a certain square,
Or court, or lane,—in short no matter where;
Time,—early morning, dear to simple souls
Who love its sunshine, and its fresh-baked rolls;
Persons,—take pity on this telltale blush,
That, like the Æthiop, whispers " Hush, oh hush!"

Delightful scene! where smiling comfort broods,
Nor business frets, nor anxious care intrudes;
O si sic omnia! were it ever so!
But what is stable in this world below!
Medio e fonte,—Virtue has her faults,—
The clearest fountains taste of Epsom salts;
We snatch the cup and lift to drain it dry,—
Its central dimple holds a drowning fly!

Strong is the pine by Maine's ambrosial streams,
But stronger augers pierce its thickest beams;
No iron gate, no spiked and panelled door,
Can keep out death, the postman, or the bore;—
O for a world where peace and silence reign,
And blunted dulness terebrates in vain!

204

—The door bell jingles,—enter Richard Fox,
And takes this letter from his leathern box.

" Dear Sir,
                In writing on a former day,
One little matter I forgot to say ;
I now inform you in a single line,
On Thursday next our purpose is to *dine.*
The act of feeding, as you understand,
Is but a fraction of the work in hand ;
Its nobler half is that ethereal meat
The papers call ' the intellectual treat ' ;
Songs, speeches, toasts, around the festive board,
Drowned in the juice the College pumps afford ;
For only water flanks our knives and forks,
So, sink or float, we swim without the corks.
Yours is the art, by native genius taught,
To clothe in eloquence the naked thought ;
Yours is the skill its music to prolong
Through the sweet effluence of mellifluous song ;
Yours the quaint trick to cram the pithy line
That cracks so crisply over bubbling wine ;
And since success your various gifts attends,
We,—that is I and all your numerous friends,—
Expect from you,—your single self a host,—
A speech, a song, excuse me, *and* a toast ;
Nay, not to haggle on so small a claim,
A few of each, or several of the same.
(Signed)   Yours, *most truly,* ——"

                No ! my sight must fail,—
If that ain't Judas on the largest scale !

Well, this *is* modest; nothing else than that?
My coat? my boots? my pantaloons? my hat?
My stick? my gloves? as well as all my wits,
Learning and linen,—everything that fits!
Jack, said my lady, is it grog you'll try,
Or punch, or toddy, if perhaps you're dry?
Ah, said the sailor, though I can't refuse,
You know, my lady, 'tain't for me to choose;—
I'll take the grog to finish off my lunch,
And drink the toddy while you mix the punch.

————

THE SPEECH.   (The speaker, rising to be seen,
Looks very red, because so very green.)
I rise—I rise—with unaffected fear,
(Louder!—speak louder!—who the deuce can hear?)
I rise—I said—with undisguised dismay—
—Such are my feelings as I rise, I say!
Quite unprepared to face this learned throng,
Already gorged with eloquence and song;
Around my view are ranged on either hand
The genius, wisdom, virtue of the land;
" Hands that the rod of empire might have swayed "
Close at my elbow stir their lemonade;
Would you like Homer learn to write and speak,
That bench is groaning with its weight of Greek;
Behold the naturalist that in his teens
Found six new species in a dish of greens;
And lo, the master in a statelier walk,
Whose annual ciphering takes a ton of chalk;

And there the linguist, that by common roots
Through all their nurseries tracks old Noah's
    shoots,—
How Shem's proud children reared the Assyrian piles,
While Ham's were scattered through the Sandwich
    Isles !

—Fired at the thought of all the present shows,
My kindling fancy down the future flows ;
I see the glory of the coming days
O'er Time's horizon shoot its streaming rays ;
Near and more near the radiant morning draws
In living lustre (rapturous applause) ;
From east to west the blazing heralds run,
Loosed from the chariot of the ascending sun,
Through the long vista of uncounted years
In cloudless splendor (three tremendous cheers).
My eye prophetic, as the depths unfold,
Sees a new advent of the age of gold ;
While o'er the scene new generations press,
New heroes rise the coming time to bless,—
Not such as Homer's, who, we read in Pope,
Dined without forks and never heard of soap,—
Not such as May to Marlborough Chapel brings,
Lean, hungry, savage, anti-everythings,
Copies of Luther in the pasteboard style,—
But genuine articles,—the true Carlyle ;
While far on high the blazing orb shall shed
Its central light on Harvard's holy head,
And Learning's ensigns ever float unfurled
Here in the focus of the new-born world !

The speaker stops, and, trampling down the pause,
Roars through the hall the thunder of applause,
One stormy gust of long suspended Ahs!
One whirlwind chaos of insane hurrahs!

THE SONG.   But this demands a briefer line,—
A shorter muse and not the old long Nine;—
Long metre answers for a common song,
Though common metre does not answer long.

> She came beneath the forest dome
>   To seek its peaceful shade,
> An exile from her ancient home,—
>   A poor forsaken maid;
> No banner, flaunting high above,
>   No blazoned cross, she bore;
> One holy book of light and love
>   Was all her worldly store.

> The dark brown shadows passed away,
>   And wider spread the green,
> And, where the savage used to stray,
>   The rising mart was seen;
> So, when the laden winds had brought
>   Their showers of golden rain,
> Her lap some precious gleanings caught,
>   Like Ruth's amid the grain.

> But wrath soon gathered uncontrolled
>   Among the baser churls,
> To see her ankles red with gold,
>   Her forehead white with pearls;

" Who gave to thee the glittering bands
    That lace thine azure veins?
Who bade thee lift those snow-white hands
    We bound in gilded chains?"

These are the gems my children gave,
    The stately dame replied;
The wise, the gentle, and the brave,
    I nurtured at my side;
If envy still your bosom stings,
    Take back their rims of gold;
My sons will melt their wedding rings,
    And give a hundred-fold!

THE TOAST.—Oh, tell me, ye who thoughtless ask
Exhausted nature for a threefold task,
In wit and pathos if one share remains,
A safe investment for an ounce of brains?
Hard is the job to launch the desperate pun,
A pun-job dangerous as the Indian one.
Turned by the current of some stronger wit
Back from the object that you mean to hit,
Like the strange missile which the Australian
    throws,
Your verbal *boomerang* slaps you on the nose.
One vague inflection spoils the whole with doubt,
One trivial letter ruins all, left out;
A knot can choke a felon into clay,
A not will save him, spelt without the k;
The smallest word has some unguarded spot,
And danger lurks in i without a dot.

14

Thus great Achilles, who had shown his zeal
In healing wounds, died of a wounded heel;
Unhappy chief, who, when in childhood doused,
Had saved his bacon, had his feet been soused!
Accursed heel that killed a hero stout!
Oh, had your mother known that you were out,
Death had not entered at the trifling part
That still defies the small chirurgeon's art
With corns and bunions,—not the glorious John
Who wrote the book we all have pondered on,—
But other bunions, bound in fleecy hose,
To " Pilgrim's Progress " unrelenting foes!

A health, unmingled with the reveller's wine,
To him whose title is indeed divine;
Truth's sleepless watchman on her midnight tower,
Whose lamp burns brightest when the tempests
    lower.
Oh, who can tell with what a leaden flight
Drag the long watches of his weary night;
While at his feet the hoarse and blinding gale
Strews the torn wreck and bursts the fragile sail,
When stars have faded, when the wave is dark,
When rocks and sands embrace the foundering
    bark,
And still he pleads with unavailing cry,
Behold the light, O wanderer, look or die!

A health, fair Themis! Would the enchanted vine
Wreathed its green tendrils round this cup of
    thine;

If Learning's radiance fill thy modern court,
Its glorious sunshine streams through Blackstone's
    port !
Lawyers are thirsty, and their clients too,
Witness at least, if memory serve me true,
Those old tribunals, famed for dusty suits,
Where men sought justice ere they brushed their
    boots ;—
And what can match, to solve a learned doubt,
The warmth within that comes from "cold with-
    out " ?

Health to the art whose glory is to give
The crowning boon that makes it life to live.
Ask not her home ;—the rock where Nature flings
Her arctic lichen, last of living things,
The gardens, fragrant with the Orient's balm,
From the low jasmine to the star-like palm,
Hail her as mistress o'er the distant waves,
And yield their tribute to her wandering slaves.
Wherever, moistening the ungrateful soil,
The tear of suffering tracks the path of toil,
There, in the anguish of his fevered hours,
Her gracious finger points to healing flowers ;
Where the lost felon steals away to die,
Her soft hand waves before his closing eye ;
Where hunted misery finds his darkest lair,
The midnight taper shows her kneeling there !

Virtue,—the guide that men and nations own ;
And Law, the bulwark that protects her throne ;

And HEALTH, — to all its happiest charm that
    lends;
These and their servants, man's untiring friends;
Pour the bright lymph that Heaven itself lets
    fall,—
In one fair bumper let us toast them all!

NUX POSTCŒNATICA.

I WAS sitting with my microscope, upon my parlor
   rug,
With a very heavy quarto and a very lively bug;
The true bug had been organized with only two
   antennæ,
But the humbug in the copperplate would have
   them twice as many.

And I thought, like Dr. Faustus, of the emptiness
   of art,
How we take a fragment for the whole, and call
   the whole a part,
When I heard a heavy footstep that was loud
   enough for two,
And a man of forty entered, exclaiming,—"How
   d'ye do?"

He was not a ghost, my visitor, but solid flesh and
   bone;
He wore a Palo Alto hat, his weight was twenty
   stone;
(It's odd how hats expand their brims as riper years
   invade,
As if when life had reached its noon, it wanted them
   for shade!)

I lost my focus,—dropped my book,—the bug, who
     was a flea,
At once exploded, and commenced experiments on
     me.
They have a certain heartiness that frequently ap-
     palls,—
Those mediæval gentlemen in semilunar smalls!

"My boy," he said—(colloquial ways,—the vast,
     broad-hatted man),
"Come dine with us on Thursday next,—you must,
     you know you can;
We're going to have a roaring time, with lots of fun
     and noise,
Distinguished guests, et cetera, the JUDGE, and all
     the boys."

Not so,—I said,—my temporal bones are showing
     pretty clear
It's time to stop, just look and see that hair above
     this ear;
My golden days are more than spent,—and, what is
     very strange,
If these are real silver hairs, I'm getting lots of
     change.

Besides—my prospects—don't you know that people
     won't employ
A man that wrongs his manliness by laughing like
     a boy?

And suspect the azure blossom that unfolds upon a
    shoot,
As if wisdom's old potato could not flourish at its
    root!

It's a very fine reflection, when you're etching out
    a smile
On a copper plate of faces that would stretch at
    least a mile,
That, what with sneers from enemies, and cheapen-
    ing shrugs of friends,
It will cost you all the earnings that a month of
    labor lends!

It's a vastly pleasing prospect, when you're screw-
    ing out a laugh,
That your very next year's income is diminished by
    a half,
And a little boy trips barefoot that Pegasus may go,
And the baby's milk is watered that your Helicon
    may flow!

No;—the joke has been a good one,—but I'm get-
    ting fond of quiet,
And I don't like deviations from my customary
    diet;
So I think I will not go with you to hear the toasts
    and speeches,
But stick to old Montgomery Place, and have some
    pig and peaches.

The fat man answered :—Shut your mouth, and hear
    the genuine creed ;
The true essentials of a feast are only fun and
    feed ;
The force that wheels the planets round delights in
    spinning tops,
And that young earthquake t'other day was great
    at shaking props.

I tell you what, philosopher, if all the longest heads
That ever knocked their sinciputs in stretching on
    their beds
Were round one great mahogany, I'd beat those
    fine old folks
With twenty dishes, twenty fools, and twenty clever
    jokes !

Why, if Columbus should be there, the company
    would beg
He'd show that little trick of his of balancing the
    egg !
Milton to Stilton would give in, and Solomon to
    Salmon,
And Roger Bacon be a bore, and Francis Bacon
    gammon !

And as for all the "patronage" of all the clowns
    and boors
That squint their little narrow eyes at any freak of
    yours,

Do leave them to your prosier friends,—such fel-
    lows ought to die
When rhubarb is so very scarce and ipecac so high !

And so I come,—like Lochinvar, to tread a single
    measure,
To purchase with a loaf of bread a sugar-plum of
    pleasure,
To enter for the cup of glass that's run for after
    dinner,
Which yields a single sparkling draught, then breaks
    and cuts the winner.

Ah, that's the way delusion comes,—a glass of old
    Madeira,
A pair of visual diaphragms revolved by Jane or
    Sarah,
And down go vows and promises without the slight-
    est question
If eating words won't compromise the organs of
    digestion !

And yet, among my native shades, beside my nurs-
    ing mother,
Where every stranger seems a friend, and every
    friend a brother,
I feel the old convivial glow (unaided) o'er me steal-
    ing,—
The warm, champagny, old-particular, brandy-
    punchy feeling.

We're all alike ;—Vesuvius flings the scoriæ from
  his fountain,
But down they come in volleying rain back to the
  burning mountain ;
We leave, like those volcanic stones, our precious
  Alma Mater,
But will keep dropping in again to see the dear old
  crater.

ON LENDING A PUNCH-BOWL.

THIS ancient silver bowl of mine,—it tells of good
    old times,
Of joyous days, and jolly nights, and merry Christ-
    mas chimes ;
They were a free and jovial race, but honest, brave,
    and true,
That dipped their ladle in the punch when this old
    bowl was new.

A Spanish galleon brought the bar,—so runs the
    ancient tale ;
'Twas hammered by an Antwerp smith, whose arm
    was like a flail ;
And now and then between the strokes, for fear his
    strength should fail,
He wiped his brow, and quaffed a cup of good old
    Flemish ale.

'Twas purchased by an English squire to please his
    loving dame,
Who saw the cherubs, and conceived a longing for
    the same ;
And oft, as on the ancient stock another twig was
    found,
'Twas filled with caudle spiced and hot, and handed
    smoking round.

219

But, changing hands, it reached at length a Puritan
　　divine,
Who used to follow Timothy, and take a little wine,
But hated punch and prelacy; and so it was, per-
　　haps,
He went to Leyden, where he found conventicles and
　　schnapps.

And then, of course, you know what's next,—it left
　　the Dutchman's shore
With those that in the Mayflower came,—a hundred
　　souls and more,—
Along with all the furniture, to fill their new
　　abodes,—
To judge by what is still on hand, at least a hundred
　　loads.

'Twas on a dreary winter's eve, the night was clos-
　　ing dim,
When old Miles Standish took the bowl, and filled
　　it to the brim;
The little Captain stood and stirred the posset with
　　his sword,
And all his sturdy men at arms were ranged about
　　the board.

He poured the fiery Hollands in,—the man that
　　never feared,—
He took a long and solemn draught, and wiped his
　　yellow beard;

And one by one the musketeers,—the men that
 fought and prayed,—
All drank as 'twere their mother's milk, and not a
 man afraid.

That night, affrighted from his nest, the screaming
 eagle flew,
He heard the Pequot's ringing whoop, the soldier's
 wild halloo ;
And there the sachem learned the rule he taught to
 kith and kin,
" Run from the white man when you find he smells
 of Hollands gin ! "

A hundred years, and fifty more, had spread their
 leaves and snows,
A thousand rubs had flattened down each little
 cherub's nose ;
When once again the bowl was filled, but not in
 mirth or joy,
'Twas mingled by a mother's hand to cheer her
 parting boy.

Drink, John, she said, 'twill do you good,—poor
 child, you'll never bear
This working in the dismal trench, out in the midnight air ;
And if,—God bless me,—you were hurt, 'twould
 keep away the chill ;
So John *did* drink,—and well he wrought that
 night at Bunker's Hill !

I tell you, there was generous warmth in good old
 English cheer ;
I tell you, 'twas a pleasant thought to bring its
 symbol here.
'Tis but the fool that loves excess ;—hast thou a
 drunken soul ?
Thy bane is in thy shallow skull, not in my silver
 bowl !

I love the memory of the past,—its pressed yet
 fragrant flowers,—
The moss that clothes its broken walls,—the ivy on
 its towers,—
Nay, this poor bauble it bequeathed,—my eyes grow
 moist and dim,
To think of all the vanished joys that danced around
 its brim.

Then fill a fair and honest cup, and bear it straight
 to me ;
The goblet hallows all it holds, whate'er the liquid
 be ;
And may the cherubs on its face protect me from
 the sin,
That dooms one to those dreadful words,—" My
 dear, where *have* you been ? "

THE STETHOSCOPE SONG.

A PROFESSIONAL BALLAD.

THERE was a young man in Boston town
    He bought him a STETHOSCOPE nice and new,
All mounted and finished and polished down,
    With an ivory cap and a stopper too.

It happened a spider within did crawl,
    And spun him a web of ample size,
Wherein there chanced one day to fall
    A couple of very imprudent flies.

The first was a bottle-fly, big and blue,
    The second was smaller, and thin and long;
So there was a concert between the two,
    Like an octave flute and a tavern gong.

Now being from Paris but recently,
    This fine young man would show his skill;
And so they gave him, his hand to try,
    A hospital patient extremely ill.

Some said that his *liver* was short of *bile*,
    And some that his *heart* was over size,
While some kept arguing all the while
    He was crammed with *tubercles* up to his eyes.

223

This fine young man then up stepped he,
    And all the doctors made a pause;
Said he,—The man must die, you see,
    By the fifty-seventh of Louis's laws.

But, since the case is a desperate one,
    To explore his chest it may be well;
For, if he should die and it were not done,
    You know the *autopsy* would not tell.

Then out his stethoscope he took,
    And on it placed his curious ear;
Mon Dieu! said he, with a knowing look,
    Why, here is a sound that's mighty queer!

The *bourdonnement* is very clear,—
    Amphoric buzzing, as I'm alive!
Five doctors took their turn to hear;
    Amphoric buzzing, said all the five.

There's *empyema* beyond a doubt;
    We'll plunge a *trocar* in his side.—
The diagnosis was made out,
    They tapped the patient; so he died.

Now such as hate new-fashioned toys
    Began to look extremely glum;
They said that *rattles* were made for boys,
    And vowed that his *buzzing* was all a hum.

There was an old lady had long been sick,
    And what was the matter none did know;
Her pulse was slow, though her tongue was quick;
    To her this knowing youth must go.

So there the nice old lady sat,
    With phials and boxes all in a row;
She asked the young doctor what he was at,
    To thump her and tumble her ruffles so.

Now, when the stethoscope came out,
    The flies began to buzz and whiz;—
O ho! the matter is clear, no doubt;
    An *aneurism* there plainly is.

The *bruit de râpe* and the *bruit de scie*
    And the *bruit de diable* are all combined;
How happy Bouillaud would be,
    If he a case like this could find!

Now, when the neighboring doctors found
    A case so rare had been descried,
They every day her ribs did pound
    In squads of twenty; so she died.

Then six young damsels, slight and frail,
    Received this kind young doctor's cares;
They all were getting slim and pale,
    And short of breath on mounting stairs.

They all made rhymes with " sighs " and " skies,"
    And loathed their puddings and buttered rolls,
And dieted, much to their friends' surprise,
    On pickles and pencils and chalk and coals.

So fast their little hearts did bound,
    The frightened insects buzzed the more;
So over all their chests he found
    The *râle sifflant,* and *râle sonore.*
15

He shook his head ;—there's grave disease.—
    I greatly fear you all must die ;
A slight *post-mortem*, if you please,
    Surviving friends would gratify.

The six young damsels wept aloud,
    Which so prevailed on six young men,
That each his honest love avowed,
    Whereat they all got well again.

This poor young man was all aghast ;
    The price of stethoscopes came down ;
And so he was reduced at last
    To practise in a country town.

The doctors being very sore,
    A stethoscope they did devise,
That had a rammer to clear the bore,
    With a knob at the end to kill the flies.

Now use your ears, all you that can,
    But don't forget to mind your eyes,
Or you may be cheated, like this young man
    By a couple of silly, abnormal flies.

EXTRACTS FROM A MEDICAL POEM.

THE STABILITY OF SCIENCE.

The feeble seabirds, blinded in the storms,
On some tall lighthouse dash their little forms,
And the rude granite scatters for their pains
Those small deposits that were meant for brains.
Yet the proud fabric in the morning's sun
Stands all unconscious of the mischief done;
Still the red beacon pours its evening rays
For the lost pilot with as full a blaze,
Nay, shines, all radiance, o'er the scattered fleet
Of gulls and boobies brainless at its feet.
  I tell their fate, though courtesy disclaims
To call our kind by such ungentle names;
Yet, if your rashness bid you vainly dare,
Think of their doom, ye simple, and beware!

See where aloft its hoary forehead rears
The towering pride of twice a thousand years!
Far, far below the vast incumbent pile
Sleeps the gray rock from art's Ægean isle,
Its massive courses, circling as they rise,
Swell from the waves to mingle with the skies;
There every quarry lends its marble spoil,
And clustering ages blend their common toil;

227

The Greek, the Roman, reared its ancient walls,
The silent Arab arched its mystic halls;
In that fair niche, by countless billows laved,
Trace the deep lines that Sydenham engraved;
On yon broad front that breasts the changing swell,
Mark where the ponderous sledge of Hunter fell;
By that square buttress look where Louis stands,
The stone yet warm from his uplifted hands;
And say, O Science, shall thy life-blood freeze
When fluttering folly flaps on walls like these?

A PORTRAIT.

SIMPLE in youth, but not austere in age;
Calm, but not cold, and cheerful though a sage;
Too true to flatter, and too kind to sneer,
And only just when seemingly severe;
So gently blending courtesy and art,
That wisdom's lips seemed borrowing friendship's
    heart;
Taught by the sorrows that his age had known
In others' trials to forget his own,
As hour by hour his lengthened day declined,
The sweeter radiance lingered o'er his mind.
Cold were the lisp that spoke his early praise,
And hushed the voices of his morning days,
Yet the same accents dwelt on every tongue,
And love renewing kept him ever young.

A SENTIMENT.

Ὁ βιος βραχυς—life is but a song—
Ἡ τεχνη μαχρη—art is wondrous long;

Yet to the wise her paths are ever fair,
And Patience smiles, though Genius may despair.
Give us but knowledge, though by slow degrees,
And blend our toil with moments bright as these;
Let Friendship's accents cheer our doubtful way,
And Love's pure planet lend its guiding ray,—
Our tardy Art shall wear an angel's wings,
And life shall lengthen with the joy it brings!

A SONG OF OTHER DAYS.

As o'er the glacier's frozen sheet
    Breathes soft the Alpine rose,
So, through life's desert springing sweet,
    The flower of friendship grows;
And as, where'er the roses grow,
    Some rain or dew descends,
'Tis nature's law that wine should flow
    To wet the lips of friends.

    Then once again, before we part,
      My empty glass shall ring;
    And he that has the warmest heart
      Shall loudest laugh and sing.

They say we were not born to eat;
    But gray-haired sages think
It means,—Be moderate in your meat,
    And partly live to drink;
For baser tribes the rivers flow
    That know not wine or song;
Man wants but little drink below,
    But wants that little strong.

      Then once again, etc.

If one bright drop is like the gem
  That decks a monarch's crown,
One goblet holds a diadem
  Of rubies melted down !
A fig for Cæsar's blazing brow,
  But, like the Egyptian Queen,
Bid each dissolving jewel glow
  My thirsty lips between.

        Then once again, etc.

The Grecian's mound, the Roman's urn,
  Are silent when we call,
Yet still the purple grapes return
  To cluster on the wall ;
It was a bright Immortal's head
  They circled with the vine,
And o'er their best and bravest dead
  They poured the dark-red wine.

        Then once again, etc.

Methinks o'er every sparkling glass
  Young Eros waves his wings,
And echoes o'er its dimples pass
  From dead Anacreon's strings ;
And, tossing round its beaded brim
  Their locks of floating gold,
With bacchant dance and choral hymn
  Return the nymphs of old.

        Then once again, etc.

A welcome then to joy and mirth,
 From hearts as fresh as ours,
To scatter o'er the dust of earth
 Their sweetly mingled flowers;
'Tis Wisdom's self the cup that fills
 In spite of Folly's frown,
And Nature, from her vine-clad hills,
 That rains her life-blood down!

  Then once again, etc.

A SENTIMENT.

THE pledge of Friendship! it is still divine,
Though watery floods have quenched its burning
    wine;
Whatever vase the sacred drops may hold,
The gourd, the shell, the cup of beaten gold,
Around its brim the hand of Nature throws
A garland sweeter than the banquet's rose.
Bright are the blushes of the vine-wreathed bowl,
Warm with the sunshine of Anacreon's soul,
But dearer memories gild the tasteless wave
That fainting Sidney perished as he gave.
'Tis the heart's current lends the cup its glow,
Whate'er the fountain whence the draught may
    flow,—
The diamond dew-drops sparkling through the sand,
Scooped by the Arab in his sunburnt hand,
Or the dark streamlet oozing from the snow,
Where creep and crouch the shuddering Esqui-
    maux;—
Ay, in the stream that ere again we meet,
Shall burst the pavement, glistening at our feet,
And, stealing silent from its leafy hills,
Thread all our alleys with its thousand rills,—
In each pale draught if generous feeling blend,
And o'er the goblet friend shall smile on friend,
Even cold Cochituate every heart shall warm,
And genial Nature still defy reform!

TO AN ENGLISH FRIEND.

THE seed that wasteful Autumn cast
To waver on its stormy blast.
Long o'er the wintry desert tost,
Its living germ has never lost;
Dropped by the weary tempest's wing,
It feels the kindling ray of spring,
And starting from its dream of death,
Pours on the air its perfumed breath.

So, parted by the rolling flood,
The love that springs from common blood
Needs but a single sunlit hour
Of mingling smiles to bud and flower;
Unharmed its slumbering life has flown
From shore to shore, from zone to zone,
Where summer's falling roses stain
The tepid waves of Pontchartrain,
Or where the lichen creeps below
Katahdin's wreaths of whirling snow i
Though fiery sun and stiffening cold
May warp the fair ancestral mould,
No winter chills, no summer drains
The life-blood drawn from English veins,—
Still bearing, wheresoe'er it flows,
The love that with its fountain rose,
Unchanged by space, unwronged by time,
From age to age, from clime to clime!
234

THE PLOUGHMAN.

(ANNIVERSARY OF THE BERKSHIRE AGRICULTURAL
SOCIETY, OCT. 4TH, 1849.)

CLEAR the brown path, to meet his coulter's gleam!
Lo! on he comes, behind his smoking team,
With toil's bright dew-drops on his sun-burnt brow,
The lord of Earth, the hero of the plough!

First in the field before the reddening sun,
Last in the shadows when the day is done,
Line after line, along the bursting sod,
Marks the broad acres where his feet have trod;
Still, where he treads the stubborn clods divide,
The smooth fresh furrow opens deep and wide;
Matted and dense the tangled turf upheaves,
Mellow and dark the ridgy cornfield cleaves;
Up the steep hill-side, where the laboring train
Slants the long track that scores the level plain;
Through the moist valley, clogged with oozing clay,
The patient convoy breaks its destined way;
At every turn the loosening chains resound,
The swinging ploughshare circles glistening round,
Till the wide field one billowy waste appears,
And wearied hands unbind the panting steers.

These are the hands whose sturdy labor brings
The peasant's food, the golden pomp of kings:
235

This is the page, whose letters shall be seen
Changed by the sun to words of living green;
This is the scholar, whose immortal pen
Spells the first lesson hunger taught to men;
These are the lines, O heaven-commanded toil,
That fill thy deed,—the charter of the soil!

O gracious Mother, whose benignant breast
Wakes us to life, and lulls us all to rest,
How thy sweet features, kind to every clime,
Mock with their smile the wrinkled front of time!
We stain thy flowers,—they blossom o'er the dead;
We rend thy bosom, and it gives us bread;
O'er the red field that trampling strife has torn,
Waves the green plumage of thy tasselled corn;
Our maddening conflicts scar thy fairest plain,
Still thy soft answer is the growing grain.
Yet, O our Mother, while uncounted charms
Round the fresh clasp of thine embracing arms,
Let not our virtues in thy love decay,
And thy fond weakness waste our strength away.

No! by these hills, whose banners now displayed,
In blazing cohorts Autumn has arrayed:
By yon twin crest, amid the sinking sphere
Last to dissolve, and first to reappear;
By these fair plains the mountain circle screens,
And feeds in silence from its dark ravines;
True to their home, these faithful arms shall toil
To crown with peace their own untainted soil;

And, true to God, to freedom, to mankind,
If her chained bandogs Faction shall unbind,
These stately forms, that bending even now
Bowed their strong manhood to the humble plough,
Shall rise erect, the guardians of the land,
The same stern iron in the same right hand,
Till Gravlock thunders to the parting sun,
The sword has rescued what the ploughshare won !

A POEM

DELIVERED AT THE DEDICATION OF THE

PITTSFIELD CEMETERY.

September 9, 1850.

Angel of Death! extend thy silent reign!
Stretch thy dark sceptre o'er this new domain!
No sable car along the winding road
Has borne to earth its unresisting load;
No sudden mound has risen yet to show
Where the pale slumberer folds his arms below;
No marble gleams to bid his memory live
In the brief lines that hurrying Time can give;
Yet, O Destroyer! from thy shrouded throne
Look on our gift; this realm is all thine own!

Fair is the scene; its sweetness oft beguiled
From their dim paths the children of the wild;
The dark-haired maiden loved its grassy dells,
The feathered warrior claimed its wooded swells,
Still on its slopes the ploughman's ridges show
The pointed flints that left his fatal bow,
Chipped with rough art and slow barbarian toil,—
Last of his wrecks that strews the alien soil!

238

Here spread the fields that waved the ripened
    store
Till the brown arms of Labor held no more;
The scythe's broad meadow with its dusky blush;
The sickle's harvest with its velvet flush;
The green-haired maize, her silken tresses laid,
In soft luxuriance, on her harsh brocade;
The gourd that swells beneath her tossing plume;
The coarser wheat that rolls in lakes of bloom,—
Its coral stems and milk-white flowers alive
With the wide murmurs of the scattered hive;
The glossy apple with the pencilled streak
Of morning painted on its southern cheek;
The pear's long necklace strung with golden drops,
Arched, like the banyan, o'er its hasty props;
The humble roots that paid the laborer's care
With the cheap luxuries wealth consents to spare;
The healing herbs whose virtues could not save
The hand that reared them from the neighboring
    grave.

Yet all its varied charms, forever free
From task and tribute, Labor yields to thee;
No more when April sheds her fitful rain
The sower's hand shall cast its flying grain;
No more when Autumn strews the flaming leaves
The reaper's band shall gird its yellow sheaves;
For thee alike the circling seasons flow
Till the first blossoms heave the latest snow.
In the stiff clod below the whirling drifts,
In the loose soil the springing herbage lifts,

In the hot dust beneath the parching weeds
Life's wilting flower shall drop its shrivelled seeds;
Its germ entranced in thy unbreathing sleep
Till what thou sowest mightier angels reap!

Spirit of Beauty! let thy graces blend
With loveliest Nature all that Art can lend.
Come from the bowers where Summer's life-blood
    flows
Through the red lips of June's half-open rose,
Dressed in bright hues, the loving sunshine's dower;
For tranquil Nature owns no mourning flower.

Come from the forest where the beech's screen
Bars the fierce noonbeams with its flakes of green;
Stay the rude axe that bares the shadowy plains,
Stanch the deep wound that dries the maple's veins.

Come with the stream whose silver-braided rills
Fling their unclasping bracelets from the hills,
Till in one gleam, beneath the forest's wings,
Melts the white glitter of a hundred springs.

Come from the steeps where look majestic forth
From their twin thrones the Giants of the North
On the huge shapes that, crouching at their knees,
Stretch their broad shoulders, rough with shaggy
    trees.
Through the wide waste of ether, not in vain,
Their softened gaze shall reach our distant plain;
There, while the mourner turns his aching eyes
On the blue mounds that print the bluer skies,
Nature shall whisper that the fading view
Of mightiest grief may wear a heavenly hue.

Cherub of Wisdom ! let thy marble page
Leave its sad lesson, new to every age ;
Teach us to live, not grudging every breath
To the chill winds that waft us on to death,
But ruling calmly every pulse it warms,
And tempering gently every word it forms.

Seraph of Love ! in heaven's adoring zone,
Nearest of all around the central throne,
While with soft hands the pillowed turf we spread
That soon shall hold us in its dreamless bed,
With the low whisper—Who shall first be laid
In the dark chamber's yet unbroken shade ?—
Let thy sweet radiance shine rekindled here,
And all we cherish grow more truly dear.
Here in the gates of Death's o'erhanging vault,
Oh, teach us kindness for our brother's fault ;
Lay all our wrongs beneath this peaceful sod,
And lead our hearts to Mercy and its God.

Father of all ! in Death's relentless claim
We read Thy mercy by its sterner name ;
In the bright flower that decks the solemn bier,
We see Thy glory in its narrowed sphere ;
In the deep lessons that affliction draws,
We trace the curves of Thy encircling laws ;
In the long sigh that sets our spirits free,
We own the love that calls us back to Thee !

Through the hushed street, along the silent plain,
The spectral future leads its mourning train,
16

Dark with the shadows of uncounted bands,
Where man's white lips and woman's wringing
    hands
Track the still burden, rolling slow before,
That love and kindness can protect no more;
The smiling babe that, called to mortal strife,
Shuts its meek eyes and drops its little life;
The drooping child that prays in vain to live,
And pleads for help its parent cannot give;
The pride of beauty stricken in its flower;
The strength of manhood broken in an hour;
Age in its weakness, bowed by toil and care,
Traced in sad lines beneath its silvered hair.

The sun shall set, and heaven's resplendent
    spheres
Gild the smooth turf unhallowed yet by tears,
But ah, how soon the evening stars will shed
Their sleepless light around the slumbering dead!

Take them, O Father, in immortal trust!
Ashes to ashes, dust to kindred dust,
Till the last angel rolls the stone away,
And a new morning brings eternal day!

ASTRÆA:

THE BALANCE OF ILLUSIONS.[1]

WHAT secret charm, long whispering in mine ear,
Allures, attracts, compels, and chains me here,
Where murmuring echoes call me to resign
Their sacred haunts to sweeter lips than mine;
Where silent pathways pierce the solemn shade,
In whose still depths my feet have never strayed:
Here, in the home where grateful children meet,
And I, half alien, take the stranger's seat,
Doubting, yet hoping that the gift I bear
May keep its bloom in this unwonted air?
Hush, idle fancy, with thy needless art,
Speak from thy fountains, O my throbbing heart!

Say, shall I trust these trembling lips to tell
The fireside tale that memory knows so well?
How, in the days of Freedom's dread campaign,
A home-bred school-boy left his village plain,
Slow faring southward, till his wearied feet
Pressed the worn threshold of this fair retreat;
How, with his comely face and gracious mien,
He joined the concourse of the classic green,

[1] A poem delivered before the Phi Beta Kappa Society
of Yale College, August 14, 1850.

243

Nameless, unfriended, yet by Nature blest
With the rich tokens that she loves the best;
The flowing locks, his youth's redundant crown,
Smoothed o'er a brow unfurrowed by a frown;
The untaught smile that speaks so passing plain
A world all hope, a past without a stain;
The clear-hued cheek, whose burning current glows
Crimson in action, carmine in repose;
Gifts such as purchase, with unminted gold,
Smiles from the young and blessings from the old.

Say, shall my hand with pious love restore
The faint, far pictures time beholds no more?
How the grave Senior, he whose later fame
Stamps on our laws his own undying name,
Saw from on high, with half-paternal joy,
Some spark of promise in the studious boy,
And bade him enter, with benignant tone,
Those stately precincts which he called his own,
Where the fresh student and the youthful sage
Read by one taper from the common page;
How the true comrade, whose maturer date
Graced the large honors of his ancient State,
Sought his young friendship, which through every
        change
No time could weaken, no remove estrange;
How the great MASTER, reverend, solemn, wise,
Fixed on his face those calm, majestic eyes,
Full of grave meaning, where a child might read
The Hebraist's patience and the Pilgrim's creed,
But warm with flashes of parental fire
That drew the stripling to his second sire;

How kindness ripened, till the youth might dare
Take the low seat beside his sacred chair,
While the gray scholar, bending o'er the young,
Spelled the square types of Abraham's ancient
    tongue,
Or with mild rapture stooped devoutly o'er
His small coarse leaf, alive with curious lore;
Tales of grim judges, at whose awful beck
Flashed the broad blade across a royal neck
Or learned dreams of Israel's long-lost child
Found in the wanderer of the western wild.

Dear to his age were memories such as these,
Leaves of his June in life's autumnal breeze;
Such were the tales that won my boyish ear,
Told in low tones that evening loves to hear.

Thus in the scene I pass so lightly o'er,
Trod for a moment, then beheld no more,
Strange shapes and dim, unseen by other eyes,
Through the dark portals of the past arise;
I see no more the fair embracing throng,
I hear no echo to my saddened song,
No more I heed the kind or curious gaze,
The voice of blame, the rustling thrill of praise;
Alone, alone, the awful past I tread
White with the marbles of the slumbering dead;
One shadowy form my dreaming eyes behold
That leads my footsteps as it led of old,
One floating voice, amid the silence heard,
Breathes in my ear love's long unspoken word;—

These are the scenes thy youthful eyes have known;
My heart's warm pulses claim them as its own!
The sapling compassed in thy fingers' clasp,
My arms scarce circle in their twice-told grasp,
Yet in each leaf of yon o'ershadowing tree
I read a legend that was traced by thee.
Year after year the living wave has beat
These smooth-worn channels with its trampling feet,
Yet in each line that scores the grassy sod
I see the pathway where thy feet have trod.
Though from the scene that hears my faltering lay,
The few that loved thee long have passed away.
Thy sacred presence all the landscape fills,
Its groves and plains and adamantine hills!

Ye who have known the sudden tears that flow,—
Sad tears, yet sweet, the dews of twilight woe,—
When, led by chance, your wandering eye has
        crossed
Some poor memorial of the loved and lost,
Bear with my weakness as I look around
On the dear relics of this holy ground,
These bowery cloisters, shadowed and serene,
My dreams have pictured ere mine eyes have seen.

And oh, forgive me, if the flower I brought
Droops in my hand beside this burning thought;
The hopes and fears that marked this destined hour,
The chill of doubt, the startled throb of power,
The flush of pride, the trembling glow of shame,
All fade away and leave my FATHER's name!

WINTER is past; the heart of Nature warms
Beneath the wrecks of unresisted storms;
Doubtful at first, suspected more than seen,
The southern slopes are fringed with tender green;
On sheltered banks, beneath the dripping eaves,
Spring's earliest nurslings spread their glowing
    leaves,
Bright with the hues from wider pictures won,
White, azure, golden,—drift, or sky, or sun;—
The snowdrop, bearing on her patient breast
The frozen trophy torn from winter's crest:
The violet, gazing on the arch of blue
Till her own iris wears its deepened hue;
The spendthrift crocus, bursting through the mould
Naked and shivering with his cup of gold.
Swelled with new life, the darkening elm on high
Prints her thick buds against the spotted sky;
On all her boughs the stately chestnut cleaves
The gummy shroud that wraps her embryo leaves;
The housefly, stealing from his narrow grave,
Drugged with the opiate that November gave,
Beats with faint wing against the sunny pane,
Or crawls, tenacious, o'er its lucid plain;
From shaded chinks of lichen-crusted walls,
In languid curves, the gliding serpent crawls;
The bog's green harper, thawing from his sleep,
Twangs a hoarse note and tries a shortened leap;
On floating rails that face the softening noons
The still shy turtles range their dark platoons,
Or toiling, aimless, o'er the mellowing fields,
Trails through the grass their tessellated shields.

At last young April, ever frail and fair,
Wooed by her playmate with the golden hair,
Chased to the margin of receding floods
O'er the soft meadows starred with opening buds,
In tears and blushes sighs herself away,
And hides her cheek beneath the flowers of May,

Then the proud tulip lights her beacon blaze,
Her clustering curls the hyacinth displays,
O'er her tall blades the crested fleur-de-lis,
Like blue-eyed Pallas, towers erect and free ;
With yellower flames the lengthened sunshine
        glows,
And love lays bare the passion-breathing rose ;
Queen of the lake, along its reedy verge
The rival lily hastens to emerge,
Her snowy shoulders glistening as she strips,
Till morn is sultan of her parted lips.

Then bursts the song from every leafy glade,
The yielding season's bridal serenade ;
Then flash the wings returning summer calls
Through the deep arches of her forest halls ;
The bluebird breathing from his azure plumes
The fragrance borrowed where the myrtle blooms ;
The thrush, poor wanderer, dropping meekly down,
Clad in his remnant of autumnal brown ;
The oriole, drifting like a flake of fire
Rent by the whirlwind from a blazing spire ;
The robin, jerking his spasmodic throat,
Repeats, *staccato*, his peremptory note ;

The crackbrained bobolink courts his crazy mate,
Poised on a bulrush tipsy with his weight;
Nay, in his cage the lone canary sings,
Feels the soft air and spreads his idle wings;—

Why dream I here within these caging walls,
Deaf to her voice while blooming Nature calls;
Peering and gazing with insatiate looks
Through blinding lenses, or in wearying books?
Off, gloomy spectres of the shrivelled past,
Fly with the leaves that filled the Autumn blast!
Ye imps of Science, whose relentless chains
Lock the warm tides within these living veins,
Close your dim cavern, while its captive strays
Dazzled and giddy in the morning's blaze!

What life is this, that spreads in sudden birth
Its plumes of light around a new-born earth?
Is this the sun that brought the unwelcome day,
Pallid and glimmering with his lifeless ray,
Or through the sash that bars yon narrow cage
Slanted, intrusive, on the opened page?
Is this soft breath the same complaining gale
That filled my slumbers with its murmuring wail?
Is this green mantle of elastic sod
The same brown desert with its frozen clod,
Where the last ridges of the dingy snow
Lie till the windflower blooms unstained below?

Thus to my heart its wonted tides return
When sullen Winter breaks his crystal urn,

And o'er the turf in wild profusion showers
Its dewy leaflets and ambrosial flowers.
In vacant rapture for a while I range
Through the wide scene of universal change,
Till, as the statue in its nerves of stone
Felt the new senses wakening one by one,
Each long-closed inlet finds its destined ray
Through the dark curtain Spring has rent away.
I crush the buds the clustering lilacs bear;
The same sweet fragrance that I loved is there;
The same fresh hues each opening disk reveals;
Soft as of old each silken petal feels;
The birch's rind its flavor still retains,
Its boughs still ringing with the selfsame strains;
Above, around, rekindling Nature claims
Her glorious altars wreathed in living flames;
Undimmed, unshadowed, far as morning shines,
Feeds with fresh incense her eternal shrines.
Lost in her arms, her burning life I share,
Breathe the wild freedom of her perfumed air,
From Heaven's fair face the long-drawn shadows
    roll,
And all its sunshine floods my opening soul!

Yet in the darksome crypt I left so late,
Whose only altar is its rusted grate,—
Sepulchral, rayless, joyless, as it seems,
Shamed by the glare of May's refulgent beams,—
While the dim seasons dragged their shrouded
    train,
Its paler splendors were not quite in vain.

From these dull bars the cheerful firelight's glow
Streamed through the casement o'er the spectral
    snow;
Here, while the night-wind wreaked its frantic will
On the loose ocean and the rock-bound hill,
Rent the cracked topsail from its quivering yard,
And rived the oak a thousand storms had scarred,
Fenced by these walls the peaceful taper shone,
Nor felt a breath to swerve its trembling cone.

Not all unblest the mild interior scene
When the red curtain spread its folded screen;
O'er some light task the lonely hours were past,
And the long evening only flew too fast;
Or the wide chair its leathern arms would lend,
In genial welcome to some easy friend,
Stretched on its bosom with relaxing nerves,
Slow moulding, plastic, to its hollow curves;
Perchance indulging, if of generous creed,
In brave Sir Walter's dream-compelling weed.
Or, happier still, the evening hour would bring
To the round table its expected ring,
And while the punch bowl's sounding depths were
    stirred,—
Its silver cherubs smiling as they heard,—
O'er caution's head the blinding hood was flung,
And friendship loosed the jesses of the tongue.

Such the warm life this dim retreat has known,
Not quite deserted when its guests were flown;

Nay, filled with friends, an unobtrusive set,
Guiltless of calls and cards and etiquette,
Ready to answer, never known to ask,
Claiming no service, prompt for every task.

On those dark shelves no housewife tool profanes,
O'er his mute files the monarch folio reigns;
A mingled race, the wreck of chance and time,
That talk all tongues and breathe of every clime;
Each knows his place, and each may claim his part
In some quaint corner of his master's heart.
This old Decretal, won from Kloss's hoards,
Thick-leafed, brass-cornered, ribbed with oaken
            boards,
Stands the gray patriarch of the graver rows,
Its fourth ripe century narrowing to its close;
Not daily conned, but glorious still to view
With glistening letters wrought in red and blue.
There towers Stagira's all-embracing sage,
The Aldine anchor on his opening page;
There sleep the births of Plato's heavenly mind
In yon dark tome by jealous clasps confined,
" Olim e libris "—(dare I call it mine ?)
Of Yale's great Head and Killingworth's divine !
In those square sheets the songs of Maro fill
The silvery types of smooth-leafed Baskerville;
High over all, in compact close array,
Their classic wealth the Elzevirs display.
In lower regions of the sacred space
Range the dense volumes of a humbler race;

There grim chirurgeons all their mysteries teach
In spectral pictures, or in crabbed speech;
Harvey and Haller, fresh from Nature's page,
Shoulder the dreamers of an earlier age,
Lully and Geber, and the learned crew
That loved to talk of all they could not do.
Why count the rest,—those names of later days
That many love, and all agree to praise,—
Or point the titles, where a glance may read
The dangerous lines of party or of creed?
Too well, perchance, the chosen list would show
What few may care and none can claim to know.
Each has his features, whose exterior seal
A brush may copy, or a sunbeam seal
Go to his study,—on the nearest shelf
Stands the mosaic portrait of himself.

What though for months the tranquil dust de-
    scends,
Whitening the heads of these mine ancient friends,
While the damp offspring of the modern press
Flaunts on my table with its pictured dress;
Not less I love each dull familiar face,
Not less should miss it from the appointed place;
I snatch the book, along whose burning leaves
His scarlet web our wild romancer weaves,
Yet, while proud Hester's fiery pangs I share,
My old MAGNALIA must be standing *there!*

See, while I speak my fireside joys return,
The lamp rekindles and the ashes burn,

The dream of summer fades before their ray,
As in red firelight sunshine dies away.

A twofold picture ; ere the first was gone,
The deepening outline of the next was drawn,
And wavering fancy hardly dares to choose
The first or last of her dissolving views.

No Delphic sage is wanted to divine
The shape of Truth beneath my gauzy line ;
Yet there are truths,—like schoolmates, once well
        known,
But half remembered, not enough to own,—
That lost from sight in life's bewildering train,
May be, like strangers, introduced again,
Dressed in new feathers, as from time to time
May please our friends, the milliners of rhyme.

Trust not, it says, the momentary hue
Whose false complexion paints the present view ;
Red, yellow, violet, stain the rainbow's light,
The prism dissolves, and all again is white.

When o'er the street the morning peal is flung
From yon tall belfry with the brazen tongue,
Its wide vibrations, wafted by the gale,
To each far listener tell a different tale.

The sexton, stooping to the quivering floor
Till the great caldron spills its brassy roar,
Whirls the hot axle, counting, one by one,
Each dull concussion, till his task is done.

Toil's patient daughter, when the welcome note
Clangs through the silence from the steeple's throat,

Streams a white unit, to the checkered street,
Demure, but guessing whom she soon shall meet;
The bell, responsive to her secret flame,
With every note repeats her lover's name.

The lover, tenant of the neighboring lane,
Sighing, and fearing lest he sigh in vain,
Hears the stern accents, as they come and go,
Their only burden one despairing No!

Ocean's rough child, whom many a shore has
        known
Ere homeward breezes swept him to his own,
Starts at the echo as it circles round,
A thousand memories kindling with the sound;
The early favorite's unforgotten charms,
Whose blue initials stain his tawny arms;
His first farewell, the flapping canvas spread,
The seaward streamers crackling o'er his head,
His kind, pale mother, not ashamed to weep
Her first-born's bridal with the haggard deep,
While the brave father stood with tearless eye,
Smiling and choking with his last good-by.

'Tis but a wave, whose spreading circle beats,
With the same impulse, every nerve it meets,
Yet who shall count the varied shapes that ride
On the round surge of that aërial tide!

O child of earth! If floating sounds like these
Steal from thyself their power to wound or please,
If here or there thy changing will inclines,
As the bright zodiac shifts its rolling signs,

Look at thy heart, and when its depths are known,
Then try thy brother's, judging by thine own,
But keep thy wisdom to the narrow range,
While its own standards are the sport of change,
Nor ask mankind to tremble, and obey
The passing breath that holds thy passion's sway.

But how, alas! among our eager race,
Shall smiling candor show her girlish face?
What place is secret to the meddling crew,
Whose trade is settling what we all shall do?
What verdict sacred from the busy fools,
That sell the jargon of their outlaw schools?
What pulpit certain to be never vexed
With libels sanctioned by a holy text?
Where, O my country, is the spot that yields
The freedom fought for on a hundred fields?

Not one strong tyrant holds the servile chain,
Where all may vote, and each may hope to reign
One sturdy cord a single limb may bind,
And leave the captive only half confined,
But the free spirit finds its legs and wings
Tied with unnumbered Liliputian strings,
Which, like the spider's undiscovered fold,
In countless meshes round the prisoner rolled,
With silken pressure that he scarce can feel,
Clamp every fibre as in bands of steel!

Hard is the task to point in civil phrase
One's own dear people's foolish works or ways;

Woe to the friend that marks a touchy fault,
Himself obnoxious to the world's assault!
Think what an earthquake is a nation's hiss,
That takes its circuit through a land like this;
Count with the census, would you be precise,
From sea to sea, from oranges to ice;
A thousand myriads are its virile lungs,
A thousand myriads its contralto tongues!
    And oh, remember the indignant press;
Honey is bitter to its fond caress,
But the black venom that its hate lets fall
Would shame to sweetness the hyena's gall!

    Briefly and gently let the task be tried
To touch some frailties on their tender side;
Not to dilate on each imagined wrong,
And spoil at once our temper and our song,
But once or twice a passing gleam to throw
On some rank failings ripe enough to show,
Patterns of others,—made of common stuff,—
The world will furnish parallels enough,—
Such as bewilder their contracted view,
Who make one pupil do the work of two;
Who following Nature, where her tracks divide,
Drive all their passions on the narrower side,
And pour the phials of their virtuous wrath
On half mankind that take the wider path.

    Nature is liberal to her inmost soul,
She loves alike the tropic and the pole,
The storm's wild anthem, and the sunshine's calm,
— 17

The arctic fungus, and the desert palm ;
Loves them alike, and wills that each **maintain**
Its destined share of her divided reign ;
No creeping moss refuse her crystal **gem,**
No soaring pine her cloudy diadem !

Alas ! her children, borrowing but in **part**
The flowing pulses of her generous heart,
Shame their kind mother with eternal **strife**
At all the crossings of their mingled life ;
Each age, each people, finds its ready **shifts**
To quarrel stoutly o'er her choicest gifts.

History can tell of early ages dim,
When man's chief glory was in strength of **limb ;**
Then the best patriot gave the hardest **knocks,**
The height of virtue was to fell an ox ;
Ill fared the babe of questionable mould,
Whom its stern father happened to behold ;
In vain the mother with her ample vest
Hid the poor nursling on her throbbing **breast ;**
No tears could save him from the kitten's **fate,**
To live an insult to the warlike state.

This weakness passed, and nations owned **once**
    more,
Man was still human, measuring five feet **four,**
The anti-cripples ceased to domineer,
And owned Napleon worth a grenadier.

In these mild times the ancient bully's **sport**
Would lead its hero to a well-known court ;

Olympian athletes, though the pride of Greece,
Must face the Justice if they broke the peace,
And valor find some inconvenient checks,
If strolling Theseus met Policeman X.

Perhaps too far in these considerate days
Has Patience carried her submissive ways;
Wisdom has taught us to be calm and meek,
To take one blow and turn the other cheek;
It is not written what a man shall do,
If the rude caitiff strike the other too?

Land of our fathers, in thine hour of need
God helped thee, guarded by the passive creed!
As the lone pilgrim trusts to beads and cowl,
When through the forest rings the gray wolf's howl;
As the deep galleon trusts her gilded prow
When the black corsair slants athwart her bow;
As the poor pheasant, with his peaceful mien,
Trusts to his feathers, shining golden-green,
When the dark plumage with the crimson beak
Has rustled shadowy from its splintered peak;
So trust thy friends, whose idle tongues would charm
The lifted sabre from thy foeman's arm,
Thy torches ready for the answering peal
From bellowing fort and thunder-freighted keel!

Yet when thy champion's stormy task is done,
The frigate silenced and the fortress won,
When toil-worn valor claims his laurel wreath,
His reeking cutlass slumbering in its sheath,

The fierce declaimer shall be heard once more,
Whose twang was smothered by the conflict's **roar**;
Heroes shall fall that strode unharmed away
Through the red heaps of many a doubtful day,
Hacked in his sermons, riddled in his prayers,
The broadcloth slashing what the broad**sword**
     spares!

Untaught by trial, ignorance might suppose
That all our fighting must be done with blows;
Alas! not so ; between the lips and brain
A dread artillery masks its loaded train ;
The smooth portcullis of the smiling face
Veils the grim battery with deceptive grace,
But in the flashes of its opened fire,
Truth, Honor, Justice, Peace, and Love expire.

Yon whey-faced brother, who delights **to wear**
A weedy flux of ill-conditioned hair,
Seems of the sort that in a crowded place
One elbows freely into smallest space ;
A timid creature, lax of knee and hip,
Whom small disturbance whitens round the **lip**;
One of those harmless spectacled machines,
Ignored by waiters **when** they call for greens,
Whom schoolboys question if their walk **transcends**
The last advices of maternal friends,
Whom John, obedient to his master's sign,
Conducts, laborious, up to ninety-nine,
While Peter, glistening with luxurious scor**n**,
Husks his white ivories like an ear of corn;

Dark in the brow and bilious in the cheek,
Whose yellowish linen flowers but once a week,
Conspicuous, annual, in their threadbare suits,
And the laced high-lows which they call their boots.
Well mayst thou *shun* that dingy front severe,
But him, O stranger, him thou canst not *fear!*

Be slow to judge, and slower to despise,
Man of broad shoulders and heroic size!
The tiger, writhing from the boa's rings,
Drops at the fountain where the cobra stings.
In that lean phantom, whose extended glove
Points to the text of universal love,
Behold the master that can tame thee down
To crouch, the vassal of his Sunday frown;
His velvet throat against thy corded wrist,
His loosened tongue against thy doubled fist!

The MORAL BULLY, though he never swears,
Nor kicks intruders down his entry stairs,
Though meekness plants his backward sloping hat,
And non-resistance ties his white cravat,
Though his black broadcloth glories to be seen
In the same plight with Shylock's gabardine,
Hugs the same passion to his narrow breast,
That heaves the cuirass on the trooper's chest,
Hears the same hell-hounds yelling in his rear,
That chase from port the maddened buccaneer,
Feels the same comfort while his acrid words
Turn the sweet milk of kindness into curds,
Or with grim logic prove, beyond debate,
That all we love is worthiest of our hate,

As the scarred ruffian of the pirates' deck,
When his long swivel rakes the staggering wreck!

Heaven keep us all! Is every rascal clown,
Whose arm is stronger, free to knock us down?
Has every scarecrow, whose cachectic soul
Seems fresh from Bedlam, airing on parole,
Who, though he carries but a doubtful trace
Of angel visits on his hungry face,
From lack of marrow or the coin to pay,
Has dogged some vices in a shabby way,
The right to stick us with his cut-throat terms,
And bait his homilies with his brother worms?

If generous fortune give me leave to choose
My saucy neighbors barefoot or in shoes,
I leave the hero blustering while he dares
On platforms furnished with posterior stairs,
Till prudence drives him to his " earnest " legs
With large bequest of disappointed eggs,
And take the brawler whose unstudied dress
Becomes him better, and protects him less ;
Give me the bullying of the scoundrel crew,
If swaggering virtue won't insult me too!
Come, let us breathe ; a something not divine
Has mingled, bitter, with the flowing line.
Pause for a moment, while our soul forgets
The noisy tribe in panta-loons or -lets ;
Nor pass, ungrateful, by the debt we owe
To those who teach us half of all we know,
Not in rude license, or unchristian scorn,
But hoping, loving, pitying, while they warn!

Sweep out the pieces !   Round a careless **room**
The feather duster follows up the broom ;
If the last target took a round of grape
To knock its beauty something out of **shape,**
The next asks only, if the listener **please,**
A schoolboy's blowpipe and a gill of **peas.**

This creeping object, caught upon the **brink**
Of an old teacup, filled with muddy **ink,**
Lives on a leaf that buds from time to **time**
In certain districts of a temperate clime.
O'er this he toils in silent corners snug,
And leaves a track behind him, like a **slug ;**
The leaves he stains a humbler tribe **devours,**
Thrown off in monthly or in weekly **showers ;**
Himself kept savage on a starving fare,
Of such exuviæ as his friends can spare.

Let the bug drop, and view him if we **can**
In his true aspect as a *quasi* man.
The little wretch, whose terebrating **powers**
Would bore a Paixhan in a dozen **hours,**
Is called a CRITIC by the heavy **friends**
That help to pay his minus dividends.

The pseudo-critic-editorial race
Owns no allegiance but the law of **place ;**
Each to his region sticks through thick **and thin,**
Stiff as a beetle spiked upon a pin.
Plant him in Boston, and his sheet **he fills**
With all the slipslop of his **threefold hills,**

Talks as if Nature kept her choicest smiles
Within his radius of a dozen miles,
And nations waited till his next Review
Had made it plain what Providence must do.
Would you believe him, water is not damp
Except in buckets with the Hingham stamp,
And Heaven should build the walls of Paradise
Of Quincy granite lined with Wenham ice.

But Hudson's banks, with more congenial skies
Swell the small creature to alarming size;
A gayer pattern wraps his flowery chest,
A sham more brilliant sparkles on his breast,
An eyeglass, hanging from a gilded chain,
Taps the white leg that trips his rakish cane;
Strings of new names, the glories of the age,
Hang up to dry on his exterior page,
Titanic pygmies, shining lights obscure,
His favored sheets have managed to secure,
Whose wide renown beyond their own abode
Extends for miles along the Harlaem road;
New radiance lights his patronizing smile,
New airs distinguish his patrician style,
New sounds are mingled with his fatal hiss,
Oftenest, "*provincial*" and "*metropolis*."

He cry "*provincial*," with imperious brow!
The half-bred rogue, that groomed his mother's cow!
Fed on coarse tubers and Æolian beans
Till clownish manhood crept among his teens,
When, after washing and unheard-of pains
To lard with phrases his refractory brains,

A third-rate college licked him to the shape,
Not of the scholar, but the scholar's ape!

God bless Manhattan!   Let her fairly claim,
With all the honors due her ancient name,
Worth, wisdom, wealth, abounding and to spare,
Rags, riots, rogues, at least her honest share;
But not presume, because, by sad mischance,
The mobs of Paris wring the neck of France,
Fortune has ordered she shall turn the poise
Of thirty Empires with her Bowery boys!

The poorest hamlet on the mountain's side
Looks on her glories with a sister's pride;
When the first babes her fruitful ship-yards wean,
Play round the breasts of Ocean's conquered queen,
The shout of millions, borne on every breeze,
Sweeps with EXCELSIOR o'er the enfranchised seas!

Yet not too rashly let her think to bind
Beneath her circlet all the nation's mind;
Our star-crowned mother, whose informing soul
Clings to no fragment, but pervades the whole,
Views with a smile the clerk of Maiden Lane,
Who takes her ventral ganglion for her brain!
No fables tell us of Minervas born
From bags of cotton or from sacks of corn;
The halls of Leyden Science used to cram,
While dulness snored in purse-proud Amsterdam!

But those old burghers had a foggy clime,
And better luck may come the second time;

What though some churls of doubtful sense declare
That poison lurks in her commercial air,
Her buds of genius dying premature,
From some malaria draining cannot cure ;
Nay, that so dangerous is her golden soil,
Whate'er she borrows, she contrives to spoil ;
That drooping minstrels in a few brief years
Lose their sweet voice, the gift of other spheres ;
That wafted singing from their native shore,
They touch the Battery, and are heard no more ;—
By those twinned waves that wear the varied gleams
Beryl or sapphire mingles in their streams,
Till the fair sisters o'er her yellow sands,
Clasping their soft and snowy ruffled hands,
Lay on her footstool with their silver keys
Strength from the mountains, freedom from the
        seas,—
Some future day may see her rise sublime
Above her counters,—only give her time !

When our first Soldiers' swords of honor gild
The stately mansions that her tradesmen build ;
When our first Statesmen take the Broadway
        track ;
Our first Historians following at their back ;
When our first Painters, dying, leave behind
On her proud walls the shadows of their mind ;
When our first Poets flock from farthest scenes
To take in hand her pictured Magazines ;
When our first Scholars are content to dwell
Where their own printers teach them how to spell ;

When world-known Science crowds toward **her**
   gates,
Then shall the children of our hundred States
Hail her a true METROPOLIS of men,
The nation's centre.   Then, and not till then!

  The song is failing.   Yonder changing tower
Shakes in its cup the more than brimming **hour**;
The full-length gallery which the fates deny,
A colored Moral briefly must supply.

  No life worth naming ever comes to good
If always nourished on the selfsame food;
The creeping mite may live so if he please,
And feed on Stilton till he turns to cheese,
But cool Magendie proves beyond a doubt,
If mammals try it, that their eyes drop out.

  No reasoning natures find it safe to feed
For their sole diet on a single creed;
It chills their hearts, alas! it fills their lungs,
And spoils their eyeballs while it spares **their**
   tongues.

  When the first larvæ on the elm are seen,
The crawling wretches, like its leaves, are **green**;
Ere chill October shakes the latest down,
They, like the foliage, change their tint to **brown**;
On the blue flower a bluer flower you spy,
You stretch to pluck it—'tis a butterfly;
The flattened tree-toads so resemble bark,
They're hard to find as Ethiops in the dark;

The woodcock, stiffening to fictitious mud,
Cheats the young sportsman thirsting for his blood.
So by long living on a single lie,
Nay, on one truth, will creatures get its dye;
Red, yellow, green, they take their subject's hue,—
Except when squabbling turns them black and blue!

The song is passing.   Let its meaning rise
To loftier notes before its echo dies,
Nor leave, ungr cious, in its parting train
A trivial flourish or discordant strain.

These lines may teach, rough-spoken though they be,
Thy gentle creed, divinest Charity!
Truth is at heart not always as she seems,
Judged by our sleeping or our waking dreams.

We trust and doubt, we question and believe,
From life's dark threads a trembling faith to weave,
Frail as the web that misty night has spun,
Whose dew-gemmed awnings glitter in the sun.
Though Sovereign Wisdom, at His creatures' call,
Has taught us much, He has not taught us all;
When Sinai's summit was Jehovah's throne,
The chosen Prophet knew His voice alone;
When Pilate's hall that awful question heard,
The Heavenly Captive answered not a word.

Eternal Truth!   Beyond our hopes and fears
Sweep the vast orbits of thy myriad spheres!

From age to age while History carves sublime
On her waste rock the flaming curves of time,
How the wild swayings of our planet show
That worlds unseen surround the world we know!

The song is hushed. Another moment parts
This breathing zone, this belt of living hearts;
Ah, think not thus the parting moment ends
The soul's embrace of new-discovered friends.

Sleep on my heart, thou long-expected hour,
Time's new-born daughter, with thine infant dower,
One sad, sweet look from those expiring charms
The clasping centuries strangle in their arms,
Dreams of old halls, and shadowy arches green,
And kindly faces loved as soon as seen!

Sleep, till the fires of manhood fade away,
The sprinkled locks have saddened into gray,
And age, oblivious, blends thy memories old
With hoary legends that his sire has told!

AGNES.

PART FIRST.

THE KNIGHT.

THE tale I tell is gospel true,
    As all the bookmen know,
And pilgrims who have strayed to view
    The wrecks still left to show.

The old, old story,—fair, and young,
    And fond,—and not too wise,—
That matrons tell, with sharpened tongue,
    To maids with downcast eyes.

Ah! maidens err and matrons warn
    Beneath the coldest sky;
Love lurks amid the tasselled corn
    As in the bearded rye!

But who would dream our sober sires
    Had learned the old world's ways,
And warmed their hearths with lawless fires
    In Shirley's homespun days?

'Tis like some poet's pictured trance
   His idle rhymes recite,—
This old New-England-born romance
   Of Agnes and the Knight;

Yet, known to all the country round,
   Their home is standing still,
Between Wachusett's lonely mound
   And Shawmut's threefold hill.

—One hour we rumble on the rail,
   One half-hour guide the rein,
We reach at last, o'er hill and dale,
   The village on the plain.

With blackening wall and mossy roof,
   With stained and warping floor,
A stately mansion stands aloof
   And bars its haughty door.

This lowlier portal may be tried,
   That breaks the gable wall;
And lo! with arches opening wide,
   Sir Harry Frankland's hall!

'Twas in the second George's day
   They sought the forest shade,
The knotted trunks they cleared away,
   The massive beams they laid,

They piled the rock-hewn chimney tall,
   They smoothed the terraced ground,

They reared the marble-pillared wall
　　That fenced the mansion round.

Far stretched beyond the village bound
　　The Master's broad domain;
With page and valet, horse and hound,
　　He kept a goodly train.

And, all the midland county through,
　　The ploughman stopped to gaze
Whene'er his chariot swept in view
　　Behind the shining bays,

With mute obeisance, grave and slow,
　　Repaid by nod polite,—
For such the way with high and low
　　Till after Concord fight.

Nor less to courtly circles known
　　That graced the three-hilled town
With far-off splendors of the Throne,
　　And glimmerings from the Crown;

Wise Phipps, who held the seals of state
　　For Shirley over sea;
Brave Knowles, whose press-gang moved of late
　　The King Street mob's decree;

And judges grave, and colonels grand,
　　Fair dames and stately men,
The mighty people of the land,
　　The "World" of there and then.

'Twas strange no Chloe's "beauteous Form,"
　　And " Eyes ' cœlestial Blew,"
This Strephon of the West could warm,
　　No Nymph his Heart subdue!

Perchance he wooed as gallants use,
　　Whom fleeting loves enchain,
But still unfettered, free to choose,
　　Would brook no bridle-rein.

He saw the fairest of the fair,
　　But smiled alike on all;
No band his roving foot might snare,
　　No ring his hand enthrall.

PART SECOND.

THE MAIDEN.

WHY seeks the knight that rocky cape
　　Beyond the Bay of Lynn?
What chance his wayward course may shape
　　To reach its village inn?

No story tells; whate'er we guess,
　　The past lies deaf and still,
But Fate, who rules to blight or bless,
　　Can lead us where she will.

Make way!　Sir Harry's coach and four,
　　And liveried grooms that ride!

18

They cross the ferry, touch the shore
　　On Winnisimmet's side.

They hear the wash on Chelsea Beach,—
　　The level marsh they pass,
Where miles on miles the desert reach
　　Is rough with bitter grass.

The shining horses foam and pant,
　　And now the smells begin
Of fishy Swampscot, salt Nahant,
　　And leather-scented Lynn.

Next, on their left, the slender spires,
　　And glittering vanes, that crown
The home of Salem's frugal sires,
　　The old, witch-haunted town.

So onward, o'er the rugged way
　　That runs through rocks and sand,
Showered by the tempest-driven spray,
　　From bays on either hand,

That shut between their outstretched arms
　　The crews of Marblehead,
The lords of ocean's watery farms,
　　Who plough the waves for bread.

At last the ancient inn appears,
　　The spreading elm below,
Whose flapping sign these fifty years
　　Has seesawed to and fro.

How fair the azure fields in sight
   Before the low-browed inn!
The tumbling billows fringe with light
   The crescent shore of Lynn;

Nahant thrusts outward through the waves
   Her arm of yellow sand,
And breaks the roaring surge that braves
   The gauntlet on her hand;

With eddying whirl the waters lock
   Yon treeless mound forlorn,
The sharp-winged sea-fowl's breeding-rock,
   That fronts the Spouting Horn;

Then free the white-sailed shallops glide,
   And wide the ocean smiles,
Till, shoreward bent, his streams divide
   The two bare Misery Isles.

The master's silent signal stays
   The wearied cavalcade;
The coachman reins his smoking bays
   Beneath the elm-tree's shade.

A gathering on the village green!
   The cocked-hats crowd to see,
On legs in ancient velveteen,
   With buckles at the knee!

A clustering round the tavern-door
   Of square-toed village boys,

Still wearing, as their grandsires wore,
   The old-world corduroys!

A scampering at the " Fountain " inn,—
   A rush of great and small,—
With hurrying servants' mingled din
   And screaming matron's call!

Poor Agnes! with her work half done
   They caught her unaware;
As, humbly, like a praying nun,
   She knelt upon the stair;

Bent o'er the steps, with lowliest mien
   She knelt, but not to pray,—
Her little hands must keep them clean,
   And wash their stains away.

A foot, an ankle, bare and white
   Her girlish shapes betrayed,—
" Ha! Nymphs and Graces! " spoke the Knight;
   " Look up, my beauteous Maid! "

She turned,—a reddening rose in bud,
   Its calyx half withdrawn,—
Her cheek on fire with damasked blood
   Of girlhood's glowing dawn!

He searched her features through and through,
   As royal lovers look
On lowly maidens, when they woo
   Without the ring and book.

" Come hither, Fair one! Here, my Sweet!
   Nay, prithee, look not down!
Take this to shoe those little feet,"—
   He tossed a silver crown.

A sudden paleness struck her brow,—
   A swifter flush succeeds;
It burns her cheek; it kindles now
   Beneath her golden beads.

She flitted, but the glittering eye
   Still sought the lovely face.
Who was she? What, and whence? and why
   Doomed to such menial place?

A skipper's daughter,—so they said,—
   Left orphan by the gale
That cost the fleet of Marblehead
   And Gloucester thirty sail.

Ah! many a lonely home is found
   Along the Essex shore,
That cheered its goodman outward bound,
   And sees his face no more!

" Not so," the matron whispered,—" sure
   No orphan girl is she,—
The Surraige folk are deadly poor
   Since Edward left the sea,

" And Mary, with her growing brood,
   Has work enough to do

To find the children clothes and food
　　With Thomas, John, and Hugh.

" This girl of Mary's, growing tall,—
　　(Just turned her sixteenth year,)—
To earn her bread and help them all,
　　Would work as housemaid here."

So Agnes, with her golden beads,
　　And naught beside as dower,
Grew at the wayside with the weeds,
　　Herself a garden-flower.

'Twas strange, 'twas sad,—so fresh, so fair!
　　Thus Pity's voice began.
Such grace! an angel's shape and air!
　　The half-heard whisper ran.

For eyes could see in George's time,
　　As now in later days,
And lips could shape, in prose and rhyme,
　　The honeyed breath of praise.

No time to woo!　The train must go
　　Long ere the sun is down,
To reach, before the night-winds blow,
　　The many-steepled town.

'Tis midnight,—street and square are still:
　　Dark roll the whispering waves

That lap the piers beneath the hill
　　Ridged thick with ancient graves.

Ah, gentle sleep! thy hand will smooth
　　The weary couch of pain,
When all thy poppies fail to soothe
　　The lover's throbbing brain!

'Tis morn,—the orange-mantled sun
　　Breaks through the fading gray,
And long and loud the Castle gun
　　Peals o'er the glistening bay.

"Thank God 'tis day!" With eager eye
　　He hails the morning's shine:—
"If art can win, or gold can buy,
　　The maiden shall be mine!"

PART THIRD.

THE CONQUEST.

"Who saw this hussy when she came?
　　What is the wench, and who?"
They whisper. "Agnes,—is her name?
　　Pray what has she to do?"

The housemaids parley at the gate,
　　The scullions on the stair,

And in the footmen's grave debate
    The butler deigns to share.

Black Dinah, stolen when a child,
    And sold on Boston pier,
Grown up in service, petted, spoiled,
    Speaks in the coachman's ear:

" What, all this household at his will?
    And all are yet too few?
More servants, and more servants still,—
    This pert young madam too!"

" *Servant!* fine servant!" laughed aloud
    The man of coach and steeds;
" She looks too fair, she steps too proud,
    This girl with golden beads!

" I tell you, you may fret and frown,
    And call her what you choose,
You'll find my Lady in her gown,
    Your Mistress in her shoes!"

Ah, gentle maidens, free from blame,
    God grant you never know
The little whisper, loud with shame,
    That makes the world your foe!

Why tell the lordly flatterer's art,
    That won the maiden's ear,—

The fluttering of the frightened heart,
  The blush, the smile, the tear?

Alas! it were the saddening tale
  That every language knows,—
The wooing wind, the yielding sail,
  The sunbeam and the rose.

And now the gown of sober stuff
  Has changed to fair brocade,
With broidered hem, and hanging cuff,
  And flower of silken braid;

And clasped around her blanching wrist
  A jewelled bracelet shines,
Her flowing tresses' massive twist
  A glittering net confines;

And mingling with their truant wave
  A fretted chain is hung;
But ah! the gift her mother gave,—
  Its beads are all unstrung!

Her place is at the master's board,
  Where none disputes her claim;
She walks beside the mansion's lord,
  His bride in all but name.

The busy tongues have ceased to talk,
  Or speak in softened tone,

So gracious in her daily walk
　　The angel light has shown.

No want that kindness may relieve
　　Assails her heart in vain,
The lifting of a ragged sleeve
　　Will check her palfrey's rein.

A thoughtful calm, a quiet grace
　　In every movement shown,
Reveal her moulded for the place
　　She may not call her own.

And, save that on her youthful brow
　　There broods a shadowy care,
No matron sealed with holy vow
　　In all the land so fair!

———

PART FOURTH.

THE RESCUE.

A SHIP comes foaming up the bay,
　　Along the pier she glides;
Before her furrow melts away,
　　A courier mounts and rides.

" Haste, Haste, post Haste! " the letters bear;
　　" Sir Harry Frankland, These."

Sad news to tell the loving pair!
   The knight must cross the seas.

"Alas! we part!"—the lips that spoke
   Lost all their rosy red,
As when a crystal cup is broke,
   And all its wine is shed.

"Nay, droop not thus,—where'er," he cried,
   "I go by land or sea,
My love, my life, my joy, my pride,
   Thy place is still by me!"

Through town and city, far and wide,
   Their wandering feet have strayed,
From Alpine lake to ocean tide,
   And cold Sierra's shade.

At length they see the waters gleam
   Amid the fragrant bowers
Where Lisbon mirrors in the stream
   Her belt of ancient towers.

Red is the orange on its bough,
   To-morrow's sun shall fling
O'er Cintra's hazel-shaded brow
   The flush of April's wing.

The streets are loud with noisy mirth,
   They dance on every green;

The morning's dial marks the birth
　　Of proud Braganza's queen.

At eve beneath their pictured dome
　　The gilded courtiers throng;
The broad moidores have cheated Rome
　　Of all her lords of song.

Ah! Lisbon dreams not of the day—
　　Pleased with her painted scenes—
When all her towers shall slide away
　　As now these canvas screens!

The spring has passed, the summer fled,
　　And yet they linger still,
Though autumn's rustling leaves have spread
　　The flank of Cintra's hill.

The town has learned their Saxon name,
　　And touched their English gold,
Nor tale of doubt nor hint of blame
　　From over sea is told.

Three hours the first November dawn
　　Has climbed with feeble ray
Through mists like heavy curtains drawn
　　Before the darkened day.

How still the muffled echoes sleep!
　　Hark! hark! a hollow sound,—

A noise like chariots rumbling deep
   Beneath the solid ground.

The channel lifts, the water slides
   And bares its bar of sand,
Anon a mountain billow strides
   And crashes o'er the land.

The turrets lean, the steeples reel
   Like masts on ocean's swell,
And clash a long discordant peal,
   The death-doomed city's knell.

The pavement bursts, the earth upheaves
   Beneath the staggering town!
The turrets crack—the castle cleaves—
   The spires come rushing down.

Around, the lurid mountains glow
   With strange unearthly gleams;
While black abysses gape below,
   Then close in jagged seams.

The earth has folded like a wave,
   And thrice a thousand score,
Clasped, shroudless, in their closing grave,
   The sun shall see no more!

And all is over. Street and square
   In ruined heaps are piled;
Ah! where is she, so frail, so fair,
   Amid the tumult wild?

Unscathed, she treads the wreck-piled street,
   Whose narrow gaps afford
A pathway for her bleeding feet,
   To seek her absent lord.

A temple's broken walls arrest
   Her wild and wandering eyes;
Beneath its shattered portal pressed,
   Her lord unconscious lies.

The power that living hearts obey
   Shall lifeless blocks withstand?
Love led her footsteps where he lay,—
   Love nerves her woman's hand:

One cry,—the marble shaft she grasps,—
   Up heaves the ponderous stone:—
He breathes,—her fainting form he clasps,—
   Her life has bought his own!

PART FIFTH.

THE REWARD.

How like the starless night of death
   Our being's brief eclipse,
When faltering heart and failing breath
   Have bleached the fading lips!

She lives! What guerdon shall repay
   His debt of ransomed life?

One word can charm all wrongs away,—
 The sacred name of WIFE!

The love that won her girlish charms
 Must shield her matron fame,
And write beneath the Frankland arms
 The village beauty's name.

Go, call the priest! no vain delay
 Shall dim the sacred ring!
Who knows what change the passing day
 The fleeting hour, may bring?

Before the holy altar bent,
 There kneels a goodly pair;
A stately man, of high descent,
 A woman, passing fair.

No jewels lend the blinding sheen
 That meaner beauty needs,
But on her bosom heaves unseen
 A string of golden beads.

The vow is spoke,—the prayer is said,—
 And with a gentle pride
The Lady Agnes lifts her head,
 Sir Harry Frankland's bride.

No more her faithful heart shall bear
 Those griefs so meekly borne,—

The passing sneer, the freezing stare,
　The icy look of scorn;

No more the blue-eyed English dames
　Their haughty lips shall curl,
Whene'er a hissing whisper names
　The poor New-England girl.

But stay!—his mother's haughty brow,—
　The pride of ancient race,—
Will plighted faith, and holy vow,
　Win back her fond embrace?

Too well she knew the saddening tale
　Of love no vow had blest,
That turned his blushing honors pale
　And stained his knightly crest.

They seek his Northern home,—alas!
　He goes alone before;—
His own dear Agnes may not pass
　The proud, ancestral door.

He stood before the stately dame;
　He spoke; she calmly heard,
But not to pity, nor to blame;
　She breathed no single word.

He told his love,—her faith betrayed;
　She heard with tearless eyes;

Could she forgive the erring maid?
   She stared in cold surprise.

How fond her heart, he told,—how **true;**
   The haughty eyelids fell;—
The kindly deeds she loved to do;
   She murmured, " It is well."

But when he told that fearful **day,**
   And how her feet were led
To where entombed in life he lay,
   The breathing with the dead,

And how she bruised her tender **breasts**
   Against the crushing stone,
That still the strong-armed clown **protests**
   No man can lift alone,—

O then the frozen spring was broke;
   By turns she wept and smiled;—
" Sweet Agnes! " so the mother spoke,
   " God bless my angel child!

" She saved thee from the jaws of death,—
   'Tis thine to right her wrongs;
I tell thee,—I, who gave thee breath,—
   To her thy life belongs! "

Thus Agnes won her noble **name,**
   Her lawless lover's hand;
The lowly maiden so became
   A lady in the land!

19

PART SIXTH.

CONCLUSION.

THE tale is done; it little needs
    To track their after ways,
And string again the golden beads
    Of love's uncounted days.

They leave the fair ancestral isle
    For bleak New England's shore;
How gracious is the courtly smile
    Of all who frowned before!

Again through Lisbon's orange bowers
    They watch the river's gleam,
And shudder as her shadowy towers
    Shake in the trembling stream.

Fate parts at length the fondest pair;
    His cheek, alas! grows pale;
The breast that trampling death could spare
    His noiseless shafts assail.

He longs to change the heaven of blue
    For England's clouded sky,—
To breathe the air his boyhood knew;
    He seeks them but to die.

—Hard by the terraced hill-side town,
    Where healing streamlets run,

Still sparkling with their old renown,—
  The " Waters of the Sun,"—

The Lady Agnes raised the stone
  That marks his honored grave,
And there Sir Harry sleeps alone
  By Wiltshire Avon's wave.

The home of early love was dear;
  She sought its peaceful shade,
And kept her state for many a year,
  With none to make afraid.

At last the evil days were come
  That saw the red cross fall;
She hears the rebel's rattling drum,—
  Farewell to Frankland Hall!

—I tell you, as my tale began,
  The Hall is standing still;
And you, kind listener, maid or man,
  May see it if you will.

The box is glistening huge and green,
  Like trees the lilacs grow,
Three elms high-arching still are seen,
  And one lies stretched below.

The hangings, rough with velvet flowers,
  Flap on the latticed wall;

And o'er the mossy ridge-pole towers
   The rock-hewn chimney tall.

The doors on mighty hinges clash
   With massive bolt and bar,
The heavy English-moulded sash
   Scarce can the night-winds jar.

Behold the chosen room he sought
   Alone, to fast and pray,
Each year, as chill November brought
   The dismal earthquake day.

There hung the rapier blade he wore,
   Bent in its flattened sheath;
The coat the shrieking woman tore
   Caught in her clenching teeth;—

The coat with tarnished silver lace
   She snapped at as she slid,
And down upon her death-white face
   Crashed the huge coffin's lid.

A graded terrace yet remains;
   If on its turf you stand
And look along the wooded plains
   That stretch on either hand,

The broken forest walls define
   A dim, receding view,

Where, on the far horizon's line
　He cut his vista through.

If further story you shall crave,
　Or ask for living proof,
Go see old Julia, born a slave
　Beneath Sir Harry's roof.

She told me half that I have told,
　And she remembers well
The mansion as it looked of old
　Before its glories fell;—

The box, when round the terraced square
　Its glossy wall was drawn;
The climbing vines, the snow-balls fair,
　The roses on the lawn.

And Julia says, with truthful look
　Stamped on her wrinkled face,
That in her own black hands she took
　The coat with silver lace.

And you may hold the story light,
　Or, if you like, believe;
But there it was, the woman's bite,—
　A mouthful from the sleeve.

Now go your ways:—I need not tell
　The moral of my rhyme;
But, youths and maidens, ponder well,
　This tale of olden time!

PICTURES FROM OCCASIONAL POEMS.

1850–56.

SPRING.

WINTER is past; the heart of Nature warms
Beneath the wrecks of unresisted storms;
Doubtful at first, suspected more than seen,
The southern slopes are fringed with tender green;
On sheltered banks, beneath the dripping eaves,
Spring's earliest nurslings spread their glowing
    leaves,
Bright with the hues from wider pictures won,
White, azure, golden,—drift, or sky, or sun;—
The snowdrop, bearing on her patient breast
The frozen trophy torn from Winter's crest;
The violet, gazing on the arch of blue
Till her own iris wears its deepened hue;
The spendthrift crocus, bursting through the mould
Naked and shivering with his cup of gold.
Swelled with new life, the darkening elm on high
Prints her thick buds against the spotted sky;
On all her boughs the stately chestnut cleaves
The gummy shroud that wraps her embryo leaves;

The house-fly, stealing from his narrow grave,
Drugged with the opiate that November gave,
Beats with faint wing against the sunny pane,
Or crawls, tenacious, o'er its lucid plain;
From shaded chinks of lichen-crusted walls,
In languid curves, the gliding serpent crawls;
The bog's green harper, thawing from his sleep,
Twangs a hoarse note and tries a shortened leap;
On floating rails that face the softening noons
The still shy turtles range their dark platoons,
Or, toiling aimless o'er the mellowing fields,
Trail through the grass their tessellated shields.

At last young April, ever frail and fair,
Wooed by her playmate with the golden hair,
Chased to the margin of receding floods
O'er the soft meadows starred with opening buds,
In tears and blushes sighs herself away,
And hides her cheek beneath the flowers of May.

Then the proud tulip lights her beacon blaze,
Her clustering curls the hyacinth displays,
O'er her tall blades the crested fleur-de-lis,
Like blue-eyed Pallas, towers erect and free;
With yellower flames the lengthened sunshine glows,
And love lays bare the passion-breathing rose;
Queen of the lake, along its reedy verge
The rival lily hastens to emerge,
Her snowy shoulders glistening as she strips,
Till morn is sultan of her parted lips.

Then bursts the song from every leafy glade,
The yielding season's bridal serenade;
Then flash the wings returning Summer calls
Through the deep arches of her forest halls;—
The bluebird, breathing from his azure plumes
The fragrance borrowed where the myrtle blooms;
The thrush, poor wanderer, dropping meekly down,
Clad in his remnant of autumnal brown;
The oriole, drifting like a flake of fire
Rent by the whirlwind from a blazing spire.
The robin, jerking his spasmodic throat,
Repeats, imperious, his *staccáto* note;
The crack-brained bobolink courts his crazy mate,
Poised on a bulrush tipsy with his weight;
Nay, in his cage the lone canary sings,
Feels the soft air, and spreads his idle wings.

Why dream I here within these caging walls,
Deaf to her voice, while blooming Nature calls;
Peering and gazing with insatiate looks
Through blinding lenses, or in wearying books?
Off, gloomy spectres of the shrivelled past!
Fly with the leaves that filled the autumn blast!
Ye imps of Science, whose relentless chains
Lock the warm tides within these living veins,
Close your dim cavern, while its captive strays
Dazzled and giddy in the morning's blaze!

THE STUDY.

YET in the darksome crypt I left so late,
Whose only altar is its rusted grate,—
Sepulchral, rayless, joyless as it seems,
Shamed by the glare of May's refulgent beams,—
While the dim seasons dragged their shrouded train,
Its paler splendors were not quite in vain.
From these dull bars the cheerful firelight's glow
Streamed through the casement o'er the spectral
snow;
Here, while the night-wind wreaked its frantic will
On the loose ocean and the rock-bound hill,
Rent the cracked topsail from its quivering yard,
And rived the oak a thousand storms had scarred,
Fenced by these walls the peaceful taper shone,
Nor felt a breath to slant its trembling cone.

Not all unblest the mild interior scene
When the red curtain spread its falling screen;
O'er some light task the lonely hours were past,
And the long evening only flew too fast;
Or the wide chair its leathern arms would lend
In genial welcome to some easy friend,
Stretched on its bosom with relaxing nerves,
Slow moulding, plastic, to its hollow curves;
Perchance indulging, if of generous creed,
In brave Sir Walter's dream-compelling weed.

Or, happier still, the evening hour would bring
To the round table its expected ring,
And while the punch-bowl's sounding depths were
    stirred,—
Its silver cherubs smiling as they heard,—
Our hearts would open, as at evening's hour
The close-sealed primrose frees its hidden flower.

Such the warm life this dim retreat has known,
Not quite deserted when its guests were flown;
Nay, filled with friends, an unobtrusive set,
Guiltless of calls and cards and etiquette,
Ready to answer, never known to ask,
Claiming no service, prompt for every task.

On those dark shelves no housewife hand profanes,
O'er his mute files the monarch folio reigns;
A mingled race, the wreck of chance and time,
That talk all tongues and breathe of every clime;
Each knows his place, and each may claim his part
In some quaint corner of his master's heart.
This old Decretal, won from Kloss's hoards,
Thick-leaved, brass-cornered, ribbed with oaken
    boards,
Stands the gray patriarch of the graver rows,
Its fourth ripe century narrowing to its close;
Not daily conned, but glorious still to view,
With glistening letters wrought in red and blue.
There towers Stagira's all-embracing sage,
The Aldine anchor on his opening page;
There sleep the births of Plato's heavenly mind,
In yon dark tomb by jealous clasps confined,

" Olim e libris "—(dare I call it mine?)
Of Yale's grave Head and Killingworth's divine!
In those square sheets the songs of Maro fill
The silvery types of smooth-leaved Baskerville;
High over all, in close, compact array,
Their classic wealth the Elzevirs display.
In lower regions of the sacred space
Range the dense volumes of a humbler race;
There grim chirurgeons all their mysteries teach
In spectral pictures, or in crabbed speech;
Harvey and Haller, fresh from Nature's page,
Shoulder the dreamers of an earlier age,
Lully and Geber, and the learned crew
That loved to talk of all they could not do.
Why count the rest,—those names of later days
That many love, and all agree to praise,—
Or point the titles, where a glance may read
The dangerous lines of party or of creed?
Too well, perchance, the chosen list would show
What few may care and none can claim to know.
Each has his features, whose exterior seal
A brush may copy, or a sunbeam steal;
Go to his study,—on the nearest shelf
Stands the mosaic portrait of himself.

What though for months the tranquil dust descends,
Whitening the heads of these mine ancient friends,
While the damp offspring of the modern press
Flaunts on my table with its pictured dress;
Not less I love each dull familiar face,
Nor less should miss it from the appointed place;

I snatch the book, along whose burning leaves
His scarlet web our wild romancer weaves,
Yet, while proud Hester's fiery pangs I share,
My old MAGNALIA must be standing *there!*

THE BELLS.

WHEN o'er the street the morning peal is flung
From you tall belfry with the brazen tongue,
Its wide vibrations, wafted by the gale,
To each far listener tell a different tale.

The sexton, stooping to the quivering floor
Till the great caldron spills its brassy roar,
Whirls the hot axle, counting, one by one,
Each dull concussion, till his task is done.

Toil's patient daughter, when the welcome note
Clangs through the silence from the steeple's throat,
Streams, a white unit, to the checkered street,
Demure, but guessing whom she soon shall meet;
The bell, responsive to her secret flame,
With every note repeats her lover's name.

The lover, tenant of the neighboring lane,
Sighing, and fearing lest he sigh in vain,
Hears the stern accents, as they come and go,
Their only burden one despairing No!

Ocean's rough child, whom many a shore has known
Ere homeward breezes swept him to his own,
Starts at the echo as it circles round,
A thousand memories kindling with the sound;

The early favorite's unforgotten charms,
Whose blue initials stain his tawny arms;
His first farewell, the flapping canvas spread,
The seaward streamers crackling o'er his head,
His kind, pale mother, not ashamed to weep
Her first-born's bridal with the haggard deep,
While the brave father stood with tearless eye,
Smiling and choking with his last good by.

'Tis but a wave, whose spreading circle beats,
With the same impulse, every nerve it meets,
Yet who shall count the varied shapes that ride
On the round surge of that aerial tide!

O child of earth! If floating sounds like these
Steal from thyself their power to wound or please,
If here or there thy changing will inclines,
As the bright zodiac shifts its rolling signs,
Look at thy heart, and when its depths are known,
Then try thy brother's, judging by thine own,
But keep thy wisdom to the narrower range,
While its own standards are the sport of change,
Nor count us rebels when we disobey
The passing breath that holds thy passion's sway.

NON-RESISTANCE.

PERHAPS too far in these considerate days
Has patience carried her submissive ways;
Wisdom has taught us to be calm and meek,
To take one blow, and turn the other cheek;

It is not written what a man shall do,
If the rude caitiff strike the other too!

Land of our fathers, in thine hour of need
God help thee, guarded by the passive creed!
As the lone pilgrim trusts to beads and cowl,
When through the forest rings the gray wolf's howl
As the deep galleon trusts her gilded prow
When the black corsair slants athwart her bow;
As the poor pheasant, with his peaceful mien,
Trusts to his feathers, shining golden-green,
When the dark plumage with the crimson beak
Has rustled shadowy from its splintered peak;
So trust thy friends, whose babbling tongues would
        charm
The lifted sabre from thy foeman's arm,
Thy torches ready for the answering peal
From bellowing fort and thunder freighted keel!

THE MORAL BULLY.

Yon whey-faced brother, who delights to wear
A weedy flux of ill-conditioned hair,
Seems of the sort that in a crowded place
One elbows freely into smallest space;
A timid creature, lax of knee and hip,
Whom small disturbance whitens round the lip;
One of those harmless spectacled machines,
The Holy-Week of Protestants convenes;

Whom schoolboys question if their walk transcends
The last advices of maternal friends;
Whom John, obedient to his master's sign,
Conducts, laborious, up to *ninety-nine,*
While Peter, glistening with luxurious scorn,
Husks his white ivories like an ear of corn;
Dark in the brow and bilious in the cheek,
Whose yellowish linen flowers but once a week,
Conspicuous, annual, in their threadbare suits,
And the laced high-lows which they call their boots.
Well mayst thou *shun* that dingy front severe,
But him, O stranger, him thou canst not *fear!*

Be slow to judge, and slower to despise,
Man of broad shoulders and heroic size!
The tiger, writhing from the boa's rings,
Drops at the fountain where the cobra stings.
In the lean phantom, whose extended glove
Points to the text of universal love,
Behold the master that can tame thee down
To crouch, the vassal of his Sunday frown;
His velvet throat against thy corded wrist,
His loosened tongue against thy doubled fist!

The MORAL BULLY, though he never swears,
Nor kicks intruders down his entry stairs,
Though meekness plants his backward-sloping hat,
And non-resistance ties his white cravat,
Though his black broadcloth glories to be seen
In the same plight with Shylock's gaberdine,

Hugs the same passion to his narrow breast
That heaves the cuirass on the trooper's chest,
Hears the same hell-hounds yelling in his rear
That chase from port the maddened buccaneer,
Feels the same comfort while his acrid words
Turn the sweet milk of kindness into curds,
Or with grim logic prove, beyond debate,
That all we love is worthiest of our hate,
As the scarred ruffian of the pirate's deck,
When his long swivel rakes the staggering wreck!

Heaven keep us all! Is every rascal clown
Whose arm is stronger free to knock us down?
Has every scarecrow, whose cachectic soul
Seems fresh from Bedlam, airing on parole,
Who, though he carries but a doubtful trace
Of angel visits on his hungry face,
From lack of marrow or the coins to pay,
Has dodged some vices in a shabby way,
The right to stick us with his cut-throat terms,
And bait his homilies with his brother worms?

THE MIND'S DIET.

No life worth naming ever comes to good
If always nourished on the self-same food;
The creeping mite may live so if he please,
And feed on Stilton till he turns to cheese,
But cool Magendie proves beyond a doubt,
If mammals try it, that their eyes drop out.

No reasoning natures find it safe to feed,
For their sole diet, on a single creed;
It spoils their eyeballs while it spares their tongues,
And starves the heart to feed the noisy lungs.

When the first larvæ on the elm are seen,
The crawling wretches, like its leaves, are green;
Ere chill October shakes the latest down,
They, like the foliage, change their tint to brown;
On the blue flower a bluer flower you spy,
You stretch to pluck it—'t is a butterfly;
The flattened tree-toads so resemble bark,
They're hard to find as Ethiops in the dark;
The woodcock, stiffening to fictitious mud,
Cheats the young sportsman thirsting for his blood.
So by long living on a single lie,
Nay, on one truth, will creatures get its dye;
Red, yellow, green, they take their subject's hue,—
Except when squabbling turns them black and blue!

OUR LIMITATIONS.

We trust and fear, we question and believe,
From life's dark threads a trembling faith to weave,
Frail as the web that misty night has spun,
Whose dew-gemmed awnings glitter in the sun.
While the calm centuries spell their lessons out,
Each truth we conquer spreads the realm of doubt;
When Sinai's summit was Jehovah's throne,
The chosen Prophet knew his voice alone;

20

When Pilate's hall that awful question heard,
The Heavenly Captive answered not a word.

Eternal Truth! beyond our hopes and fears
Sweep the vast orbits of thy myriad spheres!
From age to age, while History carves sublime
On her waste rock the flaming curves of time,
How the wild swayings of our planet show
That worlds unseen surround the world we know!

———

THE OLD PLAYER.

The curtain rose; in thunders long and loud
The galleries rung; the veteran actor bowed.
In flaming line the telltales of the stage
Showed on his brow the autograph of age;
Pale, hueless waves amid his clustered hair,
And umbered shadows, prints of toil and care;
Round the wide circle glanced his vacant eye,—
He strove to speak,—his voice was but a sigh.

Year after year had seen its short-lived race
Flit past the scenes and others take their place;
Yet the old prompter watched his accents still,
His name still flaunted on the evening's bill.
Heroes, the monarchs of the scenic floor,
Had died in earnest and were heard no more;
Beauties, whose cheeks such roseate bloom o'erspread
They faced the footlights in unborrowed red,

Had faded slowly through successive shades
To gray duennas, foils of younger maids;
Sweet voices lost the melting tones that start
With Southern throbs the sturdy Saxon heart,
While fresh sopranos shook the painted sky
With their long, breathless, quivering locust-cry.
Yet there he stood,—the man of other days,
In the clear present's full, unsparing blaze,
As on the oak a faded leaf that clings
While a new April spreads its burnished wings.

How bright yon rows that soared in triple tier,
Their central sun the flashing chandelier!
How dim the eye that sought with doubtful aim
Some friendly smile it still might dare to claim!
How fresh these hearts! his own how worn and cold!
Such the sad thoughts that long-drawn sigh had told.

No word yet faltered on his trembling tongue;
Again, again, the crashing galleries rung.
As the old guardsman at the bugle's blast
Hears in its strain the echoes of the past;
So, as the plaudits rolled and thundered round,
A life of memories startled at the sound.

He lived again,—the page of earliest days,—
Days of small fee and parsimonious praise;
Then lithe young Romeo—hark that silvered tone,
From those smooth lips—alas! they were his own.
Then the bronzed Moor, with all his love and woe,
Told his strange tale of midnight melting snow;
And dark plumed Hamlet, with his cloak and blade,
Looked on the royal ghost, himself a shade.
All in one flash, his youthful memories came,
Traced in bright hues of evanescent flame,

As the spent swimmer's in the lifelong dream,
While the last bubble rises through the stream.

Call him not old, whose visionary brain
Holds o'er the past its undivided reign.
For him in vain the envious seasons roll
Who bears eternal summer in his soul.
If yet the minstrel's song, the poet's lay,
Spring with her birds, or children at their play,
Or maiden's smile, or heavenly dream of art,
Stir the few life-drops creeping round his heart,
Turn to the record where his years are told,—
Count his gray hairs,—they cannot make him old!
What magic power has changed the faded mime?
One breath of memory on the dust of time.
As the last window in the buttressed wall
Of some gray minster tottering to its fall,
Though to the passing crowd its hues are spread,
A dull mosaic, yellow, green, and red,
Viewed from within, a radiant glory shows
When through its pictured screen the sunlight flows,
And kneeling pilgrims on its storied pane
See angels glow in every shapeless stain;
So streamed the vision through his sunken eye,
Clad in the splendors of his morning sky.
All the wild hopes his eager boyhood knew,
All the young fancies riper years proved true,
The sweet, low-whispered words, the winning glance
From queens of song, from Houris of the dance,
Wealth's lavish gift, and Flattery's soothing phrase,
And Beauty's silence when her blush was praise,

And melting Pride, her lashes wet with tears,
Triumphs and banquets, wreaths and crowns and
    cheers,
Pangs of wild joy that perish on the tongue,
And all that poets dream, but leave unsung!
  In every heart some viewless founts are fed
From far-off hill-sides where the dews were shed;
On the worn features of the weariest face
Some youthful memory leaves its hidden trace,
As in old gardens left by exiled kings
The marble basins tell of hidden springs,
But, gray with dust, and overgrown with weeds,
Their choking jets the passer little heeds,
Till time's revenges break their seals away,
And, clad in rainbow light, the waters play.

  Good night, fond dreamer! let the curtain fall:
The world's a stage, and we are players all.
A strange rehearsal! Kings without their crowns,
And threadbare lords, and jewel-wearing clowns,
Speak the vain words that mock their throbbing
    hearts,
As Want, stern prompter! spells them out their parts.
The tinselled hero whom we praise and pay
Is twice an actor in a twofold play.
We smile at children when a painted screen
Seems to their simple eyes a real scene;
Ask the poor hireling, who has left his throne
To seek the cheerless home he calls his own,
Which of his double lives most real seems,
The world of solid fact or scenic dreams?

Canvas, or clouds,—the foot-lights, or the spheres,—
The play of two short hours, or seventy years?
   Dream on! Though Heaven may woo our open
     eyes,
Through their closed lids we look on fairer skies;
Truth is for other worlds, and hope for this;
The cheating future lends the present's bliss;
Life is a running shade, with fettered hands,
That chases phantoms over shifting sands;
Death a still spectre on a marble seat,
With ever clutching palms and shackled feet;
The airy shapes that mock life's slender chain,
The flying joys he strives to clasp in vain,
Death only grasps; to live is to pursue,—
Dream on! there's nothing but illusion true!

————

THE ISLAND RUIN.

Ye that have faced the billows and the spray
Of good St. Botolph's island-studded bay,
As from the gliding bark your eye has scanned
The beaconed rocks, the wave-girt hills of sand,
Have ye not marked one elm-o'ershadowed isle,
Round as the dimple chased in beauty's smile,—
A stain of verdure on an azure field,
Set like a jewel in a battered shield?
Fixed in the narrow gorge of Ocean's path,
Peaceful it meets him in his hour of wrath;

When the mailed Titan, scourged by hissing gales,
Writhes in his glistening coat of clashing scales;
The storm-beat island spreads its tranquil green,
Calm as an emerald on an angry queen.

So fair when distant should be fairer near;
A boat shall waft us from the outstretched pier.
The breeze blows fresh; we reach the island's edge,
Our shallop rustling through the yielding sedge.

No welcome greets us on the desert isle;
Those elms, far-shadowing, hide no stately pile:
Yet these green ridges mark an ancient road;
And lo! the traces of a fair abode;
The long gray line that marks a garden-wall,
And heaps of fallen beams,—fire-branded all.

Who sees unmoved, a ruin at his feet,
The lowliest home where human hearts have beat?
Its hearth-stone, shaded with the bistre stain
A century's showery torrents wash in vain;
Its starving orchard, where the thistle blows
And mossy trunks still mark the broken rows;
Its chimney-loving poplar, oftenest seen
Next an old roof, or where a roof has been;
Its knot-grass, plantain,—all the social weeds,
Man's mute companions, following where he leads;
Its dwarfed, pale flowers, that show their straggling
    heads,
Sown by the wind from grass-choked garden-beds;
Its woodbine, creeping where it used to climb;
Its roses, breathing of the olden time;
All the poor shows the curious idler sees,
As life's thin shadows waste by slow degrees,

Till naught remains, the saddening tale to tell,
Save home's last wrecks,—the cellar and the well!
    And whose the home that strews in black decay
The one green-glowing island of the bay?
Some dark-browed pirate's, jealous of the fate
That seized the strangled wretch of " Nix's Mate"?
Some forger's, skulking in a borrowed name,
Whom Tyburn's dangling halter yet may claim?
Some wan-eyed exile's, wealth and sorrow's heir,
Who sought a lone retreat for tears and prayer?
Some brooding poet's, sure of deathless fame,
Had not his epic perished in the flame?
Or some gray wooer's, whom a girlish frown
Chased from his solid friends and sober town?
Or some plain tradesman's, fond of shade and ease,
Who sought them both beneath these quiet trees?
Why question mutes no question can unlock,
Dumb as the legend on the Dighton rock?
One thing at least these ruined heaps declare,—
They were a shelter once; a man lived there.

    But where the charred and crumbling records fail,
Some breathing lips may piece the half-told tale;
No man may live with neighbors such as these,
Though girt with walls of rock and angry seas,
And shield his home, his children, or his wife,
His ways, his means, his vote, his creed, his life,
From the dread sovereignty of Ears and Eyes
And the small member that beneath them lies.

    They told strange things of that mysterious man;
Believe who will, deny them such as can;
Why should we fret if every passing sail
Had its old seaman talking on the rail?

The deep-sunk schooner stuffed with Eastern lime,
Slow wedging on, as if the waves were slime;
The knife-edged clipper with her ruffled spars,
The pawing steamer with her mane of stars,
The bull-browed galliot butting through the stream,
The wide-sailed yacht that slipped along her beam,
The deck-piled sloops, the pinched chebacco-boats,
The frigate, black with thunder-freighted throats,
All had their talk about the lonely man;
And thus, in varying phrase, the story ran.

His name had cost him little care to seek,
Plain, honest, brief, a decent name to speak,
Common, not vulgar, just the kind that slips
With least suggestion from a stranger's lips.
His birthplace England, as his speech might show,
Or his hale cheek, that wore the red-streak's glow;
His mouth sharp-moulded; in its mirth or scorn
There came a flash as from the milky corn,
When from the ear you rip the rustling sheath,
And the white ridges show their even teeth.
His stature moderate, but his strength confessed,
In spite of broadcloth, by his ample breast;
Full-armed, thick-handed; one that had been strong,
And might be dangerous still, if things went wrong.
He lived at ease beneath his elm-trees' shade,
Did naught for gain, yet all his debts were paid;
Rich, so 't was thought, but careful of his store;
Had all he needed, claimed to have no more.

But some that lingered round the isle at night
Spoke of strange stealthy doings in their sight;
Of creeping lonely visits that he made
To nooks and corners, with a torch and spade.

Some said they saw the hollow of a cave;
One, given to fables, swore it was a grave;
Whereat some shuddered, others boldly cried,
Those prowling boatmen lied, and knew they lied.

They said his house was framed with curious cares,
Lest some old friend might enter unawares;
That on the platform at his chamber's door
Hinged a loose square that opened through the floor;
Touch the black silken tassel next the bell,
Down, with a crash, the flapping trap-door fell;
Three stories deep the falling wretch would strike,
To writhe at leisure on a boarder's pike.

By day armed always; double-armed at night,
His tools lay round him; wake him such as might.
A carbine hung beside his India fan,
His hand could reach a Turkish ataghan;
Pistols, with quaint-carved stocks and barrels gilt,
Crossed a long dagger with a jewelled hilt;
A slashing cutlass stretched along the bed;—
All this was what those lying boatmen said.

Then some were full of wondrous stories told
About old chests and cupboards full of gold;
Of the wedged ingots and the silver bars
That cost old pirates ugly sabre-scars;
How his laced wallet often would disgorge
The fresh-faced guinea of an English George,
Or sweated ducat, palmed by Jews of yore,
Or double Joe, or Portuguese moidore,
And how his finger wore a rubied ring
Fit for the white-necked play-girl of a king.
But these fine legends, told with staring eyes,
Met with small credence from the old and wise.

Why tell each idle guess, each whisper vain?
Enough: the scorched and cindered beams remain.
He came, a silent pilgrim to the West,
Some old-world mystery throbbing in his breast;
Close to the thronging mart he dwelt alone;
He lived; he died. The rest is all unknown.

Stranger, whose eyes the shadowy isle survey,
As the black steamer dashes through the bay,
Why ask his buried secret to divine?
He was thy brother; speak, and tell us thine!

THE BANKER'S DINNER.

THE Banker's dinner is the stateliest feast
The town has heard of for a year, at least;
The sparry lustres shed their broadest blaze,
Damask and silver catch and spread the rays;
The florist's triumphs crown the daintier spoil
Won from the sea, the forest, or the soil;
The steaming hot-house yields its largest pines,
The sunless vaults unearth their oldest wines.
With one admiring look the scene survey,
And turn a moment from the bright display.

Of all the joys of earthly pride or power,
What gives most life, worth living, in an hour?
When Victory settles on the doubtful fight
And the last foeman wheels in panting flight,

No thrill like this is felt beneath the sun;
Life's sovereign moment is a battle won.

But say what next?   To shape a Senate's choice
By the strong magic of the master's voice;
To ride the stormy tempest of debate
That whirls the wavering fortunes of the state.

Third in the list, the happy lover's prize
Is won by honeyed words from women's eyes.
If some would have it first instead of third,
So let it be,—I answer not a word.

The fourth,—sweet readers, let the thoughtless half
Have its small shrug and inoffensive laugh;
Let the grave quarter wear its virtuous frown,
The stern half-quarter try to scowl us down;
But the last eighth, the choice and sifted few,
Will hear my words, and, pleased, confess them true.

Among the great whom Heaven has made to shine,
How few have learned the art of arts,—to dine!
Nature, indulgent to our daily need,
Kind-hearted mother! taught us all to feed;
But the chief art,—how rarely Nature flings
This choicest gift among her social kings!
Say, man of truth, has life a brighter hour
Than waits the chosen guest who knows his power?

He moves with ease, itself an angel charm,—
Lifts with light touch my lady's jewelled arm,
Slides to his seat, half leading and half led,
Smiling but quiet till the grace is said,
Then gently kindles, while by slow degrees
Creep softly out the little arts that please;

Bright looks, the cheerful language of the eye,
The neat, crisp question and the gay reply,—
Talk light and airy, such as well may pass
Between the rested fork and lifted glass;—
With play like this the earlier evening flies,
Till rustling silks proclaim the ladies rise.

His hour has come,—he looks along the chairs,
As the Great Duke surveyed his iron squares.
—That's the young traveller,—isn't much to show,—
Fast on the road, but at the table slow.
—Next him,—you see the author in his look,—
His forehead lined with wrinkles like a book,—
Wrote the great history of the ancient Huns,—
Holds back to fire among the heavy guns.
—O, there's our poet seated at his side,
Beloved of ladies, soft, cerulean-eyed.
Poets are prosy in their common talk,
As the fast trotters, for the most part, walk.
—And there's our well-dressed gentleman, who sits,
By right divine, no doubt, among the wits,
Who airs his tailor's patterns when he walks,
The man that often speaks, but never talks.
Why should he talk, whose presence lends a grace
To every table where he shows his face?
He knows the manual of the silver fork,
Can name his claret—if he sees the cork,—
Remark that " White-top " was considered fine,
But swear the " Juno " is the better wine;—
Is not this talking?   Ask Quintilian's rules;
If they say No, the town has many fools.
—Pause for a moment,—for our eyes behold
The plain unsceptred king, the man of gold,

The thrice illustrious threefold millionaire;
Mark his slow-creeping, dead, metallic stare;
His eyes, dull glimmering, like the balance-pan
That weighs its guinea as he weighs his man.
—Who's next?   An artist, in a satin tie
Whose ample folds defeat the curious eye.
—And there's the cousin,—must be asked, you
      know,—
Looks like a spinster at a baby-show.
Hope he is cool,—they set him next the door,—
And likes his place, between the gap and bore.
—Next comes a Congress-man, distinguished guest!
We don't count him,—they asked him with the rest;
And then some white cravats, with well-shaped ties,
And heads above them which their owners prize.

   Of all that cluster round the genial board,
Not one so radiant as the banquet's lord.
Some say they fancy, but they know not why,
A shade of trouble brooding in his eye,
Nothing, perhaps,—the rooms are over-hot,—
Yet see his cheek,—the dull-red burning spot,—
Taste the brown sherry which he does not pass,—
Ha!   That is brandy; see him fill his glass!
   But not forgetful of his feasting friends,
To each in turn some lively word he sends;
See how he throws his baited lines about,
And plays his men as anglers play their trout.
   With the dry sticks all bonfires are begun;
Bring the first fagot, proser number one!
A question drops among the listening crew
And hits the traveller, pat on Timbuctoo.

We're on the Niger, somewhere near its source,—
Not the least hurry, take the river's course
Through Kissi, Foota, Kankan, Bammakoo,
Bambarra, Sego, so to Timbuctoo,
Thence down to Youri;—stop him if we can,
We can't fare worse,—wake up the Congress-man!
The Congress-man, once on his talking legs,
Stirs up his knowledge to its thickest dregs.
Tremendous draught for dining men to quaff!
Nothing will choke him but a purpling laugh.
A word,—a shout,—a mighty roar,—'tis done;
Extinguished; lassoed by a treacherous pun.

A laugh is priming to the loaded soul;
The scattering shots become a steady roll,
Broke by sharp cracks that run along the line,
The light artillery of the talker's wine.
The kindling goblets flame with golden dews,
The hoarded flasks their tawny fire diffuse,
And the Rhine's breast-milk gushes cold and bright,
Pale as the moon and maddening as her light;
With crimson juice the thirsty southern sky
Sucks from the hills where buried armies lie,
So that the dreamy passion it imparts
Is drawn from heroes' bones and lovers' hearts.

But lulls will come; the flashing soul transmits
Its gleams of light in alternating fits.
The shower of talk that rattled down amain
Ends in small patterings like an April's rain;
The voices halt; the game is at a stand;
Now for a solo from the master-hand!
'Tis but a story,—quite a simple thing,—

An *aria* touched upon a single string,
But every accent comes with such a grace
The stupid servants listen in their place,
Each with his waiter in his lifted hands,
Still as a well-bred pointer when he stands.
A query checks him: " Is he quite exact ? "—
(This from a grizzled, square-jawed man of fact.)
The sparkling story leaves him to his fate,
Crushed by a witness, smothered with a date,
As a swift river, sown with many a star,
Runs brighter, rippling on a shallow bar.
The smooth divine suggests a graver doubt;
A neat quotation bowls the parson out;
Then, sliding gayly from his own display,
He laughs the learned dulness all away.

So, with the merry tale and jovial song,
The jocund evening whirls itself along,
Till the last chorus shrieks its loud *encore,*
And the white neckcloths vanish through the door.

One savage word!—The menials know its tone,
And slink away; the master stands alone.
" Well played, by—"; breathe not what were best
    unheard;
His goblet shivers while he speaks the word,—
" If wine tells truth,—and so have said the wise,—
It makes me laugh to think how brandy lies!
Bankrupt to-morrow,—millionaire to-day,—
The farce is over,—now begins the play ! "
The spring he touches lets a panel glide;
An iron closet lurks beneath the slide,

Bright with such treasures as a search might bring
From the deep pockets of a truant king.
Two diamonds, eyeballs of a God of bronze,
Bought from his faithful priest, a pious Bonze;
A string of brilliants; rubies, three or four;
Bags of old coin and bars of virgin ore;
A jewelled poniard and a Turkish knife,
Noiseless and useful if we come to strife.

Gone! As a pirate flies before the wind,
And not one tear for all he leaves behind!
From all the love his better years have known
Fled like a felon,—ah! but not alone!
The chariot flashes through a lantern's glare,—
O the wild eyes! the storm of sable hair!
Still to his side the broken heart will cling,—
The bride of shame,—the wife without the ring:
Hark, the deep oath,—the wail of frenzied woe,—
Lost! lost to hope of Heaven and peace below!

He kept his secret; but the seed of crime
Bursts of itself in God's appointed time.
The lives he wrecked were scattered far and wide;
One never blamed nor wept,—she only died.
None knew his lot, though idle tongues would say
He sought a lonely refuge far away,
And there, with borrowed name and altered mien,
He died unheeded, as he lived unseen.
The moral market had the usual chills
Of Virtue suffering from protested bills:
The White Cravats, to friendship's memory true,
Sighed for the past, surveyed the future too;

21

Their sorrow breathed in one expressive line,—
" Gave pleasant dinners; who has got his wine ? "

THE MYSTERIOUS ILLNESS.

WHAT ailed young Lucius ?   Art had vainly tried
To guess his ill, and found herself defied.
The Augur plied his legendary skill;
Useless; the fair young Roman languished still.
His chariot took him every cloudless day
Along the Pincian Hill or Appian Way;
They rubbed his wasted limbs with sulphurous oil,
Oozed from the far-off Orient's heated soil;
They led him tottering down the steamy path
Where bubbling•fountains filled the thermal bath;
Borne in his litter to Egeria's cave,
They washed him, shivering, in her icy wave.
They sought all curious herbs and costly stones,
They scraped the moss that grew on dead men's bones,
They tried all cures the votive tablets taught,
Scoured every place whence healing drugs were
          brought,
O'er Thracian hills his breathless couriers ran,
His slaves waylaid the Syrian caravan.

At last a servant heard a stranger speak
A new chirurgeon's name; a clever Greek,
Skilled in his art; from Pergamus he came
To Rome but lately; GALEN was the name.
The Greek was called: a man with piercing eyes,
Who must be cunning, and who might be wise.

He spoke but little,—if they pleased, he said,
He'd wait awhile beside the sufferer's bed.
So by his side he sat, serene and calm,
His very accents soft as healing balm;
Not curious seemed, but every movement spied,
His sharp eyes searching where they seemed to
          glide;
Asked a few questions,—what he felt, and where?
" A pain just here," " A constant beating there."
Who ordered bathing for his aches and ails?
" Charmis, the water-doctor from Marseilles."
What was the last prescription in his case?
" A draught of wine with powdered chrysoprase."
Had he no secret grief he nursed alone?
A pause; a little tremor; answer,—" None."

    Thoughtful, a moment, sat the cunning leech,
And muttered " Eros ! " in his native speech.

    In the broad atrium various friends await
The last new utterance from the lips of fate;
Men, matrons, maids, they talk the question o'er,
And, restless, pace the tessellated floor.
Not unobserved the youth so long had pined,
By gentle-hearted dames and damsels kind;
One with the rest, a rich Patrician's pride,
The lady Hermia, called " the golden-eyed; "
The same the old Proconsul fain must woo,
Whom, one dark night, a masked sicarius slew;
The same black Crassus over roughly pressed
To hear his suit,—the Tiber knows the rest.
(Crassus was missed next morning by his set;
Next week the fishers found him in their net.)

She with the others paced the ample hall,
Fairest, alas! and saddest of them all.

At length the Greek declared, with puzzled face,
Some strange enchantment mingled in the case,
And naught would serve to act as counter-charm
Save a warm bracelet from a maiden's arm.
Not every maiden's,—many might be tried;
Which not in vain, experience must decide.
Were there no damsels willing to attend
And do such service for a suffering friend?

The message passed among the waiting crowd,
First in a whisper, then proclaimed aloud.
Some wore no jewels; some were disinclined,
For reasons better guessed at than defined;
Though all were saints,—at least professed to be,—
The list all counted, there were named but three.

The leech, still seated by the patient's side,
Held his thin wrist, and watched him, eagle-eyed.

Aurelia first, a fair-haired Tuscan girl,
Slipped off her golden asp, with eyes of pearl.
His solemn head the grave physician shook;
The waxen features thanked her with a look.

Olympia next, a creature half divine,
Sprung from the blood of old Evander's line,
Held her white arm, that wore a twisted chain
Clasped with an opal-sheeny cymophane.
In vain, O daughter! said the baffled Greek.
The patient sighed the thanks he could not speak.

Last, Hermia entered; look, that sudden start!
The pallium heaves above his leaping heart;
The beating pulse, the cheek's rekindled flame,

Those quivering lips, the secret all proclaim.
The deep disease long throbbing in the breast,
The dread enchantment, all at once confessed!
The case was plain; the treatment was begun;
And Love soon cured the mischief he had done.

Young Love, too oft thy treacherous bandage slips
Down from the eyes it blinded to the lips!
Ask not the Gods, O youth, for clearer sight,
But the bold heart to plead thy cause aright.
And thou, fair maiden, when thy lovers sigh,
Suspect thy flattering ear, but trust thine eye,
And learn this secret from the tale of old:
No love so true as love that dies untold.

A MOTHER'S SECRET.

How sweet the sacred legend—if unblamed
In my slight verse such holy things are named—
Of Mary's secret hours of hidden joy,
Silent, but pondering on her wondrous boy!
Ave, Maria! Pardon, if I wrong
Those heavenly words that shame my earthly song!

The choral host had closed the Angels' strain
Sung to the listening watch on Bethlehem's plain,
And now the shepherds, hastening on their way,
Sought the still hamlet where the Infant lay.
They passed the fields that gleaning Ruth toiled
        o'er,—
They saw afar the ruined threshing-floor

Where Moab's daughter, homeless and forlorn,
Found Boaz slumbering by his heaps of corn;
And some remembered how the holy scribe,
Skilled in the lore of every jealous tribe,
Traced the warm blood of Jesse's royal son
To that fair alien, bravely wooed and won.
So fared they on to seek the promised sign
That marked the anointed heir of David's line.

At last, by forms of earthly semblance led,
They found the crowded inn, the oxen's shed.
No pomp was there, no glory shone around
On the coarse straw that strewed the reeking ground;
One dim retreat a flickering torch betrayed,—
In that poor cell the Lord of Life was laid!

The wondering shepherds told their breathless tale
Of the bright choir that woke the sleeping vale;
Told how the skies with sudden glory flamed,
Told how the shining multitude proclaimed
" Joy, joy to earth! Behold the hallowed morn!
In David's city Christ the Lord is born!
' Glory to God! ' let angels shout on high,
' Good will to men! ' the listening earth reply! "

They spoke with hurried words and accents wild;
Calm in his cradle slept the heavenly child.
No trembling word the mother's joy revealed,—
One sigh of rapture, and her lips were sealed;
Unmoved she saw the rustic train depart,
But kept their words to ponder in her heart.

Twelve years had passed; the boy was fair and tall,
Growing in wisdom, finding grace with all.
The maids of Nazareth, as they trooped to fill

Their balanced urns beside the mountain rill,—
The gathered matrons, as they sat and spun,—
Spoke in soft words of Joseph's quiet son.
No voice had reached the Galilean vale
Of star-led kings, or awe-struck shepherd's tale;
In the meek, studious child they only saw
The future Rabbi, learned in Israel's law.

So grew the boy, and now the feast was near
When at the Holy Place the tribes appear.
Scarce had the home-bred child of Nazareth seen
Beyond the hills that girt the village green,
Save when at midnight, o'er the starlit sands,
Snatched from the steel of Herod's murdering bands,
A babe, close folded to his mother's breast,
Through Edom's wilds he sought the sheltering West.

Then Joseph spake: " Thy boy hath largely grown;
Weave him fine raiment, fitting to be shown;
Fair robes beseem the pilgrim, as the priest:
Goes he not with us to the holy feast ? "

And Mary culled the flaxen fibres white;
Till eve she spun; she spun till morning light.
The thread was twined; its parting meshes through
From hand to hand her restless shuttle flew,
Till the full web was wound upon the beam;
Love's curious toil,—a vest without a seam !

They reach the Holy Place, fulfil the days
To solemn feasting given, and grateful praise.
At last they turn, and far Moriah's height
Melts in the southern sky and fades from sight.
All day the dusky caravan has flowed
In devious trails along the winding road;

(For many a step their homeward path attends,
And all the sons of Abraham are as friends.)
Evening has come,—the hour of rest and joy,—
Hush! Hush! That whisper,—" Where is Mary's
    boy ? "

O weary hour! O aching days that passed
Filled with strange fears each wilder than the last,—
The soldier's lance, the fierce centurion's sword,
The crushing wheels that whirl some Roman lord,
The midnight crypt that sucks the captive's breath,
The blistering sun on Hinnom's vale of death!

Thrice on his cheek had rained the morning light;
Thrice on his lips the mildewed kiss of night,
Crouched by a sheltering column's shining plinth,
Or stretched beneath the odorous terebinth.

At last, in desperate mood, they sought once more
The Temple's porches, searched in vain before;
They found him seated with the ancient men,—
The grim old rufflers of the tongue and pen,—
Their bald heads glistening as they clustered near,
Their gray beards slanting as they turned to hear,
Lost in half-envious wonder and surprise
That lips so fresh should utter words so wise.

And Mary said,—as one who, tried too long,
Tells all her grief and half her sense of wrong,—
" What is this thoughtless thing which thou hast
    done ?
Lo, we have sought thee sorrowing, O my son ! "

Few words he spake, and scarce of filial tone,
Strange words, their sense a mystery yet unknown;
Then turned with them and left the holy hill,

To all their mild commands obedient still.
   The tale was told to Nazareth's sober men,
And Nazareth's matrons told it oft again,
The maids retold it at the fountain's side,
The youthful shepherds doubted or denied;
It passed around among the listening friends,
With all that fancy adds and fiction lends,
Till newer marvels dimmed the young renown
Of Joseph's son, who talked the Rabbis down.
   But Mary, faithful to its lightest word,
Kept in her heart the sayings she had heard,
Till the dread morning rent the Temple's veil,
And shuddering earth confirmed the wondrous tale.

Youth fades; love droops; the leaves of friendship
     fall;
A mother's secret hope outlives them all.

THE DISAPPOINTED STATESMAN.

Who of all statesmen is his country's pride,
Her councils' prompter and her leaders' guide?
He speaks; the nation holds its breath to hear;
He nods, and shakes the sunset hemisphere.
Born where the primal fount of Nature springs
By the rule cradles of her throneless kings,
In his proud eye her royal signet flames,
By his own lips her Monarch she proclaims.
   Why name his countless triumphs, whom to meet
Is to be famous, envied in defeat?

The keen debaters, trained to brawls and strife,
Who fire one shot, and finish with the knife,
Tried him but once, and, cowering in their shame,
Ground their hacked blades to strike at meaner game.
The lordly chief, his party's central stay,
Whose lightest word a hundred votes obey,
Found a new listener seated at his side,
Looked in his eye, and felt himself defied,
Flung his rash gauntlet on the startled floor,
Met the all-conquering, fought—and ruled no more.

　　See where he moves, what eager crowds attend!
What shouts of thronging multitudes ascend!
If this is life,—to mark with every hour
The purple deepening in his robes of power,
To see the painted fruits of honor fall
Thick at his feet, and choose among them all,
To hear the sounds that shape his spreading name
Peal through the myriad organ-stops of fame,
Stamp the lone isle that spots the seaman's chart,
And crown the pillared glory of the mart,
To count as peers the few supremely wise
Who mark their planet in the angel's eyes,—
If this is life—

　　　　　　What savage man is he
Who strides alone beside the sounding sea?
Alone he wanders by the murmuring shore,
His thoughts as restless as the waves that roar;
Looks on the sullen sky as stormy-browed
As on the waves yon tempest-brooding cloud,
Heaves from his aching breast a wailing sigh,
Sad as the gust that sweeps the clouded sky.

Ask him his griefs; what midnight demons plough
The lines of torture on his lofty brow;
Unlock those marble lips and bid them speak
The mystery freezing in his bloodless cheek.

His secret? Hid beneath a flimsy word;
One foolish whisper that ambition heard;
And thus it spake: " Behold yon gilded chair,
The world's one vacant throne,—thy place is there!

Ah, fatal dream! What warning spectres meet
In ghastly circle round its shadowy seat!
Yet still the Tempter murmurs in his ear
The maddening taunt he cannot choose but hear:
" Meanest of slaves, by Gods and men accurst,
He who is second when he might be first!
Climb with bold front the ladder's topmost round,
Or chain thy creeping footsteps to the ground! "

Illustrious Dupe! Have those majestic eyes
Lost their proud fire for such a vulgar prize?
Art thou the last of all mankind to know
That party-fights are won by aiming low?
Thou, stamped by Nature with her royal sign,
That party-hirelings hate a look like thine?
Shake from thy sense the wild delusive dream!
Without the purple, art thou not supreme?
And soothed by love unbought, thy heart shall own
A nation's homage nobler than its throne!

THE SECRET OF THE STARS.

Is man's the only throbbing heart that hides
The silent spring that feeds its whispering tides?
Speak from thy caverns, mystery-breeding Earth,
Tell the half-hinted story of thy birth,
And calm the noisy champions who have thrown
The book of types against the book of stone!

Have ye not secrets, ye refulgent spheres,
No sleepless listener of the starlight hears?
In vain the sweeping equatorial pries
Through every world-sown corner of the skies,
To the far orb that so remotely strays
Our midnight darkness is its noonday blaze;
In vain the climbing soul of creeping man
Metes out the heavenly concave with a span,
Tracks into space the long-lost meteor's trail,
And weighs an unseen planet in the scale;
Still o'er their doubts the wan-eyed watchers sigh,
And Science lifts her still unanswered cry:
" Are all these worlds, that speed their circling flight,
Dumb, vacant, soulless,—baubles of the night?
Warmed with God's smile and wafted by his breath,
To weave in ceaseless round the dance of Death?
Or rolls a sphere in each expanding zone,
Crowned with a life as varied as our own? "

MAKER of earth and stars!   If thou hast taught
By what thy voice hath spoke, thy hand hath wrought,

By all that Science proves, or guesses true,
More than thy Poet dreamed, thy Prophet knew,—
The heavens still bow in darkness at thy feet,
And shadows veil thy cloud-pavilioned seat!
　Not for ourselves we ask thee to reveal
One awful word beneath the future's seal;
What thou shalt tell us, grant us strength to **bear**;
What thou withholdest is thy single care.
Not for ourselves; the present clings too fast,
Moored to the mighty anchors of the past;
But when, with angry snap, some cable parts,
The sound re-echoing in our startled hearts,—
When, through the wall that clasps the harbor **round**,
And shuts the raving ocean from its bound,
Shattered and rent by sacrilegious hands,
The first mad billow leaps upon the sands,—
Then to the Future's awful page we turn,
And what we question hardly dare to learn.
　Still let us hope! for while we seem to tread
The time-worn pathway of the nations dead,
Though Sparta laughs at all our warlike deeds,
And buried Athens claims our stolen creeds,
Though Rome, a spectre on her broken throne,
Beholds our eagle and recalls her own,
Though England fling her pennons on the **breeze**
And reign before us Mistress of the seas,—
While calm-eyed History tracks us circling round
Fate's iron pillar where they all were bound,
She sees new beacons crowned with brighter **flame**
Than the old watch-fires, like, but not the same!
Still in our path a larger curve she finds,

The spiral widening as the chain unwinds!
No shameless haste shall spot with bandit-crime
Our destined empire snatched before its time.
Wait,—wait, undoubting, for the winds have caught
From our bold speech the heritage of thought;
No marble form that sculptured truth can wear
Vies with the image shaped in viewless air;
And thought unfettered grows through speech to
        deeds,
As the broad forest marches in its seeds.
What though we perish ere the day is won?
Enough to see its glorious work begun!
The thistle falls before a trampling clown,
But who can chain the flying thistle-down?
Wait while the fiery seeds of freedom fly,
The prairie blazes when the grass is dry!

What arms might ravish, leave to peaceful arts,
Wisdom and love shall win the roughest hearts;
So shall the angel who has closed for man
The blissful garden since his woes began
Swing wide the golden portals of the West,
And Eden's secret stand at length confessed!

TO GOVERNOR SWAIN.

DEAR GOVERNOR, if my skiff might brave
The winds that lift the ocean wave,
The mountain stream that loops and swerves
Through my broad meadow's channelled curves

Should waft me on from bound to bound
To where the River weds the Sound,
The Sound should give me to the Sea,
That to the Bay, the Bay to Thee.

It may not be; too long the track
To follow down or struggle back.
The sun has set on fair Naushon
Long ere my western blaze is gone;
The ocean disk is rolling dark
In shadows round your swinging bark,
While yet the yellow sunset fills
The stream that scarfs my spruce-clad hills;
The day-star wakes your island deer
Long ere my barn-yard chanticleer;
Your mists are soaring in the blue
While mine are sparks of glittering dew.

It may not be; O would it might,
Could I live o'er that glowing night!
What golden hours would come to life,
What goodly feats of peaceful strife,—
Such jests, that, drained of every joke,
The very bank of language broke,—
Such deeds, that laughter nearly died
With stitches in his belted side;
While Time, caught fast in pleasure's **chain**,
His double goblet snapped in twain,
And stood with half in either hand,—
Both brimming full,—but not of sand!

It may not be; I strive in vain
To break my slender household chain,—
Three pairs of little clasping hands,
One voice, that whispers, not commands.
Even while my spirit flies away,
My gentle jailers murmur nay;
All shapes of elemental wrath
They raise along my threatened path;
The storm grows black, the waters rise,
The mountains mingle with the skies,
The mad tornado scoops the ground,
The midnight robber prowls around,—
Thus, kissing every limb they tie,
They draw a knot and heave a sigh,
Till, fairly netted in the toil,
My feet are rooted to the soil.
Only the soaring wish is free!—
And that, dear Governor, flies to thee!

PITTSFIELD, 1851

VIGNETTES.

1853.

AFTER A LECTURE ON WORDSWORTH.

COME, spread your wings, as I spread mine,
    And leave the crowded hall
For where the eyes of twilight shine
    O'er evening's western wall.

These are the pleasant Berkshire hills,
   Each with its leafy crown;
Hark! from their sides a thousand rills
   Come singing sweetly down.

A thousand rills; they leap and shine,
   Strained through the shadowy nooks,
Till, clasped in many a gathering twine,
   They swell a hundred brooks.

A hundred brooks, and still they run
   With ripple, shade, and gleam,
Till, clustering all their braids in one,
   They flow a single stream.

A bracelet spun from mountain mist,
   A silvery sash unwound,
With ox-bow curve and sinuous twist
   It writhes to reach the Sound.

This is my bark,—a pigmy's ship;
   Beneath a child it rolls;
Fear not,—one body makes it dip,
   But not a thousand souls.

Float we the grassy banks between;
   Without an oar we glide;
The meadows, drest in living green,
   Unroll on either side.

—Come, take the book we love so well,
   And let us read and dream
22

We see whate'er its pages tell,
    And sail an English stream.

Up to the clouds the lark has sprung,
    Still trilling as he flies;
The linnet sings as there he sung;
    The unseen cuckoo cries,

And daisies strew the banks along,
    And yellow kingcups shine,
With cowslips, and a primrose throng,
    And humble celandine.

Ah foolish dream! when Nature nursed
    Her daughter in the West,
The fount was drained that opened first;
    She bared her other breast.

On the young planet's orient shore
    Her morning hand she tried;
Then turned the broad medallion o'er
    And stamped the sunset side.

Take what she gives, her pine's tall stem,
    Her elm with hanging spray;
She wears her mountain diadem
    Still in her own proud way.

Look on the forests' ancient kings,
    The hemlock's towering pride:
Yon trunk had thrice a hundred rings
    And fell before it died.

Nor think that Nature saves her bloom
    And slights our grassy plain;
For us she wears her court costume,—
    Look on its broidered train;

The lily with the sprinkled dots,
    Brands of the noontide beam;
The cardinal, and the blood-red spots,
    Its double in the stream,

As if some wounded eagle's breast,
    Slow throbbing o'er the plain,
Had left its airy path impressed
    In drops of scarlet rain.

And hark! and hark! the woodland rings;
    There thrilled the thrush's soul;
And look! that flash of flamy wings,—
    The fire-plumed oriole!

Above, the hen-hawk swims and swoops,
    Flung from the bright, blue sky;
Below, the robin hops, and whoops
    His piercing, Indian cry.

Beauty runs virgin in the woods
    Robed in her rustic green,
And oft a longing thought intrudes,
    As if we might have seen

Her every finger's every joint
    Ringed with some golden line,

Poet whom Nature did anoint!
　　Had our wild home been thine.

Yet think not so; Old England's blood
　　Runs warm in English veins;
But wafted o'er the icy flood
　　Its better life remains:

Our children know each wild-wood smell,
　　The bayberry and the fern,
The man who does not know them well
　　Is all too old to learn.

Be patient!　On the breathing page
　　Still pants our hurried past;
Pilgrim and soldier, saint and sage,—
　　The poet comes the last!

Though still the lark-voiced matins ring
　　The world has known so long;
The wood-thrush of the West shall sing
　　Earth's last sweet even-song!

AFTER A LECTURE ON MOORE.

SHINE soft, ye trembling tears of light
　　That strew the mourning skies;
Hushed in the silent dews of night
　　The harp of Erin lies.

What though her thousand years have past
    Of poets, saints, and kings,—
Her echoes only hear the last
    That swept those golden strings.

Fling o'er his mound, ye star-lit bowers,
    The balmiest wreaths ye wear,
Whose breath has lent your earth-born flowers
    Heaven's own ambrosial air.

Breathe, bird of night, thy softest tone,
    By shadowy grove and rill;
Thy song will soothe us while we own
    That his was sweeter still.

Stay, pitying Time, thy foot for him
    Who gave thee swifter wings,
Nor let thine envious shadow dim
    The light his glory flings.

If in his cheek unholy blood
    Burned for one youthful hour,
'Twas but the flushing of the bud
    That blooms a milk-white flower.

Take him, kind mother, to thy breast,
    Who loved thy smiles so well,
And spread thy mantle o'er his rest
    Of rose and asphodel.

—The bark has sailed the midnight sea,
    The sea without a shore,

That waved its parting sign to thee,—
  "A health to thee, Tom Moore!"

And thine, long lingering on the strand,
  Its bright-hued streamers furled,
Was loosed by age, with trembling hand,
  To seek the silent world.

Not silent! no, the radiant stars
  Still singing as they shine,
Unheard through earth's imprisoning bars,
  Have voices sweet as thine.

Wake, then, in happier realms above
  The songs of bygone years,
Till angels learn those airs of love
  That ravished mortal ears!

AFTER A LECTURE ON KEATS.

"Purpureos spargam flores."

THE wreath that star-crowned Shelley gave
Is lying on thy Roman grave,
Yet on its turf young April sets
Her store of slender violets;
Though all the Gods their garlands shower,
I too may bring one purple flower.
—Alas! what blossom shall I bring,
That opens in my Northern spring?

The garden beds have all run wild,
So trim when I was yet a child;
Flat plantains and unseemly stalks
Have crept across the gravel walks;
The vines are dead, long, long ago,
The almond buds no longer blow.
No more upon its mound I see
The azure, plume-bound fleur-de-lis;
Where once the tulips used to show,
In straggling tufts the pansies grow;
The grass has quenched my white-rayed gem,
The flowering " Star of Bethlehem,"
Though its long blade of glossy green
And pallid stripe may still be seen.
Nature, who treads her nobles down,
And gives their birthright to the clown,
Has sown her base-born weedy things
Above the garden's queens and kings.
—Yet one sweet flower of ancient race
Springs in the old familiar place.
When snows were melting down the vale,
And Earth unlaced her icy mail,
And March his stormy trumpet blew,
And tender green came peeping through,
I loved the earliest one to seek
That broke the soil with emerald beak,
And watch the trembling bells so blue
Spread on the column as it grew.
Meek child of earth! thou wilt not shame
The sweet, dead poet's holy name;
The God of music gave thee birth

Called from the crimson-spotted earth,
Where, sobbing his young life away,
His own fair Hyacinthus lay.
—The hyacinth my garden gave
Shall lie upon that Roman grave!

———

AFTER A LECTURE ON SHELLEY.

ONE broad, white sail in Spezzia's treacherous bay;
    On comes the blast; too daring bark, beware!
The cloud has clasped her; lo! it melts away;
    The wide, waste waters, but no sail is there.

Morning: a woman looking on the sea;
    Midnight: with lamps the long verandah burns;
Come, wandering sail, they watch, they burn for thee!
    Suns come and go, alas! no bark returns.

And feet are thronging on the pebbly sands,
    And torches flaring in the weedy caves,
Where'er the waters lay with icy hands
    The shapes uplifted from their coral graves.

Vainly they seek; the idle quest is o'er;
    The coarse, dark women, with their hanging locks,
And lean, wild children gather from the shore
    To the black hovels bedded in the rocks.

But Love still prayed, with agonizing wail,
    " One, one last look, ye heaving waters, yield! "

Till Ocean, clashing in his jointed mail,
   Raised the pale burden on his level shield.

Slow from the shore the sullen waves retire;
   His form a nobler element shall claim;
Nature baptized him in ethereal fire,
   And Death shall crown him with a wreath of flame.

Fade, mortal semblance, never to return;
   Swift is the change within thy crimson shroud;
Seal the white ashes in the peaceful urn;
   All else has risen in yon silvery cloud.

Sleep where thy gentle Adonais lies,
   Whose open page lay on thy dying heart,
Both in the smile of those blue-vaulted skies,
   Earth's fairest dome of all divinest art.

Breathe for his wandering soul one passing sigh,
   O happier Christian, while thine eye grows dim,—
In all the mansions of the house on high,
   Say not that Mercy has not one for him!

AT THE CLOSE OF A COURSE OF LECTURES.

As the voice of the watch to the mariner's dream;
As the footstep of Spring on the ice-girdled stream,
There comes a soft footstep, a whisper, to me,—
The vision is over,—the rivulet free!

We have trod from the threshold of turbulent March,
Till the green scarf of April is hung on the larch,
And down the bright hill-side that welcomes the day,
We hear the warm panting of beautiful May.

We will part before Summer has opened her wing,
And the bosom of June swells the bodice of Spring,
While the hope of the season lies fresh in the bud,
And the young life of Nature runs warm in our blood.

It is but a word, and the chain is unbound,
The bracelet of steel drops unclasped to the ground;
No hand shall replace it,—it rests where it fell,—
It is but one word that we all know too well.

Yet the hawk with the wildness untamed in his eye,
If you free him, stares round ere he springs to the
        sky;
The slave whom no longer his fetters restrain
Will turn for a moment and look at his chain.

Our parting is not as the friendship of years,
That chokes with the blessing it speaks through its
        tears;
We have walked in a garden, and, looking around,
Have plucked a few leaves from the myrtles we found.

But now at the gate of the garden we stand,
And the moment has come for unclasping the hand;
Will you drop it like lead, and in silence retreat
Like the twenty crushed forms from an omnibus seat?

Nay! hold it one moment,—the last we may share,—
I stretch it in kindness, and not for my fare;
You may pass through the doorway in rank or in file,
If your ticket from Nature is stamped with a smile.

For the sweetest of smiles is the smile as we part,
When the light round the lips is a ray from the heart;
And lest a stray tear from its fountain might swell,
We will seal the bright spring with a quiet farewell.

THE HUDSON.

AFTER A LECTURE AT ALBANY.

'Twas a vision of childhood that came with its dawn,
Ere the curtain that covered life's day-star was
        drawn;
The nurse told the tale when the shadows grew long,
And the mother's soft lullaby breathed it in song.

" There flows a fair stream by the hills of the
        west,"—
She sang to her boy as he lay on her breast;
" Along its smooth margin thy fathers have played;
Beside its deep waters their ashes are laid."

I wandered afar from the land of my birth,
I saw the old rivers, renowned upon earth,
But fancy still painted that wide-flowing stream
With the many-hued pencil of infancy's dream.

I saw the green banks of the castle-crowned Rhine,
Where the grapes drink the moonlight and change it
to wine;
I stood by the Avon, whose waves as they glide
Still whisper his glory who sleeps at their side.

But my heart would still yearn for the sound of the
waves
That sing as they flow by my forefathers' graves;
If manhood yet honors my cheek with a tear,
I care not who sees it,—no blush for it here!

Farewell to the deep-bosomed stream of the West!
I fling this loose blossom to float on its breast;
Nor let the dear love of its children grow cold,
Till the channel is dry where its waters have rolled!

DECEMBER, 1854.

A POEM

FOR THE MEETING OF THE AMERICAN MEDICAL ASSOCIATION AT NEW YORK, MAY 5, 1853.

I HOLD a letter in my hand,—
A flattering letter—more's the pity,—
By some contriving junto planned,
And signed *per order of Committee;*
It touches every tenderest spot,—
My patriotic predilections,
My well known—something—don't ask what,
My poor old songs, my kind affections.

They make a feast on Thursday next,
  And hope to make the feasters merry;
They own they're something more perplexed
  For poets than for port and sherry;—
They want the men of—(word torn out);
  Our friends will come with anxious faces
(To see our blankets off, no doubt,
  And trot us out and show our paces).

They hint that papers by the score
  Are rather musty kind of rations;
They don't exactly mean a bore,
  But only trying to the patience;
That such as—you know who I mean—
  Distinguished for their—what d'ye call 'em—
Should bring the dews of Hippocrene
  To sprinkle on the faces solemn.

—The same old story; that's the chaff
  To catch the birds that sing the ditties;
Upon my soul, it makes me laugh
  To read these letters from Committees!
They're all *so* loving and *so* fair,—
  All for *your* sake such kind compunction,—
'T would save your carriage half its wear
  To touch its wheels with such an unction!

Why, who am I, to lift me here
  And beg such learned folk to listen,—
To ask a smile, or coax a tear
  Beneath these stoic lids to glisten?

As well might some arterial thread
    Ask the whole frame to feel it gushing,
While throbbing fierce from heel to head
    The vast aortic tide was rushing.

As well some hair-like nerve might strain
    To set its special streamlet going,
While through the myriad-channelled brain
    The burning flood of thought was flowing;
Or trembling fibre strive to keep
    The springing haunches gathered shorter,
While the scourged racer, leap on leap,
    Was stretching through the last hot quarter!

Ah me! you take the bud that came
    Self-sown in your poor garden's borders,
And hand it to the stately dame
    That florists breed for, all she orders;
She thanks you—it was kindly meant—
    (A pale affair, not worth the keeping,)—
*Good morning;—*and your bud is sent
    To join the tea-leaves used for sweeping.

Not always so, kind hearts and true,—
    For such I know are round me beating;
Is not the bud I offer you,—
    Fresh gathered for the hour of meeting,—
Pale though its outer leaves may be,
    Rose-red in all its inner petals,
Where the warm life we cannot see—
    The life of love that gave it—settles?

We meet from regions far away,
　　Like rills from distant mountains streaming;
The sun is on Francisco's bay
　　O'er Chesapeake the lighthouse gleaming;
While summer girds the still bayou
　　In chains of bloom, her bridal token,
Monadnock sees the sky grow blue,
　　His crystal bracelet yet unbroken.

Yet Nature bears the self-same heart
　　Beneath her russet-mantled bosom,
As where with burning lips apart
　　She breathes, and white magnolias blossom;
The self-same founts her chalice fill
　　With showery sunlight running over,
On fiery plain and frozen hill,
　　On myrtle-beds and fields of clover.

I give you *Home!* its crossing lines
　　United in one golden suture,
And showing every day that shines
　　The present growing to the future,—
A flag that bears a hundred stars,
　　In one bright ring, with love for centre,
Fenced round with white and crimson bars,
　　No prowling treason dares to enter!

O brothers, home may be a word
　　To make affection's living treasure—
The wave an angel might have stirred—
　　A stagnant pool of selfish pleasure;

Home!   It is where the day-star springs
And where the evening sun reposes,
Where'er the eagle spreads his wings,
From northern pines to southern roses!

THE NEW EDEN.

(Meeting of the berkshire horticultural society, at stockbridge, sept. 13, 1854.)

Scarce could the parting ocean close,
Seamed by the Mayflower's cleaving bow,
When o'er the rugged desert rose
The waves that tracked the Pilgrim's plough.

Then sprang from many a rock-strewn field
The rippling grass, the nodding grain,
Such growths as English meadows yield
To scanty sun and frequent rain.

But when the fiery days were done,
And Autumn brought his purple haze,
Then, kindling in the slanted sun,
The hill-sides gleamed with golden maize.

The food was scant, the fruits were few:
A red-streak glistened here and there;
Perchance in statelier precincts grew
Some stern old Puritanic pear.

Austere in taste, and tough at core,
Its unrelenting bulk was shed,

To ripen in the Pilgrim's store
  When all the summer sweets were fled.

Such was his lot, to front the storm
  With iron heart and marble brow,
Nor ripen till his earthly form
  Was cast from life's autumnal bough.

—But ever on the bleakest rock
  We bid the brightest beacon glow,
And still upon the thorniest stock
  The sweetest roses love to blow.

So on our rude and wintry soil
  We feed the kindling flame of art,
And steal the tropic's blushing spoil
  To bloom on Nature's ice-clad heart.

See how the softening Mother's breast
  Warms to her children's patient wiles,—
Her lips by loving Labor pressed
  Break in a thousand dimpling smiles,

From when the flushing bud of June
  Dawns with its first auroral hue,
Till shines the rounded harvest-moon,
  And velvet dahlias drink the dew.

Nor these the only gifts she brings;
  Look where the laboring orchard groans,
And yields its beryl-threaded strings
  For chestnut burs and hemlock cones.

23

Dear though the shadowy maple be,
  And dearer still the whispering pine,
Dearest yon russet-laden tree
  Browned by the heavy rubbing kine!

There childhood flung its rustling stone,
  There venturous boyhood learned to climb,—
How well the early graft was known
  Whose fruit was ripe ere harvest time!

Nor be the Fleming's pride forgot,
  With swinging drops and drooping bells,
Freckled and splashed with streak and spot,
  On the warm-breasted, sloping swells;

Nor Persia's painted garden-queen,—
  Frail Houri of the trellised wall,—
Her deep-cleft bosom scarfed with green,—
  Fairest to see, and first to fall.

———

—When man provoked his mortal doom,
  And Eden trembled as he fell,
When blossoms sighed their last perfume,
  And branches waved their long farewell,

One sucker crept beneath the gate,
  One seed was wafted o'er the wall,
One bough sustained his trembling weight;
  These left the garden,—these were all.

And far o'er many a distant zone
  These wrecks of Eden still are flung:

The fruits that Paradise hath known
   Are still in earthly gardens hung.

Yes, by our own unstoried stream
   The pink-white apple-blossoms burst
That saw the young Euphrates gleam,—
   That Gihon's circling waters nursed.

For us the ambrosial pear displays
   The wealth its arching branches hold,
Bathed by a hundred summer days
   In floods of mingling fire and gold.

And here, where beauty's cheek of flame
   With morning's earliest beam is fed,
The sunset-painted peach may claim
   To rival its celestial red.

———

—What though is some unmoistened vale
   The summer leaf grow brown and sere,
Say, shall our star of promise fail
   That circles half the rolling sphere,

From beaches salt with bitter spray,
   O'er prairies green with softest rain,
And ridges bright with evening's ray,
   To rocks that shade the stormless main?

If by our slender-threaded streams
   The blade and leaf and blossom die,

If, drained by noontide's parching beams,
　　The milky veins of Nature dry,

See, with her swelling bosom bare,
　　Yon wild-eyed Sister in the West,—
The ring of Empire round her hair,
　　The Indian's wampum on her breast!

We saw the August sun descend,
　　Day after day, with blood-red stain,
And the blue mountains dimly blend
　　With smoke-wreaths from the burning plain;

Beneath the hot Sirocco's wings
　　We sat and told the withering hours,
Till Heaven unsealed its hoarded springs,
　　And bade them leap in flashing showers.

Yet in our Ishmael's thirst we knew
　　The mercy of the Sovereign hand
Would pour the fountain's quickening dew
　　To feed some harvest of the land.

No flaming swords of wrath surround
　　Our second Garden of the Blest;
It spreads beyond its rocky bound,
　　It climbs Nevada's glittering crest.

God keep the tempter from its gate!
　　God shield the children, lest they fall
From their stern father's free estate,—
　　Till Ocean is its only wall!

SEMICENTENNIAL CELEBRATION OF THE NEW ENGLAND SOCIETY,

NEW YORK, DEC. 22, 1855.

NEW England, we love thee; no time can erase
From the hearts of thy children the smile on thy face.
'Tis the mother's fond look of affection and pride,
As she gives her fair son to the arms of his bride.

His bride may be fresher in beauty's young flower;
She may blaze in the jewels she brings with her dower.
But passion must chill in Time's pitiless blast;
The one that first loved us will love to the last.

You have left the dear land of the lake and the hill,
But its winds and its waters will talk with you still.
" Forget not," they whisper, " your love is our debt,"
And echo breathes softly, " We never forget."

The banquet's gay splendors are gleaming around,
But your hearts have flown back o'er the waves of
        the Sound;
They have found the brown home where their pulses
        were born;
They are throbbing their way through the trees and
        the corn.

There are roofs you remember,—their glory is fled;
There are mounds in the churchyard,—one sigh for
        the dead.

There are wrecks, there are ruins, all scattered
          around ;
But Earth has no spot like that corner of ground.

Come, let us be cheerful,—remember last night,
How they cheered us, and—never mind—meant it
          all right ;
To-night, we harm nothing,—we love in the lump;
Here's a bumper to Maine, in the juice of the pump!

Here's to all the good people, wherever they be,
Who have grown in the shade of the liberty-tree ;
We all love its leaves, and its blossoms and fruit,
But pray have a care of the fence round its root.

We should like to talk big; it's a kind of a right,
When the tongue has got loose and the waistband
          grown tight ;
But, as pretty Miss Prudence remarked to her beau,
On its own heap of compost, no biddy should crow.

Enough ! There are gentlemen waiting to talk,
Whose words are to mine as the flower to the stalk.
Stand by your old mother whatever befall ;
God bless all her children ! Good night to you all !

ODE FOR WASHINGTON'S BIRTHDAY.

CELEBRATION OF THE MERCANTILE LIBRARY ASSOCIA-
TION. FEBRUARY 22, 1856.

WELCOME to the day returning,
          Dearer still as ages flow,

While the torch of Faith is burning,
   Long as Freedom's altars glow!
See the throneless Conqueror seated,
   Slumbering on a mother's breast;
For the arm he stretched to save us,
   Be its morn forever blest!

Hear the tale of youthful glory,
   While of Britain's rescued band
Friend and foe repeat the story,
   Spread his fame o'er sea and land,
Where the red cross proudly streaming,
   Flaps above the frigate's deck,
Where the golden lilies, gleaming,
   Star the watch-towers of Quebec.

Look! The shadow on the dial
   Marks the hour of deadlier strife;
Days of terror, years of trial,
   Scourge a nation into life.
Lo, the youth, become her leader!
   All her baffled tyrants yield;
Through his arm the Lord hath freed her;
   Crown him on the tented field!

Vain is Empire's mad temptation;
   Not for him an earthly crown!
He whose sword hath freed a nation
   Strikes the offered sceptre down.
See the thorneless Conqueror seated,
   Ruler by a people's choice;
See the Patriot's task completed;
   Hear the Father's dying voice!

" By the name that you inherit,
    By the sufferings you recall,
Cherish the fraternal spirit;
    Love your country first of all!
Listen not to idle questions
    If its bands may be united;
Doubt the patriot whose suggestions
    Strive a nation to divide! "

Father! We, whose ears have tingled
    With the discord-notes of shame,—
We, whose sires their blood have mingled
    In the battle's thunder-flame,—
Gathering, while this holy morning
    Lights the land from sea to sea,
Hear thy counsel, heed thy warning;
    Trust us, while we honor thee!

CLASS OF '29.

FOR THURSDAY, NOVEMBER 6, 1856.

You'LL believe me, dear boys, 'tis a pleasure to rise
With a welcome like this in your darling old eyes,
To meet the same smiles and to hear the same tone
Which have greeted me oft in the years that have
    flown.

Were I gray as the grayest old rat in the wall,
My locks would turn brown at the sight of you all;

If my heart were as dry as the shell on the sand,
It would fill like the goblet I hold in my hand.

There are noontides of autumn, when summer returns,
Though the leaves are all garnered and sealed in
    their urns,
And the bird on his perch that was silent so long
Believes the sweet sunshine and breaks into song.

We have caged the young birds of our beautiful June:
Their plumes are still bright and their voices in tune;
One moment of sunshine from faces like these,
And they sing as they sung in the green-growing trees.

The voices of morning! How sweet is their thrill
When the shadows have turned, and the evening grows
    still!
The text of our lives may get wiser with age,
But the print was so fair on its twentieth page!

Look off from your goblet and up from your plate,
Come, take the last journal and glance at its date,—
Then think what we fellows should say and should do,
If the 6 were a 9, and the 5 were a 2.

Ah no! For the shapes that would meet with us here
From the far land of shadows are ever too dear!
Though youth flung around us its pride and its
    charms,
We should see but the comrades we clasped in our
    arms.

A health to our future,—a sigh for our past!
We love, we remember, we hope to the last;
And for all the base lies that the almanacs hold,
While we've youth in our hearts, we can never grow
    old.

FOR THE MEETING OF THE BURNS CLUB.

1856.

THE mountains glitter in the snow
    A thousand leagues asunder;
Yet here, amid the banquet's glow,
    I hear their voice of thunder;
Each giant's ice-bound goblet clinks;
    A flowing stream is summoned;
Wachusett to Ben Nevis drinks;
    Monadnock to Ben Lomond!

Though years have clipped the eagle's plume
    That crowned the chieftain's bonnet,
The sun still sees the heather bloom,
    The silver mists lie on it;
With tartan kilt and philibeg,
    What stride was ever bolder
Than his who showed the naked leg
    Beneath the plaided shoulder?

The echoes sleep on Cheviot's hills,
    That heard the bugles blowing

When down their sides the crimson rills
　　With mingled blood were flowing;
The hunts where gallant hearts were game,
　　The slashing on the border,
The raid that swooped with sword and flame,
　　Give place to " law and order."

Not while the rocking steeples reel
　　With midnight tocsins ringing,
Not while the crashing war-notes peal,
　　God sets his poets singing;
The bird is silent in the night,
　　Or shrieks a cry of warning
While fluttering round the beacon-light,—
　　But hear him greet the morning!

The lark of Scotia's morning sky!
　　Whose voice may sing his praises?
With Heaven's own sunlight in his eye,
　　He walked among the daisies,
Till through the cloud of fortune's wrong
　　He soared to fields of glory;
But left his land her sweetest song
　　And earth her saddest story.

'Tis not the forts the builder piles
　　That chain the earth together;
The wedded crowns, the sister isles,
　　Would laugh at such a tether ;
The kindling thought, the throbbing words,
　　That set the pulses beating,

Are stronger than the myriad swords
  Of mighty armies meeting.

Thus while within the banquet glows,
  Without, the wild winds whistle,
We drink a triple health,—the Rose,
  The Shamrock, and the Thistle!
Their blended hues shall never fade
  Till War has hushed his cannon,—
Close-twined as ocean-currents braid
  The Thames, the Clyde, the Shannon!

FOR THE BURNS CENTENNIAL CELEBRATION.

JANUARY 25, 1859.

His birthday.—Nay, we need not speak
  The name each heart is beating,—
Each glistening eye and flushing cheek
  In light and flame repeating!

We come in one tumultuous tide,—
  One surge of wild emotion,—
As crowding through the Frith of Clyde
  Rolls in the Western Ocean;

As when yon cloudless, quartered moon
  Hangs o'er each storied river,

The swelling breasts of Ayr and Doon
  With sea-green wavelets quiver.

The century shrivels like a scroll,—
  The past becomes the present,—
And face to face, and soul to soul,
  We greet the monarch-peasant.

While Shenstone strained in feeble flights
  With Corydon and Phillis,—
While Wolfe was climbing Abraham's heights
  To snatch the Bourbon lilies,—

Who heard the wailing infant's cry,
  The babe beneath the shieling,
Whose song to-night in every sky
  Will shake earth's starry ceiling,—

Whose passion-breathing voice ascends
  And floats like incense o'er us,
Whose ringing lay of friendship blends
  With labor's anvil chorus?

We love him, not for sweetest song,
  Though never tone so tender;
We love him, even in his wrong,—
  His wasteful self-surrender.

We praise him, not for gifts divine,—
  His Muse was born of woman,—
His manhood breathes in every line,—
  Was ever heart more human?

We love him, praise him, just for this:
   In every form and feature,
Through wealth and want, through woe and
      bliss,
   He saw his fellow-creature!

No soul could sink beneath his love,—
   Not even angel blasted;
No mortal power could soar above
   The pride that all outlasted!

Ay! Heaven had set one living man
   Beyond the pedant's tether,—
His virtues, frailties, HE may scan,
   Who weighs them all together!

I fling my pebble on the cairn
   Of him, though dead, undying;
Sweet Nature's nursling, bonniest bairn
   Beneath her daisies lying.

The waning suns, the wasting globe,
   Shall spare the minstrel's story,—
The centuries weave his purple robe,
   The mountain-mist of glory!

BIRTHDAY OF DANIEL WEBSTER.

JANUARY 18, 1856.

WHEN life hath run its largest round
   Of toil and triumph, joy and woe,
How brief a storied page is found
   To compass all its outward show!

The world-tried sailor tires and droops;
  His flag is rent, his keel forgot;
His farthest voyages seem but loops
  That float from life's entangled knot.

But when within the narrow space
  Some larger soul hath lived and wrought,
Whose sight was open to embrace
  The boundless realms of deed and thought,—

When, stricken by the freezing blast,
  A nation's living pillars fall,
How rich the storied page, how vast,
  A word, a whisper can recall!

No medal lifts its fretted face,
  Nor speaking marble cheats your eye,
Yet, while these pictured lines I trace,
  A living image passes by:

A roof beneath the mountain pines;
  The cloisters of a hill-girt plain;
The front of life's embattled lines;
  A mound beside the heaving main.

These are the scenes: a boy appears;
  Set life's round dial in the sun,
Count the swift arc of seventy years,
  His frame is dust; his task is done.

Yet pause upon the noontide hour,
  Ere the declining sun has laid

His bleaching rays on manhood's power,
   And look upon the mighty shade.

No gloom that stately shape can hide,
   No change uncrown its brow; behold!
Dark, calm, large-fronted, lightning-eyed,
   Earth has no double from its mould!

Ere from the fields by valor won
   The battle-smoke had rolled away,
And bared the blood-red setting sun,
   His eyes were opened on the day.

His land was but a shelving strip
   Black with the strife that made it **free;**
He lived to see its banners dip
   Their fringes in the Western sea.

The boundless prairies learned his name,
   His words the mountain echoes knew,
The Northern breezes swept his fame
   From icy lake to warm bayou.

In toil he lived; in peace he died;
   When life's full cycle was complete,
Put off his robes of power and pride,
   And laid them at his Master's feet.

His rest is by the storm-swept waves
   Whom life's wild tempests roughly tried,
Whose heart was like the streaming caves
   Of ocean, throbbing at his side.

Death's cold white hand is like the snow
    Laid softly on the furrowed hill,
It hides the broken seams below,
    And leaves the summit brighter still.

In vain the envious tongue upbraids;
    His name a nation's heart shall keep
Till morning's latest sunlight fades
    On the blue tablet of the deep!

MEETING OF THE ALUMNI OF HARVARD COLLEGE.

1857.

I THANK you, MR. PRESIDENT, you've kindly broke
        the ice;
Virtue should always be the first,—I'm only SECOND
        VICE—
(A vice is something with a screw that's made to hold
        its jaw
Till some old file has played away upon an ancient
        saw.)

Sweet brothers by the Mother's side, the babes of
        days gone by,
All nurslings of her Juno breasts whose milk is never
        dry,

24

We come again, like half-grown boys, and gather at
    her beck
About her knees, and on her lap, and clinging round
    her neck.

We find her at her stately door, and in her ancient
    chair,
Dressed in the robes of red and green she always
    loved to wear.
Her eye has all its radiant youth, her cheek its morn-
    ing flame;
We drop our roses as we go, hers flourish still the
    same.

We have been playing many an hour, and far away
    we've strayed,
Some laughing in the cheerful sun, some lingering in
    the shade;
And some have tired, and laid them down where
    darker shadows fall,—
Dear as her loving voice may be, they cannot hear its
    call.

What miles we've travelled since we shook the dew-
    drops from our shoes
We gathered on this classic green, so famed for heavy
    dues!
How many boys have joined the game, how many
    slipped away,
Since we've been running up and down, and having
    out our play!

One boy at work with book and brief, and one with
    gown and band,
One sailing vessels on the pool, one digging in the
    sand,
One flying paper kites on 'change, one planting little
    pills,—
The seeds of certain annual flowers well known as
    little bills.

What maidens met us on our way, and clasped us
    hand in hand!
What cherubs,—not the legless kind, that fly, but
    never stand!
How many a youthful head we've seen put on its
    silver crown!
What sudden changes back again to youth's em-
    purpled brown!

But fairer sights have met our eyes, and broader
    lights have shone,
Since others lit their midnight lamps where once we
    trimmed our own;
A thousand trains that flap the sky with flags of rush-
    ing fire,
And, throbbing in the Thunderer's hand, Thought's
    million-chorded lyre.

We've seen the sparks of Empire fly beyond the
    mountain bars,
Till, glittering o'er the Western wave, they joined
    the setting stars;

And ocean trodden into paths that trampling giants
    ford,
To find the planet's vertebræ and sink its spinal cord.

We've tried reform,—and chloroform,—and both
    have turned our brain;
When France called up the photograph, we roused the
    foe to pain;
Just so those earlier sages shared the chaplet of re-
    nown,—
Hers sent a bladder to the clouds, ours brought their
    lightning down.

We've seen the little tricks of life, its varnish and
    veneer,
Its stucco-fronts of character flake off and disappear;
We've learned that oft the brownest hands will heap
    the biggest pile,
And met with many a " perfect brick " beneath a
    rimless " tile."

What dreams we've had of deathless name, as scholars,
    statesmen, bards,
While Fame, the lady with the trump, held up her
    picture cards!
Till, having nearly played our game, she gayly whis-
    pered, " Ah!
I said you should be something grand,—you'll soon
    be grandpapa."

Well, well, the old have had their day, the young
    must take their turn;
There's something always to forget, and something
    still to learn;

But how to tell what's old or young, the tap-root from
     the sprigs,
Since Florida revealed her fount to Ponce de Leon
     Twiggs?

The wisest was a Freshman once, just freed from bar
     and bolt,
As noisy as a kettle-drum, as leggy as a colt;
Don't be too savage with the boys,—the Primer does
     not say
The kitten ought to go to church because " the cat
     doth prey."

The law of merit and of age is not the rule of three;
Non constat that A.M. must prove as busy as A.B.
When Wise the father tracked the son, ballooning
     through the skies,
He taught a lesson to the old,—go thou and do like
     Wise!

Now then, old boys, and reverend youth, of high or
     low degree,
Remember how we only get one annual out of three,
And such as dare to simmer down three dinners into
     one
Must cut their salads mighty short, and pepper well
     with fun.

I've passed my zenith long ago, it's time for me to
     set;
A dozen planets wait to shine, and I am lingering yet,

As sometimes in the blaze of day a milk-and-watery
    moon
Stains with its dim and fading ray the lustrous blue
    of noon.
Farewell! yet let one echo rise to shake our ancient
    hall;
God save the Queen,—whose throne is here,—the
    Mother of us all!
Till dawns the great Commencement-day on every
    shore and sea,
And " Expectantur " all mankind, to take their last
    Degree!

———

THE PARTING SONG.

FESTIVAL OF THE ALUMNI, 1857.

THE noon of summer sheds its ray
    On Harvard's holy ground;
The Matron calls, the sons obey,
    And gather smiling round.
CHORUS.—Then old and young together stand,
    The sunshine and the snow,
        As heart to heart and hand in hand,
    We sing before we go!

Her hundred opening doors have swung;
    Through every storied hall
The pealing echoes loud have rung,
    " Thrice welcome one and all! "
        Then old and young, etc.

We floated through her peaceful bay,
    To sail life's stormy seas;
But left our anchor where it lay
    Beneath her green old trees.
        Then old and young, etc.

'As now we lift its lengthening chain,
    That held us fast of old,
The rusted rings grow bright again,—
    Their iron turns to gold.
        Then old and young, etc.

Though scattered ere the setting sun,
    As leaves when wild winds blow,
Our home is here, our hearts are one,
    Till Charles forgets to flow.
        Then old and young, etc.

BOSTON COMMON.—THREE PICTURES.

(FOR THE FAIR IN AID OF THE FUND TO PROCURE
BALL'S STATUE OF WASHINGTON.)

1630.

'ALL overgrown with bush and fern,
    And straggling clumps of tangled trees,
With trunks that lean and boughs that turn,
    Bent eastward by the mastering breeze,—

With spongy bogs that drip and fill
  A yellow pond with muddy rain,
Beneath the shaggy southern hill
  Lies wet and low the Shawmut plain.
And hark! the trodden branches crack;
  A crow flaps off with startled scream;
A straying woodchuck canters back;
  A bittern rises from the stream;
Leaps from his lair a frightened deer;
  An otter plunges in the pool;—
Here comes old Shawmut's pioneer,
  The parson on his brindled bull!

1774.

THE streets are thronged with trampling feet,
  The northern hill is ridged with graves,
But night and morn the drum is beat
  To frighten down the " rebel knaves."
The stones of King Street still are red,
  And yet the bloody red-coats come:
I hear their pacing sentry's tread,
  The click of steel, the tap of drum,
And over all the open green,
  Where grazed of late the harmless kine,
The cannon's deepening ruts are seen,
  The war-horse stamps, the bayonets shine.
The clouds are dark with crimson rain
  Above the murderous hireling's den,
And soon their whistling showers shall stain
  The pipe-clayed belts of Gage's men.

186.....

AROUND the green, in morning light,
    The spired and palaced summits blaze,
And, sunlike, from her Beacon-height
    The dome-crowned city spreads her rays;
They span the waves, they belt the plains,
    They skirt the roads with bands of white,
Till with a flash of gilded panes
    Yon farthest hill-side bounds the sight.
Peace, Freedom, Wealth! no fairer view,
    Though with the wild-bird's restless wings
We sailed beneath the noontide's blue
    Or chased the moonlight's endless rings!
Here, fitly raised by grateful hands
    His holiest memory to recall,
The Hero's, Patriot's image stands;
    He led our sires who won them all!

November 14, 1859,

LATTER-DAY WARNINGS.

WHEN legislators keep the law,
    When banks dispense with bolts and locks,
When berries—whortle, rasp, and straw—
    Grow bigger *downwards* through the box,—

When he that selleth house or land
    Shows leak in roof or flaw in right,—
When haberdashers choose the stand
    Whose window hath the broadest light,—

When preachers tell us all they think,
 And party leaders all they mean,—
When what we pay for, that we drink,
 From real grape and coffee-bean,—

When lawyers take what they would give,
 And doctors give what they would take,—
When city fathers eat to live,
 Save when they fast for conscience' sake,—

When one that hath a horse on sale
 Shall bring his merit to the proof,
Without a lie for every nail
 That holds the iron on the hoof,—

When in the usual place for rips
 Our gloves are stitched with special care,
And guarded well the whalebone tips
 Where first umbrellas need repair,—

When Cuba's weeds have quite forgot
 The power of suction to resist,
And claret-bottles harbor not
 Such dimples as would hold your fist,—

When publishers no longer steal,
 And pay for what they stole before,—
When the first locomotive's wheel
 Rolls through the Hoosac tunnel's bore;—

Till then let Cumming blaze away,
 And Miller's saints blow up the globe;
But when you see that blessed day,
 Then order your ascension robe!

PROLOGUE.

A Prologue? Well, of course the ladies know;—
I have my doubts. No matter,—here we go!
What is a Prologue? Let our Tutor teach:
Pro means beforehand; *logos* stands for speech.
'Tis like the harper's prelude on the strings,
The prima donna's courtesy ere she sings:—
Prologues in metre are to other *pros*
As worsted stockings are to engine-hose.

"The world's a stage,"—as Shakespeare said, one
    day;
The stage a world—was what he meant to say.
The outside world's a blunder, that is clear;
The real world that Nature meant is here.
Here every foundling finds its lost mamma;
Each rogue, repentant, melts his stern papa;
Misers relent, the spendthrift's debts are paid,
The cheats are taken in the traps they laid;
One after one the troubles all are past
Till the fifth act comes right side up at last,
When the young couple, old folks, rogues, and all,
Join hands, *so* happy at the curtain's fall.
Here suffering virtue ever finds relief,
And black-browed ruffians always come to grief.
When the lorn damsel, with a frantic screech,
And cheeks as hueless as a brandy-peach,
Cries, "Help, kyind Heaven!" and drops upon her
    knees
On the green—baize,—beneath the (canvas) trees,—

See to her side avenging Valor fly:—
"Ha! Villain! Draw! Now, Terraitorr, yield or
    die!"
When the poor hero flounders in despair,
Some dear lost uncle turns up millionnaire,
Clasps the young scapegrace with paternal joy,
Sobs on his neck, "*My boy!* MY BOY!! **MY
    BOY!!!**"

Ours, then, sweet friends, the real world to-night.
Of love that conquers in disaster's spite.
Ladies attend! While woful cares and doubt
Wrong the soft passion in the world without,
Though fortune scowl, though prudence interfere,
One thing is certain: Love will triumph here!
Lords of creation, whom your ladies rule,—
The world's great masters, when you're out of
    school,—
Learn the brief moral of our evening's play:
Man has his will,—but woman has her way!
While man's dull spirit toils in smoke and fire,
Woman's swift instinct threads the electric wire,—
The magic bracelet stretched beneath the waves
Beats the black giant with his score of slaves.
All earthly powers confess your sovereign art
But that one rebel,—woman's wilful heart.
All foes you master; but a woman's wit
Lets daylight through you ere you know you're hit.
So, just to picture what her art can do,
Hear an old story, made as good as new.

Rudolph, professor of the headsman's trade,
Alike was famous for his arm and blade.

One day a prisoner Justice had to kill
Knelt at the block to test the artist's skill.
Bare-armed, swart-visaged, gaunt, and shaggy-browed,
Rudolph the headsman rose above the crowd.
His falchion lightened with a sudden gleam,
As the pike's armor flashes in the stream.
He sheathed his blade; he turned as if to go;
The victim knelt, still waiting for the blow.
"Why strikest not? Perform thy murderous act,"
The prisoner said. (His voice was slightly cracked.)
"Friend, I *have* struck," the artist straight replied;
"Wait but one moment, and yourself decide."
He held his snuff-box,—"Now then, if you please!"
The prisoner sniffed, and, with a crashing sneeze,
Off his head tumbled,—bowled along the floor,—
Bounced down the steps;—the prisoner said no more!

Woman! thy falchion is a glittering eye;
If death lurk in it, O, how sweet to die!
Thou takest hearts as Rudolph took the head;
We die with love, and never dream we're dead!

THE OLD MAN OF THE SEA.

A NIGHTMARE DREAM BY DAYLIGHT.

Do you know the Old Man of the Sea, of the Sea?
  Have you met with that dreadful old man?
If you have n't been caught, you will be, you will be;
  For catch you he must and he can.

He doesn't hold on by your throat, by your throat,
   As of old in the terrible tale;
But he grapples you tight by the coat, by the coat,
   Till its buttons and button-holes fail.

There's the charm of a snake in his eye, in his eye,
   And a polypus-grip in his hand;
You cannot go back, nor get by, nor get by,
   If you look at the spot where he stands.

O, you're grabbed!   See his claw on your sleeve, on
     your sleeve!
   It is Sinbad's Old Man of the Sea!
You're a Christian, no doubt you believe, you believe:
   You're a martyr, whatever you be!

—Is the breakfast-hour past?   They must wait, they
     must wait,
   While the coffee boils sullenly down,
While the Johnny-cake burns on the grate, on the
     grate,
   And the toast is done frightfully brown.

—Yes, your dinner will keep; let it cool, let it cool,
   And Madam may worry and fret,
And children half-starved go to school, go to school;
   He can't think of sparing you yet.

—Hark! the bell for the train!   "Come along! come
     along!
   For there isn't a second to lose."

" ALL ABOARD ! " (He holds on.)   " Fsht ! ding-dong !
        Fsht ! ding-dong ! "—
    You can follow on foot, if you choose.

—There's a maid with a cheek like a peach, like a
        peach,
    That is waiting for you in the church ;—
But he clings to your side like a leech, like a leech,
    And you leave your lost bride in the lurch.

—There's a babe in a fit,—hurry quick ! hurry quick !
    To the doctor's as fast as you can !
The baby is off, while you stick, while you stick,
    In the grip of the dreadful Old Man !

—I have looked on the face of the Bore, of the Bore ;
    The voice of the Simple I know ;
I have welcomed the Flat at my door, at my door ;
    I have sat by the side of the Slow ;

I have walked like a lamb by the friend, by the friend,
    That stuck to my skirts like a burr ;
I have borne the stale talk without end, without end,
    Of the sitter whom nothing could stir :

But my hamstrings grow loose, and I shake, and I
        shake,
    At the sight of the dreadful Old Man ;
Yea, I quiver and quake, and I take, and I take,
    To my legs with what vigor I can !

O the dreadful Old Man of the Sea, of the Sea!
    He's come back like the Wandering Jew!
He has had his cold claw upon me, upon me,—
    And be sure that he'll have it on you!

———

ODE FOR A SOCIAL MEETING.

WITH SLIGHT ALTERATIONS BY A TEETOTALER.

COME! fill a fresh bumper,—for why should we go

While the ~~nectar~~ [logwood] still reddens our cups as they flow?

Pour out the ~~rich juices~~ [decoction] still bright with the sun,

Till o'er the brimmed crystal the ~~rubies~~ [dye-stuff] shall run.

The ~~purple-globed clusters~~ [half-ripened apples] their life-dews have bled;

How sweet is the ~~breath~~ [taste] of the ~~fragrance they shed~~ [sugar of lead]!

For summer's ~~last roses~~ [rank poisons] lie hid in the ~~wines~~ [wines!!!]

That were garnered by ~~maidens who laughed thro'~~ [stable-boys smoking long]

~~the vines.~~ [nines]

Then a ~~smile~~ [scowl], and a ~~glass~~ [howl], and a ~~toast~~ [scoff], and a ~~cheer~~ [sneer],

For ~~all the good wine, and we've some of it here~~ [strychnine and whiskey, and ratsbane and beer]!

In cellar, in pantry, in attic, in hall,

~~Long live the gay servant that laughs for us all!~~ [Down, down with the tyrant that masters us all!]

THE DEACON'S MASTERPIECE:

OR THE WONDERFUL "ONE-HOSS SHAY."

A LOGICAL STORY.

HAVE you heard of the wonderful one-hoss shay,
That was built in such a logical way
It ran a hundred years to a day,
And then, of a sudden, it——ah, but stay,
I'll tell you what happened without delay,
Scaring the parson into fits,
Frightening people out of their wits,—
Have you ever heard of that, I say?

Seventeen hundred and fifty-five.
Georgius Secundus was then alive,—
Snuffy old drone from the German hive.
That was the year when Lisbon-town
Saw the earth open and gulp her down,
And Braddock's army was done so brown,
Left without a scalp to its crown.
It was on the terrible Earthquake-day
That the Deacon finished the one-hoss shay.

Now in building of chaises, I tell you what,
There is always *somewhere* a weakest spot,—
In hub, tire, felloe, in spring or thill,
In panel, or crossbar, or floor, or sill,
In screw, bolt, thoroughbrace,—lurking still,
Find it somewhere you must and will,—
Above or below, or within or without,—
25

And that's the reason, beyond a doubt,
A chaise *breaks down*, but doesn't *wear out.*

But the Deacon swore, (as Deacons do,
With an " I dew vum," or an " I tell *yeou,*")
He would build one shay to beat the taown
'n' the keounty 'n' all the kentry raoun';
It should be so built that it *couldn'* break daown:
—" Fur," said the Deacon, " 't 's mighty plain
Thut the weakes' place mus' stan' the strain;
'n' the way t' fix it, uz I maintain,
                    Is only jest
T' make that place uz strong uz the rest."

So the Deacon inquired of the village folk
Where he could find the strongest oak,
That couldn't be split nor bent nor broke,—
That was for spokes and floor and sills;
He sent for lancewood to make the thills;
The crossbars were ash, from the straightest trees;
The panels of white-wood, that cuts like cheese,
But lasts like iron for things like these;
The hubs of logs from the " Settler's ellum,"—
Last of its timber,—they couldn't sell 'em,
Never an axe had seen their chips,
And the wedges flew from between their lips,
Their blunt ends frizzled like celery-tips;
Step and prop-iron, bolt and screw,
Spring, tire, axle, and linchpin too,
Steel of the finest, bright and blue;
Thoroughbrace bison-skin, thick and wide;

Boot, top, dasher, from tough old hide
Found in the pit when the tanner died.
That was the way he " put her through."—
" There ! " said the Deacon, " naow she'll dew ! "

Do ! I tell you, I rather guess
She was a wonder, and nothing less !
Colts grew horses, beards turned gray,
Deacon and deaconess dropped away,
Children and grandchildren—where were they ?
But there stood the stout old one-hoss shay
As fresh as on Lisbon-earthquake-day !

EIGHTEEN HUNDRED ;—it came and found
The Deacon's masterpiece strong and sound.
Eighteen hundred increased by ten ;—
" Hahnsum kerridge " they called it then.
Eighteen hundred and twenty came ;—
Running as usual ; much the same.
Thirty and forty at last arrive,
And then come fifty, and FIFTY-FIVE.

Little of all we value here
Wakes on the morn of its hundredth year
Without both feeling and looking queer.
In fact, there's nothing that keeps its youth,
So far as I know, but a tree and truth.
(This is a moral that runs at large;
Take it.—You're welcome.—No extra charge.)

FIRST OF NOVEMBER,—the Earthquake-day.—
There are traces of age in the one-hoss shay,

A general flavor of mild decay,
But nothing local as one may say.
There couldn't be,—for the Deacon's art
Had made it so like in every part
That there wasn't a chance for one to start.
For the wheels were just as strong as the thills,
And the floor was just as strong as the sills,
And the panels just as strong as the floor,
And the whippletree neither less nor more,
And the back-crossbar as strong as the fore,
And spring and axle and hub *encore.*
And yet, *as a whole,* it is past a doubt
In another hour it will be *worn out!*

First of November, 'Fifty-five!
This morning the parson takes a drive.
Now, small boys, get out of the way!
Here comes the wonderful one-hoss shay,
Drawn by a rat-tailed, ewe-necked bay.
"Huddup!" said the parson.—Off went they.

The parson was working his Sunday's text,—
Had got to *fifthly,* and stopped perplexed
At what the—Moses—was coming next.
All at once the horse stood still,
Close by the meet'n'-house on the hill.
—First a shiver, and then a thrill,
Then something decidedly like a spill,—
And the parson was sitting upon a rock,
At half past nine by the meet'n'-house clock,—
Just the hour of the Earthquake shock!
—What do you think the parson found,

When he got up and stared around?
The poor old chaise in a heap or mound,
As if it had been to the mill and ground!
You see, of course, if you're not a dunce,
How it went to pieces all at once,—
All at once, and nothing first,—
Just as bubbles do when they burst.

End of the wonderful one-hoss shay.
Logic is logic.   That's all I say.

ÆSTIVATION.

AN UNPUBLISHED POEM, BY MY LATE LATIN TUTOR.

In candent ire the solar splendor flames;
The foles, languescent, pend from arid rames;
His humid front the cive, anheling, wipes,
And dreams of erring on ventiferous ripes.

How dulce to vive occult to mortal eyes,
Dorm on the herb with none to supervise,
Carp the suave berries from the crescent vine,
And bibe the flow from longicaudate kine!

To me, alas! no verduous vision come,
Save yon exiguous pool's conferva-scum,—
No concave vast repeats the tender hue
That laves my milk-jug with celestial blue!

Me wretched! Let me curr to quercine shades!
Effund your albid hausts, lactiferous maids!
O, might I vole to some umbrageous clump,—
Depart,—be off,—excede,—evade,—erump!

CONTENTMENT.

" Man wants but little here below."

LITTLE I ask; my wants are few;
 I only wish a hut of stone,
(*A very plain* brown stone will do,)
   That I may call my own;—
And close at hand is such a one,
In yonder street that fronts the sun.

Plain food is quite enough for me;
 Three courses are as good as ten;—
If nature can subsist on three,
   Thank Heaven for three. Amen!
I always thought cold victual nice;—
My *choice* would be vanilla-ice.

I care not much for gold or land;—
 Give me a mortage here and there,—
Some good bank stock,—some note of hand,
   Or trifling railroad share;—
I only ask that Fortune send
A *little* more than I shall spend.

Honors are silly toys, I know,
 And titles are but empty names;

I would, *perhaps,* be Plenipo,—
       But only near St. James;
I'm very sure I should not care
To fill our Gubernator's chair.

Jewels are baubles; 'tis a sin
   To care for such unfruitful things;—
One good-sized diamond in a pin,—
       Some, *not so large,* in rings,—
A ruby, and a pearl, or so,
Will do for me;—I laugh at show.

My dame should dress in cheap attire;
   (Good, heavy silks are never dear;)—
I own perhaps I *might* desire
       Some shawls of true Cashmere,—
Some marrowy crapes of China silk,
Like wrinkled skins on scalded milk.

I would not have the horse I drive
   So fast that folks must stop and stare;
An easy gait—two, forty-five—
       Suits me; I do not care;—
Perhaps, for just a *single spurt,*
Some seconds less would do no hurt.

Of pictures, I should like to own
   Titians and Raphaels three or four,—
I love so much their style and tone,—
       One Turner, and no more,
(A landscape,—foreground golden dirt,—
The sunshine painted with a squirt.)

Of books but few,—some fifty score
 For daily use, and bound for wear;
The rest upon an upper floor;—
  Some *little* luxury *there*
Of red morocco's gilded gleam,
And vellum rich as country cream.

Busts, cameos, gems,—such things as these,
 Which others often show for pride,
I value for their power to please,
  And selfish churls deride;—
One Stradivarius, I confess,
Two Meerschaums, I would fain possess.

Wealth's wasteful tricks I will not learn,
 Nor ape the glittering upstart fool;—
Shall not carved tables serve my turn,
  But *all* must be of buhl?
Give grasping pomp its double share,—
I ask but *one* recumbent chair.

Thus humble let me live and die,
 Nor long for Midas' golden touch;
If Heaven more generous gifts deny,
  I shall not miss them *much*,—
Too grateful for the blessing lent
Of simple tastes and mind content!

PARSON TURELL'S LEGACY:

OR, THE PRESIDENT'S OLD ARM-CHAIR.

A MATHEMATICAL STORY.

FACTS respecting an old arm-chair
At Cambridge. Is kept in the College there.
Seems but little the worse for wear.
That's remarkable when I say
It was old in President Holyoke's day.
(One of his boys, perhaps you know,
Died, *at one hundred,* years ago.)
He took lodgings for rain or shine
Under green bed-clothes in '69.

Know old Cambridge? Hope you do.—
Born there? Don't say so! I was, too.
(Born in a house with a gambrel-roof,—
Standing still, if you must have proof.—
" Gambrel?—Gambrel? "—Let me beg
You'll look at a horse's hinder leg,—
First great angle above the hoof,—
That's the gambrel; hence gambrel-roof.)
—Nicest place that ever was seen,—
Colleges red and Common green,
Sidewalks brownish with trees between.
Sweetest spot beneath the skies
When the canker-worms don't rise,—
When the dust, that sometimes flies

Into your mouth and ears and eyes,
In a quiet slumber lies,
Not in the shape of unbaked pies
Such as barefoot children prize.

A kind of harbor it seems to be,
Facing the flow of a boundless sea.
Rows of gray old Tutors stand
Ranged like rocks above the sand;
Rolling beneath them, soft and green,
Breaks the tide of bright sixteen,—
One wave, two waves, three waves, four,
Sliding up the sparkling floor:
Then it ebbs to flow no more,
Wandering off from shore to shore
With its freight of golden ore!
—Pleasant place for boys to play;—
Better keep your girls away;
Hearts get rolled as pebbles do
Which countless fingering waves pursue,
And every classic beach is strown
With heart-shaped pebbles of blood-red stone.

But this is neither here nor there;—
I'm talking about an old arm-chair.
You've heard, no doubt, of PARSON TURELL?
Over at Medford he used to dwell;
Married one of the Mather's folk;
Got with his wife a chair of oak,—
Funny old chair with seat like wedge,
Sharp behind and broad front edge,—

One of the oddest of human things,
Turned all over with knobs and rings,—
But heavy, and wide, and deep, and grand,—
Fit for the worthies of the land,—
Chief-Justice Sewell a cause to try in,
Or Cotton Mather to sit—and lie—in.
—Parson Turell bequeathed the same
To a certain student,—SMITH by name;
These were the terms, as we are told:
" Saide Smith saide Chaire to have and holde;
When he doth graduate, then to passe
To ye oldest Youth in ye Senior Classe.
On Payment of "—(naming a certain sum)—
" By him to whom ye Chaire shall come;
He to ye oldest Senior next,
And soe forever,"—(thus runs the text,)—
" But one Crown lesse then he gave to claime,
That being his Debte for use of same."

Smith transferred it to one of the BROWNS,
And took his money,—five silver crowns.
Brown delivered it up to MOORE,
Who paid, it is plain, not five, but four.
Moore made over the chair to LEE,
Who gave him crowns of silver three.
Lee conveyed it unto DREW,
And now the payment, of course, was two.
Drew gave up the chair to DUNN,—
All he got, as you see, was one.
Dunn released the chair to HALL,
And got by the bargain no crown at all.

—And now it passed to a second BROWN,
Who took it and likewise *claimed a crown.*
When *Brown* conveyed it unto WARE,
Having had one crown, to make it fair,
He paid him two crowns to take the chair;
And *Ware,* being honest, (as all Wares be,)
He paid one POTTER, who took it, three.
Four got ROBINSON; five got DIX;
JOHNSON *primus* demanded six;
And so the sum kept gathering still
Till after the battle of Bunker's Hill.
—When paper money became so cheap,
Folks wouldn't count it, but said " a heap,"
A certain RICHARDS,—the books declare,—
(A.M. in '90 ? I've looked with care
Through the Triennial,—*name not there.*)
This person, Richards, was offered then
Eight score pounds, but would have ten;
Nine, I think, was the sum he took,—
Not quite certain,—but see the book.
—By and by the wars were still,
But nothing had altered the Parson's will.
The old arm-chair was solid yet,
But saddled with such a monstrous debt!
Things grew quite too bad to bear,
Paying such sums to get rid of the chair!
But dead men's fingers hold awful tight,
And there was the will in black and white,
Plain enough for a child to spell.
What should be done no man could tell,
For the chair was a kind of nightmare curse,
And every season but made it worse.

As a last resort, to clear the doubt,
They got old GOVERNOR HANCOCK out.
The Governor came with his Light-horse Troop
And his mounted truckmen, all cock-a-hoop;
·Halberds glittered and colors flew,
French horns whinnied and trumpets blew,
The yellow fifes whistled between their teeth
And the bumble-bee bass-drums boomed beneath;
So he rode with all his band,
Till the President met him, cap in hand.
—The Governor " hefted " the crowns, and
    said,—
" A will is a will, and the Parson's dead."
The Governor hefted the crowns.   Said he,—
" There is your p'int.   And here's my fee.
These are the terms you must fulfil,—
On such conditions I BREAK THE WILL ! "
The Governor mentioned what these should be.
(Just wait a minute and then you'll see.)
The President prayed.   Then all was still,
And the Governor rose and BROKE THE WILL !
—" About those conditions ? "   Well, now you go
And do as I tell you, and then you'll know.
Once a year, on Commencement day,
If you'll only take the pains to stay,
You'll see the President in the CHAIR,
Likewise the Governor sitting there.
The President rises; both old and young
May hear his speech in a foreign tongue,
The meaning whereof, as lawyers swear,
Is this: Can I keep this old arm-chair ?

And then his Excellency bows,
As much as to say that *they* allow.
The Vice-Gub. next is called by name;
He bows like t' other, which means the same.
And all the officers round 'em bow,
As much as to say that *they* allow.
And a lot of parchments about the chair
Are handed to witnesses then and there,
And then the lawyers hold it clear
That the chair is safe for another year.

God bless you, Gentlemen! Learn to **give**
Money to colleges while you live.
Don't be silly and think you'll try
To bother the colleges, when you die,
With codicil this, and codicil that,
That Knowledge may starve while Law **grows
    fat**;
For there never was pitcher that wouldn't spill,
And there's always a flaw in a donkey's will!

DE SAUTY.

AN ELECTRO-CHEMICAL ECLOGUE.

Professor.   *Blue-Nose.*

PROFESSOR.

TELL me, O Provincial! speak, Ceruleo-Nasal!
Lives there one De Sauty extant now among you,
Whispering Boanerges, son of silent thunder,
        Holding talk with nations?

Is there a De Sauty ambulant on Tellus,
Bifid-cleft like mortals, dormient in night-cap,
Having sight, smell, hearing, food-receiving feature
      Three times daily patent?

Breathes there such a being, O Ceruleo-Nasal?
Or is he a *mythus*,—ancient word for " humbug,"—
Such as Livy told about the wolf that wet-nursed
      Romulus and Remus?

Was he born of woman, this alleged De Sauty?
Or a living product of galvanic action,
Like the *acarus* bred in Crosse's flint-solution?
      Speak, thou Cyano-Rhinal!

BLUE-NOSE.

Many things thou askest, jackknife-bearing stranger,
Much-conjecturing mortal, pork-and-treacle-waster!
Pretermit thy whittling, wheel thine ear-flap toward
      me,
      Thou shalt hear them answered.

When the charge galvanic tingled through the cable,
At the polar focus of the wire electric
Suddenly appeared a white-faced man among us:
      Called himself " DE SAUTY."

As the small opossum held in pouch maternal
Grasps the nutrient organ whence the term
    mammalia,
So the unknown stranger held the wire electric,
      Sucking in the current.

When the current strengthened, bloomed the pale-
   faced stranger,—
Took no drink nor victual, yet grew fat and rosy,—
And from time to time, in sharp articulation,
   Said, "*All right!* DE SAUTY."

From the lonely station passed the utterance, spread-
   ing
Through the pines and hemlocks to the groves of
   steeples,
Till the land was filled with loud reverberations
   Of "*All right!* DE SAUTY."

When the current slackened, drooped the mystic stran-
   ger,—
Faded, faded, faded, as the stream grew weaker,—
Wasted to a shadow, with a hartshorn odor
   Of disintegration.

Drops of deliquescence glistened on his forehead,
Whitened round his feet the dust of efflorescence,
Till one Monday morning, when the flow suspended,
   There was no De Sauty.

Nothing but a cloud of elements organic,
C. O. H. N. Ferrum, Chlor. Flu. Sil. Potassa,
Calc. Sod. Phosph. Mag. Sulphur, Mang. (?)
   Alumin. (?) Cuprum, (?)
   Such as man is made of.

Born of stream galvanic, with it he had perished!
There is no De Sauty now there is no current!
Give us a new cable, then again we'll hear him
   Cry, "*All right!* DE SAUTY."

THE OLD MAN DREAMS.

O FOR one hour of youthful joy!
    Give back my twentieth spring!
I'd rather laugh a bright-haired boy
    Than reign a gray-beard king!

Off with the wrinkled spoils of age!
    Away with learning's crown!
Tear out life's wisdom-written page,
    And dash its trophies down!

One moment let my life-blood stream
    From boyhood's fount of flame!
Give me one giddy, reeling dream
    Of life all love and fame!

—My listening angel heard the prayer,
    And, calmly smiling, said,
" If I but touch thy silvered hair,
    Thy hasty wish hath sped.

" But is there nothing in thy track
    To bid thee fondly stay,
While the swift seasons hurry back
    To find the wished-for day ? "

—Ah, truest soul of womankind!
    Without thee, what were life ?
One bliss I cannot leave behind:
    I'll take—my—precious—wife!

26

—The angel took a sapphire pen
   And wrote in rainbow dew,
" The man would be a boy again,
   And be a husband too! "

—" And is there nothing yet unsaid
   Before the change appears?
Remember, all their gifts have fled
   With those dissolving years! "

Why, yes; for memory would recall
   My fond paternal joys;
I could not bear to leave them all;
   I'll take—my—girl—and—boys!

The smiling angel dropped his pen,—
   " Why this will never do;
The man would be a boy again,
   And be a father too! "

And so I laughed,—my laughter woke
   The household with its noise,—
And wrote my dream, when morning broke,
   To please the gray-haired boys.

MARE RUBRUM.

FLASH out a stream of blood-red wine!—
   For I would drink to other days;
And brighter shall their memory shine,
   Seen flaming through its crimson blaze.

The roses die, the summers fade;
  But every ghost of boyhood's dream
By Nature's magic power is laid
  To sleep beneath this blood-red stream.

It filled the purple grapes that lay
  And drank the splendors of the sun
Where the long summer's cloudless day
  Is mirrored in the broad Garonne;
It pictures still the bacchant shapes
  That saw their hoarded sunlight shed,—
The maidens dancing on the grapes,—
  Their milk-white ankles splashed with red.

Beneath these waves of crimson lie,
  In rosy fetters prisoned fast,
Those flitting shapes that never die,
  The swift-winged visions of the past.
Kiss but the crystal's mystic rim,
  Each shadow rends its flowery chain,
Springs in a bubble from its brim
  And walks the chambers of the brain.

Poor Beauty! time and fortune's wrong
  No form nor feature may withstand,—
Thy wrecks are scattered all along,
  Like emptied sea-shells on the sand;—
Yet, sprinkled with this blushing rain,
  The dust restores each blooming girl,
As if the sea-shells moved again
  Their glistening lips of pink and pearl.

Here lies the home of schoolboy life,
　　With creaking stair and wind-swept hall,
And, scarred by many a truant knife,
　　Our old initials on the wall;
Here rest—their keen vibrations mute—
　　The shout of voices known so well,
The ringing laugh, the wailing flute,
　　The chiding of the sharp-tongued bell.

Here, clad in burning robes, are laid
　　Life's blossomed joys, untimely shed;
And here those cherished forms have strayed
　　We miss awhile, and call them dead.
What wizard fills the maddening glass?
　　What soil the enchanted clusters grew,
That buried passions wake and pass
　　In beaded drops of fiery dew?

Nay, take the cup of blood-red wine,—
　　Our hearts can boast a warmer glow,
Filled from a vintage more divine,—
　　Calmed, but not chilled by winter's snow!
To-night the palest wave we sip
　　Rich as the priceless draught shall be
That wet the bride of Cana's lip,—
　　The wedding wine of Galilee!

WHAT WE ALL THINK.

THAT age was older once than now,
　　In spite of locks untimely shed,
Or silvered on the youthful brow;
　　That babes make love and children wed.

That sunshine had a heavenly glow,
　Which faded with those " good old days "
When winters came with deeper snow,
　And autumns with a softer haze.

That—mother, sister, wife, or child—
　The " best of women " each has known.
Were schoolboys ever half so wild?
　How young the grandpapas have grown!

That *but for this* our souls were free,
　And *but for that* our lives were blest;
That in some season yet to be
　Our cares will leave us time to rest.

Whene'er we groan with ache or pain,—
　Some common ailment of the race,—
Though doctors think the matter plain,—
　That ours is " a peculiar case."

That when like babes with fingers burned
　We count one bitter maxim more,
Our lesson all the world has learned,
　And men are wiser than before.

That when we sob o'er fancied woes,
　The angels hovering overhead
Count every pitying drop that flows
　And love us for the tears we shed.

That when we stand with tearless eye
　And turn the beggar from our door,

They still approve us when we sigh,
    " Ah, had I but *one thousand more!* "

Though temples crowd the crumbled brink
    O'erhanging truth's eternal flow,
Their tablets bold with *what we think,*
    Their echoes dumb to *what we know;*

That one unquestioned text we read,
    All doubt beyond, all fear above,
Nor crackling pile nor cursing creed
    Can burn or blot it: GOD IS LOVE!

SPRING HAS COME.

INTRA MUROS.

THE sunbeams, lost for half a year,
    Slant through my pane their morning rays;
For dry northwesters cold and clear,
    The east blows in its thin blue haze.

And first the snowdrop's bells are seen,
    Then close against the sheltering wall
The tulip's horn of dusky green,
    The peony's dark unfolding ball.

The golden-chaliced crocus burns;
    The long narcissus-blades appear;
The cone-beaked hyacinth returns
    To light her blue-flamed chandelier.

The willow's whistling lashes, wrung
  By the wild winds of gusty March,
With sallow leaflets lightly strung,
  Are swaying by the tufted larch.

The elms have robed their slender spray
  With full-blown flower and embryo leaf;
Wide o'er the clasping arch of day
  Soars like a cloud their hoary chief.

See the proud tulip's flaunting cup;
  That flames in glory for an hour,—
Behold it withering,—then look up,—
  How meek the forest monarch's flower!

When wake the violets, Winter dies;
  When sprout the elm-buds, Spring is near;
When lilacs blossom, Summer cries,
  " Bud, little roses! Spring is here! "

The windows blush with fresh bouquets,
  Cut with the May-dew on their lips;
The radish all its bloom displays,
  Pink as Aurora's finger-tips.

Nor less the flood of light that showers
  On beauty's changed corolla-shades,—
The walks are gay as bridal bowers
  With rows of many-petalled maids.

The scarlet shell-fish click and clash
  In the blue barrow where they slide;

The horseman, proud of streak and splash,
    Creeps homeward from his morning ride.

Here comes the dealer's awkward string,
    With neck in rope and tail in knot,—
Rough colts, with careless country-swing,
    In lazy walk or slouching trot.

——Wild filly from the mountain-side,
    Doomed to the close and chafing thills,
Lend me thy long, untiring stride
    To seek with thee thy western hills!

I hear the whispering voice of Spring,
    The thrush's trill, the robin's cry,
Like some poor bird with prisoned wing
    That sits and sings, but longs to fly.

O for one spot of living green,—
    One little spot where leaves can grow,—
To love unblamed, to walk unseen,
    To dream above, to sleep below!

A GOOD TIME GOING!

BRAVE singer of the coming time,
    Sweet minstrel of the joyous present,
Crowned with the noblest wreath of rhyme,
    The holly-leaf of Ayrshire's peasant,
Good by! Good by!—Our hearts and hands,
    Our lips in honest Saxon phrases,

Cry, God be with him, till he stands
  His feet among the English daisies!

'Tis is here we part;—for other eyes
  The busy deck, the fluttering streamer,
The dripping arms that plunge and rise,
  The waves in foam, the ship in tremor,
The kerchiefs waving from the pier,
  The cloudy pillar gliding o'er him,
The deep blue desert, lone and drear,
  With heaven above and home before him!

His home!—the Western giant smiles,
  And twirls the spotty globe to find it;—
This little speck the British Isles?
  'Tis but a freckle,—never mind it!
He laughs, and all his prairies roll,
  Each gurgling cataract roars and chuckles,
And ridges stretched from pole to pole
  Heave till they crack their iron knuckles!

But Memory blushes at the sneer,
  And Honor turns with frown defiant,
And Freedom, leaning on her spear,
  Laughs louder than the laughing giant:
" An islet is a world," she said,
  " When glory with its dust has blended,
And Britain keeps her noble dead
  Till earth and seas and skies are rended! "

Beneath each swinging forest-bough
  Some arm as stout in death reposes,—

From wave-washed foot to heaven-kissed brow
   Her valor's life-blood runs in roses;
Nay, let our brothers of the West
   Write smiling in their florid pages,
One half her soil has walked the rest
   In poets, heroes, martyrs, sages!

Hugged in the clinging billow's clasp,
   From sea-weed fringe to mountain heather,
The British oak with rooted grasp
   Her slender handful holds together;—
With cliffs of white and bowers of green,
   And Ocean narrowing to caress her,
And hills and threaded streams between,—
   Our little mother isle, God bless her!

In earth's broad temple where we stand,
   Fanned by the eastern gales that brought us,
We hold the missal in our hand,
   Bright with the lines our Mother taught us;
Where'er its blazoned page betrays
   The glistening links of gilded fetters,
Behold, the half-turned leaf displays
   Her rubric stained in crimson letters!

Enough! To speed a parting friend
   'Tis vain alike to speak and listen;—
Yet stay,—these feeble accents blend
   With rays of light from eyes that glisten.
Good by! once more,—and kindly tell
   In words of peace the young world's story,—
And say, besides, we love too well
   Our mothers' soil, our fathers' glory!

THE LAST BLOSSOM.

THOUGH young no more, we still would dream
    Of beauty's dear deluding wiles;
The leagues of life to graybeards seem
    Shorter than boyhood's lingering miles.

Who knows a woman's wild caprice?
    It played with Gœthe's silvered hair,
And many a Holy Father's " niece "
    Has softly smoothed the papal chair.

When sixty bids us sigh in vain
    To melt the heart of sweet sixteen,
We think upon those ladies twain
    Who loved so well the tough old Dean.

We see the Patriarch's wintry face,
    The maid of Egypt's dusky glow,
And dream that Youth and Age embrace,
    As April violets fill with snow.

Tranced in her lord's Olympian smile
    His lotus-loving Memphian lies,—
The musky daughter of the Nile,
    With plaited hair and almond eyes.

Might we but share one wild caress
    Ere life's autumnal blossoms fall,
And Earth's brown, clinging lips impress
    The long cold kiss that waits us all!

My bosom heaves, remembering yet
   The morning of that blissful day,
When Rose, the flower of spring, I met,
   And gave my raptured soul away.

Flung from her eyes of purest blue,
   A lasso, with its leaping chain,
Light as a loop of larkspurs, flew
   O'er sense and spirit, heart and brain.

Thou com'st to cheer my waning age,
   Sweet vision, waited for so long!
Dove that would seek the poet's cage
   Lured by the magic breath of song!

She blushes!   Ah, reluctant maid,
   Love's *drapeau rouge* the truth has told!
O'er girlhood's yielding barricade
   Floats the great Leveller's crimson fold!

Come to my arms!—love heeds not years;
   No frost the bud of passion knows.—
Ha! what is this my frenzy hears?
   A voice behind me uttered,—Rose!

Sweet was her smile,—but not for me;
   Alas! when woman looks *too* kind,
Just turn your foolish head and see,—
   Some youth is walking close behind!

" THE BOYS."

HAS there any old fellow got mixed with the boys?
If there has, take him out, without making a noise.
Hang the Almanac's cheat and the Catalogue's spite!
Old time is a liar! We're twenty to-night!

We're twenty! We're twenty! Who says we are
    more?
He's tipsy,—young jackanapes!—show him the
    door!
" Gray temples at twenty?"—Yes! white if we
    please;
Where the snow-flakes fall thickest there's nothing can
    freeze!

Was it snowing I spoke of? Excuse the mistake!
Look close,—you will see not a sign of a flake!
We want some new garlands for those we have shed,—
And these are white roses in place of the red.

We've a trick, we young fellows, you may have been
    told,
Of talking (in public) as if we were old:—
That boy we call " Doctor," and this we call
    " Judge ";
It's a neat little fiction,—of course it's all fudge.

That fellow's the " Speaker,"—the one on the right;
" Mr. Mayor," my young one, how are you to-night?

That's our " Member of Congress," we say when we
  chaff;
There's the " Reverend " What his name?—don't
  make me laugh.

That boy with the grave mathematical look
Made believe he had written a wonderful book,
And the ROYAL SOCIETY thought it was *true!*
So they chose him right in,—a good joke it was too!

There's a boy, we pretend, with a three-decker brain,
That could harness a team with a logical chain;
When he spoke for our manhood in syllabled fire,
We called him " The Justice," but now he's " The
  Squire."

And there's a nice youngster of excellent pith,—
Fate tried to conceal him by naming him Smith;
But he shouted a song for the brave and the free,—
Just read on his medal, " My country," " of thee! "

You hear that boy laughing?—You think he's all
  fun;
But the angels laugh, too, at the good he has done;
The children laugh loud as they troop to his call,
And the poor man that knows him laughs loudest of
  all!

Yes, we're boys,—always playing with tongue or with
  pen;
And I sometimes have asked, Shall we ever be men?
Shall we always be youthful, and laughing, and gay,
Till the last dear companion drops smiling away?

Then here's to our boyhood, its gold and its gray!
The stars of its winter, the dews of its May!
And when we have done with our life-lasting toys,
Dear Father, take care of thy children, THE BOYS!

January 6, 1859.

THE OPENING OF THE PIANO.

IN the little southern parlor of the house you may
    have seen
With the gambrel-roof, and the gable looking west-
    ward to the green,
At the side toward the sunset, with the window on its
    right,
Stood the London-made piano I am dreaming of to-
    night!

Ah me! how I remember the evening when it came!
What a cry of eager voices, what a group of cheeks in
    flame,
When the wondrous box was opened that had come
    from over seas,
With its smell of mastic-varnish and its flash of ivory
    keys!

Then the children all grew fretful in the restlessness
    of joy,
For the boy would push his sister, and the sister crowd
    the boy,

Till the father asked for quiet in his grave **paternal**
    way,
But the mother hushed the tumult with the words,
    " Now, Mary, play."

For the dear soul knew that music was a very sover-
    eign balm;
She had sprinkled it over Sorrow and seen its brow
    grow calm,
In the days of slender harpsichords with tapping tink-
    ling quills,
Or carolling to her spinet with its thin metallic thrills.

So Mary, the household minstrel, who always loved
    to please,
Sat down to the new " Clementi," and struck the
    glittering keys.
Hushed were the children's voices, and every eye grew
    dim,
As, floating from lip and finger, arose the " Vesper
    Hymn."

—Catharine, child of a neighbor, curly and rosy-red,
(Wedded since, and a widow,—something like ten
    years dead,)
Hearing a gush of music such as none before,
Steals from her mother's chamber and peeps at the
    open door.
Just as the " Jubilate " in threaded whisper dies,
" Open it! open it, lady! " the little maiden cries,
(For she thought 'twas a singing creature caged in a
    box she heard,)
" Open it! open it, lady! and let me see the *bird!* "

MIDSUMMER.

Here! sweep these foolish leaves away,—
I will not crush my brains to-day!
Look! are the southern curtains drawn?
Fetch me a fan, and so begone!

Not that,—the palm-tree's rustling leaf
Brought from a parching coral-reef!
Its breath is heated;—I would swing
The broad gray plumes,—the eagle's wing.

I hate these roses' feverish blood!—
Pluck me a half-blown lily-bud,
A long-stemmed lily from the lake,
Cold as a coiling water-snake.

Rain me sweet odors on the air,
And wheel me up my Indian chair,
And spread some book not overwise
Flat out before my sleepy eyes.

—Who knows it not,—this dead recoil
Of weary fibres stretched with toil,—
The pulse that flutters faint and low
When Summer's seething breezes blow?

O Nature! bare thy loving breast,
And give thy child one hour of rest,—
One little hour to lie unseen
Beneath thy scarf of leafy green!

27

So, curtained by a singing pine,
Its murmuring voice shall blend with mine,
Till, lost in dreams, my faltering lay
In sweeter music dies away.

A PARTING HEALTH.

TO J. L. MOTLEY.

YES, we knew we must lose him,—though friend-
      ship may claim
To blend her green leaves with the laurels of fame;
Though fondly, at parting, we call him our own,
'Ts the whisper of love when the bugle has blown.

As the rider that rests with the spur on his heel,—
As the guardsman that sleeps in his corselet of steel,—
As the archer that stands with his shaft on the string,
He stoops from his toil to the garland we bring.

What pictures yet slumber unborn in his loom,
Till their warriors shall breathe and their beauties
      shall bloom,
While the tapestry lengthens the life-glowing dyes
That caught from our sunsets the stain of their
      skies!

In the alcoves of death, in the charnels of time,
Where flit the gaunt spectres of passion and crime.

There are triumphs untold, there are martyrs un-
    sung,
There are heroes yet silent to speak with his tongue!

Let us hear the proud story which time has be-
    queathed!
From lips that are warm with the freedom they
    breathed!
Let him summon its tryants, and tell us their doom,
Though he sweep the black past like Van Tromp
    with his broom!

*   *   *   *   *

The dream flashes by, for the west-winds awake
On pampas, on prairie, o'er mountain and lake,
To bathe the swift bark, life a sea-girdled shrine,
With incense they stole from the rose and the pine.

So fill a bright cup with the sunlight that gushed
When the dead summer's jewels were trampled and
    crushed:
THE TRUE KNIGHT OF LEARNING,—the world holds
    him dear,—
Love bless him, Joy crown him, God speed his career!
1857.

A GOOD-BY.

TO J. R. LOWELL.

FAREWELL, for the bark has her breast to the tide,
And the rough arms of Ocean are stretched for his
    bride;

The winds from the mountain stream over the bay;
One clasp of the hand, then away and away!

I see the tall mast as it rocks by the shore;
The sun is declining, I see it once more;
To-day like the blade in a thick-waving field,
To-morrow the spike on a Highlander's shield.

Alone, while the cloud pours its treacherous breath,
With the blue lips all round her whose kisses are
    death;
Ah, think not the breeze that is urging her sail
Has left her unaided to strive with the gale.

There are hopes that play round her, like fires on the
    mast,
That will light the dark hour till its danger has past;
There are prayers that will plead with the storm when
    it raves,
And whisper " Be still! " to the turbulent waves.

Nay, think not that Friendship has called us in vain
To join the fair ring ere we break it again;
There is strength in its circle,—you lose the bright
    star,
But its sisters still chain it, though shining afar.

I give you one health in the juice of the vine,
The blood of the vineyard shall mingle with mine;
Thus, thus let us drain the last dew-drops of gold,
As we empty our hearts of the blessings they hold.

    April 29, 1855.

AT A BIRTHDAY FESTIVAL.

TO J. R. LOWELL.

WE will not speak of years to-night,—
    For what have years to bring
But larger floods of love and light,
    And sweeter songs to sing?

We will not drown in wordy praise
    The kindly thoughts that rise;
If Friendship own one tender phrase,
    He reads it in our eyes.

We need not waste our schoolboy art
    To gild this notch of Time;—
Forgive me if my wayward heart
    Has throbbed in artless rhyme.

Enough for him the silent grasp
    That knits us hand in hand,
And he the bracelet's radiant clasp
    That locks our circling band.

Strength to his hours of manly toil!
    Peace to his starlit dreams!
Who loves alike the furrowed soil,
    The music-haunted streams!

Sweet smiles to keep forever bright
    The sunshine on his lips,

And faith that sees the ring of light
    Round nature's last eclipse!

February 22, 1859.

A BIRTHDAY TRIBUTE.

TO J. F. CLARKE.

Who is the shepherd sent to lead,
    Through pastures green, the Master's sheep?
What guileless " Israelite indeed "
    The folded flock may watch and keep?

He who with manliest spirit joins
    The heart of gentlest human mould,
With burning light and girded loins,
    To guide the flock, or watch the fold;

True to all Truth the world denies,
    Not tongue-tied for its gilded sin;
Not always right in all men's eyes,
    But faithful to the light within;

Who asks no meed of earthly fame,
    Who knows no earthly master's call,
Who hopes for man, through guilt and shame,
    Still answering, " God is over all; "

Who makes another's grief his own,
    Whose smile lends joy a double cheer;

Where lives the saint, if such be known?—
Speak softly,—such an one is here!

O faithful shepherd! thou hast borne
The heat and burden of the day;
Yet, o'er thee, bright with beams unshorn,
The sun still shows thine onward way.

To thee our fragrant love we bring,
In buds that April half displays,
Sweet first-born angels of the spring,
Caught in their opening hymn of praise.

What though our faltering accents fail,
Our captives know their message well,
Our words unbreathed their lips exhale,
And sigh more love than ours can tell.

April 4, 1860.

THE GRAY CHIEF.

FOR THE MEETING OF THE MASSACHUSETTS MEDICAL
SOCIETY.

1859.

'TIS sweet to fight our battles o'er,
And crown with honest praise
The gray old chief, who strikes no more
The blow of better days.

Before the true and trusted sage
  With willing hearts we bend,
When years have touched with hallowing age
  Our Master, Guide, and Friend.

For all his manhood's labor past,
  For love and faith long tried,
His age is honored to the last,
  Though strength and will have died.

But when, untamed by toil and strife,
  Full in our front he stands,
The torch of light, the shield of life,
  Still lifted in his hands,

No temple, though its walls resound
  With bursts of ringing cheers,
Can hold the honors that surround
  His manhood's twice-told years!

THE LAST LOOK.

W. W. SWAIN.

Behold —not him we knew!
This was the prison which his soul looked through,
  Tender, and brave, and true.

His voice no more is heard;
And his dead name—that dear familiar word—
  Lies on our lips unstirred.

He spake with poet's tongue;
Living, for him the minstrel's lyre was strung:
   He shall not die unsung!

   Grief tried his love, and pain;
And the long bondage of his martyr-chain
   Vexed his sweet soul,—in vain!

   It felt life's surges break,
As, girt with stormy seas, his island lake,
   Smiling while tempests wake.

   How can we sorrow more?
Grieve not for him whose heart had gone before
   To that untrodden shore!

   Lo, through its leafy screen,
A gleam of sunlight on a ring of green,
   Untrodden, half unseen!

   Here let his body rest,
Where the calm shadows that his soul loved best
   May slide above his breast.

   Smooth his uncurtained bed;
And if some natural tears are softly shed,
   It is not for the dead.

   Fold the green turf aright
For the long hours before the morning's light,
   And say the last Good Night!

And plant a clear white stone
Close by those mounds which hold his loved, his
    own,—
    Lonely, but not alone.

Here let him sleeping lie,
Till Heaven's bright watchers slumber in the sky,
    And Death himself shall die!

NAUSHON, September 22, 1858.

IN MEMORY OF

CHARLES WENTWORTH UPHAM, JUNIOR,

HE was all sunshine; in his face
    The very soul of sweetness shone;
Fairest and gentlest of his race;
    None like him we can call our own.

Something there was of one that died
    In her fresh spring-time long ago,
Our first dear Mary, angel-eyed,
    Whose smile it was a bliss to know.

Something of her whose love imparts
    Such radiance to her day's decline,
We feel its twilight in our hearts
    Bright as the earliest morning-shine.

Yet richer strains our eye could trace
    That made our plainer mould more fair,

That curved the lip with happier grace,
  That waved the soft and silken hair.

Dust unto dust! the lips are still
  That only spoke to cheer and bless;
The folded hands lie white and chill
  Unclasped from sorrow's last caress.

Leave him in peace; he will not heed
  These idle tears we vainly pour,
Give back to earth the fading weed
  Of mortal shape his spirit wore.

" Shall I not weep my heartstrings torn,
  My flower of love that falls half blown,
My youth uncrowned, my life forlorn,
  A thorny path to walk alone ? "

O Mary! one who bore thy name,
  Whose Friend and Master was divine,
Sat waiting silent till He came,
  Bowed down in speechless grief like thine.

" Where have ye laid him ? " " Come," they say,
  Pointing to where the loved one slept;
Weeping, the sister led the way,—
  And, seeing Mary, " Jesus wept."

He weeps with thee, with all that mourn,
  And He shall wipe thy streaming eyes
Who knew all sorrows, woman born,—
  Trust in his word; thy dead shall rise!

April 15, 1860.

MARTHA.

DIED JANUARY 7, 1861.

SEXTON! Martha's dead and gone;
    Toll the bell! toll the bell!
Her weary hands their labor cease;
Good night, poor Martha,—sleep in peace!
    Toll the bell!

Sexton! Martha's dead and gone;
    Toll the bell! toll the bell!
For many a year has Martha said,
" I'm old and poor,—would I were dead!"
    Toll the bell!

Sexton! Martha's dead and gone;
    Toll the bell! toll the bell!
She'll bring no more, by day or night,
Her basket full of linen white.
    Toll the bell!

Sexton! Martha's dead and gone;
    Toll the bell! toll the bell!
'Tis fitting she should lie below
A pure white sheet of drifted snow.
    Toll the bell!

Sexton! Martha's dead and gone;
    Toll the bell! toll the bell!
Sleep, Martha sleep, to wake in light,
Where all the robes are stainless white.
    Toll the bell!

SUN AND SHADOW.

As I look from the isle, o'er its billows of green,
   To the billows of foam-crested blue,
Yon bark, that afar in the distance is seen,
   Half dreaming, my eyes will pursue:
Now dark in the shadow, she scatters the spray
   As the chaff in the stroke of the flail;
Now white as the sea-gull, she flies on her way,
   The sun gleaming bright on her sail.

Yet her pilot is thinking of dangers to shun,—
   Of breakers that whiten and roar;
How little he cares, if in shadow or sun
   They see him who gaze from the shore!
He looks to the beacon that looms from the reef,
   To the rock that is under his lee,
As he drifts on the blast, like a wind-wafted leaf,
   O'er the gulfs of the desolate sea.

Thus drifting afar to the dim-vaulted caves
   Where life and its ventures are laid,
The dreamers who gaze while we battle the waves
   May see us in sunshine or shade;
Yet true to our course, though our shadow grow
   dark,
   We'll trim our broad sail as before,
And stand by the rudder that governs the bark,
   Nor ask how we look from the shore!

THE CHAMBERED NAUTILUS.

THIS is the ship of pearl, which, poets feign,
    Sails the unshadowed main,—
    The venturous bark that flings
On the sweet summer wind its purpled wings
In gulfs enchanted, where the Siren sings,
    And coral reefs lie bare,
Where the cold sea-maids rise to sun their streaming
    hair.

Its webs of living gauze no more unfurl;
    Wrecked is the ship of pearl!
    And every chambered cell,
Where its dim dreaming life was wont to dwell,
As the frail tenant shaped his growing shell,
    Before thee lies revealed,—
Its irised ceiling rent, its sunless crypt unsealed!

Year after year beheld the silent toil
    That spread his lustrous coil;
    Still, as the spiral grew,
He left the past year's dwelling for the new,
Stole with soft step its shining archway through,
    Built up its idle door,
Stretched in his last-found home, and knew the old no
    more.

Thanks for the heavenly message brought by thee,
    Child of the wandering sea,
    Cast from her lap, forlorn!

From thy dead lips a clearer note is born
Than ever Triton blew from wreathéd horn!
 While on mine ear it rings,
Through the deep caves of thought I hear a voice that
 sings:—

Build thee more stately mansions, O my soul,
 As the swift seasons roll!
 Leave thy low-vaulted past!
Let each new temple, nobler than the last,
Shut thee from heaven with a dome more vast,
 Till thou at length art free,
Leaving thine outgrown shell by life's unresting sea!

THE TWO ARMIES.

As Life's unending column pours,
 Two marshalled hosts are seen,—
Two armies on the trampled shores
 That Death flows black between.

One marches to the drum-beat's roll,
 The wide-mouthed clarion's bray,
And bears upon a crimson scroll,
 "Our glory is to slay."

One moves in silence by the stream,
 With sad, yet watchful eyes,
Calm as the patient planet's gleam
 That walks the clouded skies.

Along its front no sabres shine,
  No blood-red pennons wave;
Its banner bears the single line,
  "Our duty is to save."

For those no death-bed's lingering shade;
  At Honor's trumpet-call,
With knitted brow and lifted blade
  In Glory's arms they fall.

For these no clashing falchions bright,
  No stirring battle-cry;
The bloodless stabber calls by night,—
  Each answers, "Here am I!"

For those the sculptor's laurelled bust,
  The builder's marble piles,
The anthems pealing o'er their dust
  Through long cathedral aisles.

For these the blossom-sprinkled turf
  That floods the lonely graves,
When Spring rolls in her sea-green surf
  In flowery-foaming waves.

Two paths lead upward from below,
  And angels wait above,
Who count each burning life-drop's flow,
  Each falling tear of Love.

Though from the Hero's bleeding breast
  Her pulses Freedom drew,

Though the white lilies in her crest
  Sprang from that scarlet dew,—

While Valor's haughty champions wait
  Till all their scars are shown,
Love walks unchallenged through the gate,
  To sit beside the Throne!

FOR THE MEETING OF THE NATIONAL SANITARY ASSOCIATION.

1860

WHAT makes the Healing Art divine?
  The bitter drug we buy and sell,
The brands that scorch, the blades that shine,
  The scars we leave, the "cures" we tell?

Are these thy glories, holiest Art,—
  The trophies that adorn thee best,—
Or but thy triumph's meanest part,
  Where mortal weakness stands confessed?

We take the arms that Heaven supplies
  For Life's long battle with Disease,
Taught by our various need to prize
  Our frailest weapons, even these.

But ah! when Science drops her shield—
  Its peaceful shelter proved in vain—
28

And bares her snow-white arm to wield
    The sad, stern ministry of pain;

When shuddering o'er the fount of life,
    She folds her heaven-anointed wings,
To lift unmoved the glittering knife
    That searches all its crimson springs;

When, faithful to her ancient lore,
She thrusts aside her fragrant balm
For blistering juice, or cankering ore,
    And tames them till they cure or calm;

When in her gracious hand are seen
    The dregs and scum of earth and seas,
Her kindness counting all things clean
    That lend the sighing sufferer ease;

Though on the field that Death has won,
    She saves some stragglers in retreat;—
These single acts of mercy done
    Are but confessions of defeat.

What though our tempered poisons save
    Some wrecks of life from aches and ails:
Those grand specifics Nature gave
    Were never poised by weights or scales!

God lent his creatures light and air,
    And waters open to the skies;
Man locks him in a stifling lair,
    And wonders why his brother dies!

In vain our pitying tears are shed,
  In vain we rear the sheltering pile
Where Art weeds out from bed to bed
  The plagues we planted by the mile!

Be that the glory of the past;
  With these our sacred toils begin:
So flies in tatters from its mast
  The yellow flag of sloth and sin,

And lo! the starry folds reveal
  The blazoned truth we hold so dear:
To guard is better than to heal,—
  The shield is nobler than the spear!

MUSA.

O MY lost Beauty!—hast thou folded quite
  Thy wings of morning light
  Beyond those iron gates
Where Life crowds hurrying to the haggard Fates,
And Age upon his mound of ashes waits
  To chill our fiery dreams,
Hot from the heart of youth plunged in his icy
    streams?

Leave me not fading in these weeds of care,
  Whose flowers are silvered hair!
  Have I not loved thee long,

Though my young lips have often done thee wrong,
And vexed thy heaven-tuned ear with careless song?
    Ah, wilt thou yet return,
Bearing thy rose-hued torch, and bid thine altar burn?

Come to me!—I will flood thy silent shrine
    With my soul's sacred wine,
    And heap thy marble floors
As the wild spice-trees waste their fragrant stores
In leafy islands walled with madrepores
    And lapped in Orient seas,
When all their feathery palms toss, plume-like, in
    the breeze.

Come to me!—thou shalt feed on honeyed words,
    Sweeter than song of birds;—
    No wailing bulbul's throat,
No melting dulcimer's melodious note,
When o'er the midnight wave its murmurs float,
    Thy ravished sense might soothe
With flow so liquid-soft, with strain so velvet-smooth.

Thou shalt be decked with jewels, like a queen,
    Sought in those bowers of green
    Where loop the clustered vines
And the close-clinging dulcamara * twines,—
Pure pearls of Maydew where the moonlight shines,
    And Summer's fruited gems,
And coral pendants shorn from Autumn's berried
    stems.

* The " bitter-sweet " of New England is the *Celastrus scandens*,—" Bourreau des arbres " of the Canadian French.

Sit by me drifting on the sleepy waves, —
    Or stretched by grass-grown graves,
    Whose gray, high-shouldered stones,
Carved with old names Life's time-worn roll disowns,
Lean, lichen-spotted, o'er the crumbled bones
    Still slumbering where they lay
While the sad Pilgrim watched to scare the wolf
    away.

Spread o'er my couch thy visionary wing!
    Still let me dream and sing,—
    Dream of that winding shore
Where scarlet cardinals bloom—for me no more,—
The stream with heaven beneath its liquid floor,
    And clustering nenuphars
Sprinkling its mirrored blue like golden-chaliced
    stars!

Come while their balms the linden-blossoms shed!—
    Come while the rose is red,—
    While blue-eyed Summer smiles
On the green ripples round yon sunken piles
Washed by the moon-wave warm from Indian isles,
    And on the sultry air
The chestnuts spread their palms like holy men in
    prayer!

O for thy burning lips to fire my brain
    With thrills of wild, sweet pain!—
    On life's autumnal blast,
Like shrivelled leaves, youth's passion-flowers are
    cast,—

Once loving thee, we love thee to the last!—
  Behold thy new-decked shrine,
And hear once more the voice that breathed " For-
    ever thine! "

THE VOICELESS.

WE count the broken lyres that rest
  Where the sweet wailing singers slumber,
But o'er their silent sister's breast
  The wild-flowers who will stoop to number?
A few can touch the magic string,
  And noisy Fame is proud to win them:—
Alas for those that never sing,
  But die with all their music in them!

Nay, grieve not for the dead alone
  Whose song has told their hearts' sad story,—
Weep for the voiceless, who have known
  The cross without the crown of glory!
Not where Leucadian breezes sweep
  O'er Sappho's memory-haunted billow,
But where the glistening night-dews weep
  On nameless sorrow's churchyard pillow.

O hearts that break and give no sign
  Save whitening lip and fading tresses,
Till Death pours out his cordial wine
  Slow-dropped from Misery's crushing presses,—

If singing breath or echoing chord
   To every hidden pang were given,
What endless melodies were poured,
   As sad as earth, as sweet as heaven!

THE CROOKED FOOTPATH.

Ah, here it is! the sliding rail
   That marks the old remembered spot,—
The gap that struck our schoolboy trail,—
   The crooked path across the lot.

It left the road by school and church,
   A pencilled shadow, nothing more,
That parted from the silver birch
   And ended at the farm-house door.

No line or compass traced its plan;
   With frequent bends to left or right,
In aimless, wayward curves it ran,
   But always kept the door in sight.

The gabled porch, with woodbine green,—
   The broken millstone at the sill,—
Though many a rood might stretch between,
   The truant child could see them still.

No rocks across the pathway lie,—
   No fallen trunk is o'er it thrown,—
And yet it winds, we know not why,
   And turns as if for tree or stone.

Perhaps some lover trod the way
  With shaking knees and leaping heart,—
And so it often runs astray
  With sinuous sweep or sudden start.

Or one, perchance, with clouded brain
  From some unholy banquet reeled,—
And since, our devious steps maintain
  His track across the trodden field.

Nay, deem not thus,—no earthborn will
  Could ever trace a faultless line;
Our truest steps are human still,—
  To walk unswerving were divine!

Truants from love, we dream of wrath;—
  O, rather let us trust the more!
Through all the wanderings of the path,
  We still can see our Father's door!

THE TWO STREAMS.

BEHOLD the rocky wall
  That down its sloping sides
Pours the swift rain-drops, blending, as they fall,
  In rushing river-tides!

Yon stream, whose sources run
  Turned by a pebble's edge,
Is Athabasca, rolling toward the sun
  Through the cleft mountain-ledge.

The slender rill had strayed,
But for the slanting stone,
To evening's ocean, with the tangled **braid**
Of foam-flecked Oregon.

So from the heights of Will
Life's parting stream descends,
And, as a moment turns its slender rill,
Each widening torrent bends,—

From the same cradle's side,
From the same mother's knee,—
One to long darkness and the frozen tide,
One to the Peaceful Sea!

ROBINSON OF LEYDEN.

HE sleeps not here; in hope and prayer
His wandering flock had gone before,
But he, the shepherd, might not share
Their sorrows on the wintry shore.

Before the Speedwell's anchor swung,
Ere yet the Mayflower's sail was spread,
While round his feet the Pilgrims clung,
The pastor spake, and thus he said:—

" Men, brethren, sisters, children dear!
God calls you hence from over sea;

Ye may not build by Haerlem Meer,
   Nor yet along the Zuyder-Zee.

" Ye go to bear the saving word
   To tribes unnamed and shores untrod:
Heed well the lessons ye have heard
   From those old teachers taught of God.

" Yet think not unto them was lent
   All light for all the coming days,
And Heaven's eternal wisdom spent
   In making straight the ancient ways:

" The living fountain overflows
   For every flock, for every lamb,
Nor heeds, though angry creeds oppose
   With Luther's dike or Calvin's dam."

He spake: with lingering, long embrace,
   With tears of love and partings fond,
They floated down the creeping Haas,
   Along the isle of Ysselmond.

They passed the frowning towers of Briel,
   The " Hook of Holland's " shelf of sand,
And grated soon with lifting keel
   The sullen shores of Fatherland.

No home for these!—too well they knew
   The mitred king behind the throne;—
The sails were set, the pennons flew,
   And westward ho! for worlds unknown.

—And these were they who gave us birth,
　The Pilgrims of the sunset wave,
Who won for us this virgin earth,
　And freedom with the soil they gave.

The pastor slumbers by the Rhine,—
　In alien earth the exiles lie,—
Their nameless graves our holiest shrine,
　His words our noblest battle-cry!

Still cry them, and the world shall hear,
　Ye dwellers by the storm-swept sea!
Ye *have* not built by Haerlem Meer,
　Nor on the land-locked Zuyder-Zee!

SAINT ANTHONY THE REFORMER.

HIS TEMPTATION.

No fear lest praise should make us proud!
　We know how cheaply that is won;
The idle homage of the crowd
　Is proof of tasks as idly done.

A surface-smile may pay the toil
　That follows still the conquering Right,
With soft, white hands to dress the spoil
　That sun-browned valor clutched in fight.

Sing the sweet song of other days,
　Serenely placid, safely true,

And o'er the present's parching ways
   Thy verse distils like evening dew.

But speak in words of living power,—
   They fall like drops of scalding rain
That plashed before the burning shower
   Swept o'er the cities of the plain!

Then scowling Hate turns deadly pale,—
   Then Passion's half-coiled adders spring,
And, smitten through their leprous mail,
   Strike right and left in hope to sting.

If thou, unmoved by poisoning wrath,
   Thy feet on earth, thy heart above,
Canst walk in peace thy kingly path,
   Unchanged in trust, unchilled in love,—

Too kind for bitter words to grieve,
   Too firm for clamor to dismay,
When Faith forbids thee to believe,
   And Meekness calls to disobey,—

Ah, then beware of mortal pride!
   The smiling pride that calmly scorns
Those foolish fingers, crimson dyed
   In laboring on thy crown of thorns!

AVIS.

I MAY not rightly call thy name,—
   Alas! thy forehead never knew
The kiss that happier children claim,
   Nor glistened with baptismal dew.

Daughter of want and wrong and woe,
   I saw thee with thy sister-band,
Snatched from the whirlpool's narrowing flow
   By Mercy's strong yet trembling hand.

—" Avis! "—With Saxon eye and cheek,
   At once a woman and a child,
The saint uncrowned I came to seek
   Drew near to greet us,—spoke, and smiled.

God gave that sweet sad smile she wore
   All wrong to shame, all souls to win,—
A heavenly sunbeam sent before
   Her footsteps through a world of sin.

—" And who is Avis? "—Hear the tale
   The calm-voiced matrons gravely tell,—
The story known through all the vale
   Where Avis and her sisters dwell.

With the lost children running wild,
   Strayed from the hand of human care,
They find one little refuse child
   Left helpless in its poisoned lair.

The primal mark is on her face,—
   The chattel-stamp,—the pariah-stain
That follows still her hunted race,—
   The curse without the crime of Cain.

How shall our smooth-turned phrase relate
   The little suffering outcast's ail?

Not Lazarus at the rich man's gate
   So turned the rose-wreathed revellers pale.

Ah, veil the living death from sight
   That wounds our beauty-loving eye!
The children turn in selfish fright,
   The white-lipped nurses hurry by.

Take her, dread Angel! Break in love
   This bruisèd reed and make it thine!—
No voice descended from above,
   But Avis answered, " She is mine."

The task that dainty menials spurn
   The fair young girl has made her own;
Her heart shall teach, her hand shall learn
   The toils, the duties yet unknown.

So Love and Death in lingering strife
   Stand face to face from day to day,
Still battling for the spoil of Life
   While the slow seasons creep away.

Love conquers Death; the prize is won;
   See to her joyous bosom pressed
The dusky daughter of the sun,—
   The bronze against the marble breast!

Her task is done; no voice divine
   Has crowned her deeds with saintly fame.
No eye can see the aureole shine
   That rings her brow with heavenly flame.

Yet what has holy page more sweet,
　Or what had woman's love more fair,
When Mary clasped her Saviour's feet
　With flowing eyes and streaming hair?

Meek child of sorrow, walk unknown,
　The Angel of that earthly throng,
And let thine image live alone
　To hallow this unstudied song!

IRIS, HER BOOK.

I PRAY thee by the soul of her that bore thee,
By thine own sister's spirit I implore thee,
Deal gently with the leaves that lie before thee!

For Iris had no mother to infold her,
Nor ever leaned upon a sister's shoulder,
Telling the twilight thoughts that Nature told her.

She had not learned the mystery of awaking
Those chorded keys that soothe a sorrow's aching,
Giving the dumb heart voice, that else were breaking.

Yet lived, wrought, suffered. Lo, the pictured token!
Why should her fleeting day-dreams fade unspoken,
Like daffodils that die with sheaths unbroken?

She knew not love, yet lived in maiden fancies,—
Walked simply clad, a queen of high romances,
And talked strange tongues with angels in her trances.

Twin-souled she seemed, a twofold nature wearing,—
Sometimes a flashing falcon in her daring,
Then a poor mateless dove that droops despairing.

Questioning all things: Why her Lord had sent her?
What were these torturing gifts, and wherefore lent
    her?
Scornful as spirit fallen, its own tormentor.

And then all tears and anguish: Queen of Heaven,
Sweet Saints, and Thou by mortal sorrows riven,
Save me! O, save me! Shall I die forgiven?

And then——Ah, God! But nay, it little matters:
Look at the wasted seeds that autumn scatters,
The myriad germs that Nature shapes and shatters!

If she had——Well! She longed, and knew not
    wherefore.
Had the world nothing she might live to care for?
No second self to say her evening prayer for?

She knew the marble shapes that set men dreaming,
Yet with her shoulders bare and tresses streaming
Showed not unlovely to her simple seeming.

Vain? Let it be so! Nature was her teacher.
What if a lonely and unsistered creature
Loved her own harmless gift of pleasing feature,

Saying, unsaddened,—This shall soon be faded,
And double-hued the shining tresses braided,
And all the sunlight of the morning shaded?

——This her poor book is full of saddest follies,
Of tearful smiles and laughing melancholies,
With summer roses twined and wintry hollies.

In the strange crossing of uncertain chances,
Somewhere, beneath some maiden's tear-dimmed
    glances
May fall her little book of dreams and fancies.

Sweet sister! Iris, who shall never name thee,
Trembling for fear her open heart may shame thee,
Speaks from this vision-haunted page to claim thee.

Spare her, I pray thee! If the maid is sleeping,
Peace with her! she has had her hour of weeping.
No more! She leaves her memory in thy keeping

UNDER THE VIOLETS.

HER hands are cold; her face is white;
    No more her pulses come and go;
Her eyes are shut to life and light;—
    Fold the white vesture, snow on snow,
    And lay her where the violets blow.

But not beneath a graven stone,
    To plead for tears with alien eyes;
A slender cross of wood alone
    Shall say, that here a maiden lies
    In peace beneath the peaceful skies.

And gray old trees of hugest limb
  Shall wheel their circling shadows **round**
To make the scorching sunlight dim
  That drinks the greenness from the **ground,**
  And drop their dead leaves on her **mound.**

When o'er their boughs the squirrels run,
  And through their leaves the robins **call,**
And, ripening in the autumn sun,
  The acorns and the chestnuts **fall,**
  Doubt not that she will heed them **all.**

For her the morning choir shall sing
  Its matins from the branches high,
And every minstrel-voice of Spring,
  That trills beneath the April sky,
  Shall greet her with its earliest **cry.**

When, turning round their dial-track,
  Eastward the lengthening shadows **pass,**
Her little mourners, clad in black,
  The crickets, sliding through the **grass,**
  Shall pipe for her an evening mass.

At last the rootlets of the trees
  Shall find the prison where she **lies,**
And bear the buried dust they seize
  In leaves and blossoms to the skies.
  So may the soul that warmed it rise!

If any, born of kindlier blood,
  Should ask, What maiden lies **below?**

Say only this: A tender bud,
  That tried to blossom in the snow,
  Lies withered where the violets blow.

THE PROMISE.

Not charity we ask,
  Nor yet thy gift refuse;
Please thy light fancy with the easy task
  Only to look and choose.

The little-heeded toy
  That wins thy treasured gold
May be the dearest memory, holiest joy,
  Of coming years untold.

Heaven rains on every heart,
  But there its showers divide,
The drops of mercy choosing as they part
  The dark or glowing side.

One kindly deed may turn
  The fountain of thy soul
To love's sweet day-star, that shall o'er thee burn
  Long as its currents roll!

The pleasures thou hast planned,—
  Where shall their memory be
When the white angel with the freezing hand
  Shall sit and watch by thee?

Living, thou dost not live,
If mercy's spring run dry;
What Heaven has lent thee wilt thou freely give,
Dying, thou shalt not die!

HE promised even so!
To thee His lips repeat,—
Behold, the tears that soothed thy sister's woe
Have washed thy Master's feet!

March 20, 1859.

THE LIVING TEMPLE.

NOT in the world of light alone,
Where God has built his blazing throne,
Nor yet alone in earth below,
With belted seas that come and go,
And endless isles of sunlit green,
Is all thy Maker's glory seen:
Look in upon thy wondrous frame,—
Eternal wisdom still the same!

The smooth, soft air with pulse-like waves
Flows murmuring through its hidden caves,
Whose streams of brightening purple rush,
Fire with a new and liverlier blush,
While all their burden of decay
The ebbing current steals away,
And red with Nature's flame they start
From the warm fountains of the heart.

No rest that throbbing slave may ask,
Forever quivering o'er his task,

While far and wide a crimson jet
Leaps forth to fill the woven net
Which in unnumbered crossing tides
The flood of burning life divides,
Then, kindling each decaying part,
Creeps back to find the throbbing heart.

But warmed with that unchanging flame
Behold the outward moving frame,
Its living marbles jointed strong
With glistening band and silvery thong,
And linked to reason's guiding reins
By myriad rings in trembling chains,
Each graven with the threaded zone
Which claims it as the master's own.

See how yon beam of seeming white
Is braided out of seven-hued light,
Yet in those lucid globes no ray
By any chance shall break astray,
Hark how the rolling surge of sound,
Arches and spirals circling round,
Wakes the hushed spirit through thine ear
With music it is heaven to hear.

Then mark the cloven sphere that holds
All thought in its mysterious folds,
That feels sensation's faintest thrill,
And flashes forth the sovereign will;
Think on the stormy world that dwells
Locked in its dim and clustering cells!

The lightning gleams of power it sheds
Along its hollow glassy threads!

O Father! grant thy love divine
To make these mystic temples thine!
When wasting age and wearing strife
Have sapped the leaning walls of life,
When darkness gathers over all,
And the last tottering pillars fall,
Take the poor dust thy mercy warms,
And mould it into heavenly forms!

HYMN OF TRUST.

O Love Divine, that stooped to share
  Our sharpest pang, our bitterest tear,
On Thee we cast each earth-born care,
  We smile at pain while Thou art near!

Though long the weary way we tread,
  And sorrow crown each lingering year,
No path we shun, no darkness dread,
  Our hearts still whispering, Thou art near!

When drooping pleasure turns to grief,
  And trembling faith is changed to fear,
The murmuring wind, the quivering leaf,
  Shall softly tell us, Thou art near!

On Thee we fling our burdening woe,
  O Love Divine, forever dear,
Content to suffer while we know,
  Living and dying, Thou art near!

A SUN-DAY HYMN.

LORD of all being! throned afar,
Thy glory flames from sun and star;
Centre and soul of every sphere,
Yet to each loving heart how near!

Sun of our life, thy quickening ray
Sheds on our path the glow of day;
Star of our hope, thy softened light
Cheers the long watches of the night.

Our midnight is thy smile withdrawn;
Our noontide is thy gracious dawn;
Our rainbow arch thy mercy's sign;
All, save the clouds of sin, are thine!

Lord of all life, below, above,
Whose light is truth, whose warmth is love,
Before thy ever-blazing throne
We ask no lustre of our own.

Grant us thy truth to make us free,
And kindling hearts that burn for thee,
Till all thy living altars claim
One holy light, one heavenly flame!

A VOICE OF THE LOYAL NORTH.

NATIONAL FAST, JANUARY 4, 1861.

We sing " Our Country's " song to-night
  With saddened voice and eye;
Her banner droops in clouded light
  Beneath the wintry sky.
We'll pledge her once in golden wine
  Before her stars have set:
Though dim one reddening orb may shine,
  We have a Country yet.

'Twere vain to sigh o'er errors past,
  The fault of sires or sons;
Our soldier heard the threatening blast,
  And spiked his useless guns;
He saw the star-wreathed ensign fall,
  By mad invaders torn;
But saw it from the bastioned wall
  That laughed their rage to scorn!

What though their angry cry is flung
  Across the howling wave,—
They smite the air with idle tongue
  The gathering storm who brave;
Enough of speech! the trumpet rings;
  Be silent, patient, calm,—
God help them if the tempest swings
  The pine against the palm!

Our toilsome years have made us tame;
    Our strength has slept unfelt;
The furnace-fire is slow to flame
    That bids our ploughshares melt;
'T is hard to lose the bread they win
    In spite of Nature's frowns,—
To drop the iron threads we spin
    That weave our web of towns,

To see the rusting turbines stand
    Before the emptied flumes,
To fold the arms that flood the land
    With rivers from their looms,—
But harder still for those who learn
    The truth forgot so long;
When once their slumbering passions burn,
    The peaceful are the strong!

The Lord have mercy on the weak,
    And calm their frenzied ire,
And save our brothers ere they shriek,
    "We played with Northern fire!"
The eagle hold his mountain height,—
    The tiger pace his den!
Give all their country, each his right!
    God keep us all! Amen!

BROTHER JONATHAN'S LAMENT FOR SISTER CAROLINE.

SHE has gone,—she has left us in passion and
   pride,—
Our stormy-browed sister, so long at our side!
She has torn her own star from our firmament's
   glow,
And turned on her brother the face of a foe!

O Caroline, Caroline, child of the sun,
We can never forget that our hearts have been one,—
Our foreheads both sprinkled in Liberty's name,
From the fountain of blood with the finger of flame!

You were always too ready to fire at a touch;
But we said, " She is hasty,—she does not mean
   much."
We have scowled, when you uttered some turbulent
   threat;
But Friendship still whispered, " Forgive and forget! "

Has our love all died out? Have its altars grown
   cold?
Has the curse come at last which the fathers fore-
   told?
Then Nature must teach us the strength of the chain
That her petulant children would sever in vain.

They may fight till the buzzards are gorged with their
    spoil,
Till the harvest grows black as it rots in the soil,
Till the wolves and the catamounts troop from their
    caves,
And the shark tracks the pirate, the lord of the
    waves:

In vain is the strife! When its fury is past,
Their fortunes must flow in one channel at last,
As the torrents that rush from the mountains of
    snow
Roll mingled in peace through the valleys below.

Our Union is river, lake, ocean, and sky:
Man breaks not the medal, when God cuts the die!
Though darkened with sulphur, though cloven with
    steel,
The blue arch will brighten, the waters will heal!

O Caroline, Caroline, child of the sun,
There are battles with Fate that can never be won!
The star-flowering banner must never be furled,
For its blossoms of light are the hope of the world!

Go, then, our rash sister! afar and aloof,
Run wild in the sunshine away from our roof;
But when your heart aches and your feet have grown
    sore,
Remember the pathway that leads to our door!

    March, 25, 1861.

UNDER THE WASHINGTON ELM, CAMBRIDGE.

APRIL 27, 1861.

EIGHTY years have passed, and more,
    Since under the brave old tree
Our fathers gathered in arms, and swore
They would follow the sign their banners bore,
    And fight till the land was free.

Half of their work was done,
    Half is left to do,—
Cambridge, and Concord, and Lexington!
When the battle is fought and won,
    What shall be told of you?

Hark!—'t is the south-wind moans,—
    Who are the martyrs down?
Ah, the marrow was true in your children's bones
That sprinkled with blood the cursed stones
    Of the murder-haunted town!

What if the storm-clouds blow?
    What if the green leaves fall?
Better the crashing tempest's throe
Than the army of worms that gnawed below;
    Trample them one and all!

Then, when the battle is won,
And the land from traitors free,

Our children shall tell of the strife begun
When Liberty's second April sun
    Was bright on our brave old tree!

INTERNATIONAL ODE.

OUR FATHERS' LAND.*

God bless our Fathers' Land!
Keep her in heart and hand
    One with our own!
From all her foes defend,
Be her brave People's Friend,
On all her realms descend,
    Protect her Throne!

Father, with loving care
Guard Thou her kingdom's Heir,
    Guid all his ways:
Thine arm his shelter be,
From him by land and sea
Bid storm and danger flee,
    Prolong his days!

Lord, let War's tempest cease,
Fold the whole Earth in peace
    Under thy wings!

* Sung in unison by twelve hundred children of the public schools, at the visit of the Prince of Wales to Boston, October 18, 1860. Air, "God save the Queen."

Make all Thy nations one,
All hearts beneath the sun,
Till Thou shalt reign alone,
Great King of kings!

FREEDOM, OUR QUEEN.

LAND where the banners wave last in the sun,
Blazoned with star-clusters, many in one,
Floating o'er prairie and mountain and sea;
Hark! 't is the voice of thy children to thee!

Here at thine altar our vows we renew
Still in thy cause to be loyal and true,—
True to thy flag on the field and the wave,
Living to honor it, dying to save!

Mother of heroes! if perfidy's blight
Fall on a star in thy garland of light,
Sound but one bugle-blast! Lo! at the sign
Armies all panoplied wheel into line!

Hope of the world! thou hast broken its chains,—
Wear thy bright arms while a tyrant remains,
Stand for the right till the nations shall own
Freedom their sovereign, with Law for her throne!

Freedom! sweet Freedom! our voices resound,
Queen by God's blessing, unsceptred, uncrowned!

Freedom, sweet Freedom, our pulses repeat,
Warm with her life-blood, as long as they beat!

Fold the broad banners-stripes over her breast,—
Crown her with star-jewels Queen of the West!
Earth for her heritage, God for her friend,
She shall reign over us, world without end!

ARMY HYMN.

" Old Hundred."

O LORD of Hosts! Almighty King!
Behold the sacrifice we bring!
To every arm Thy strength impart,
Thy spirit shed through every heart!

Wake in our breasts the living fires,
The holy faith that warmed our sires;
Thy hand hath made our Nation free;
To die for her is serving Thee.

Be Thou a pillared flame to show
The midnight snare, the silent foe;
And when the battle thunders loud,
Still guide us in its moving cloud.

God of all Nations! Sovereign Lord!
In Thy dread name we draw the sword,
We lift the starry flag on high
That fills with light our stormy sky.

From treason's rent, from murder's stain,
Guard Thou its folds till Peace shall reign,—
Till fort and field, till shore and sea,
Join our loud anthem, PRAISE TO THEE!

PARTING HYMN.

" Dundee."

FATHER of Mercies, Heavenly Friend,
   We seek Thy gracious throne;
To Thee our faltering prayers ascend,
   Our fainting hearts are known!

From blasts that chill, from suns that smite,
   From every plague that harms;
In camp and march, in siege and fight,
   Protect our men-at-arms!

Though from our darkened lives they take
   What makes our life most dear,
We yield them for their country's sake
   With no relenting tear.

Our blood their flowing veins will shed,
   Their wounds our breasts will share;
O, save us from the woes we dread,
   Or grant us strength to bear!

Let each unhallowed cause that brings
   The stern destroyer cease,

Thy flaming angel fold his wings,
And seraphs whisper Peace!

Thine are the sceptre and the sword,
Stretch forth Thy mighty hand,—
Reign Thou our kingless nation's Lord,
Rule Thou our throneless land!

THE FLOWER OF LIBERTY.

WHAT flower is this that greets the morn,
Its hues from Heaven so freshly born?
With burning star and flaming band
It kindles all the sunset land:
O tell us what its name may be,—
Is this the Flower of Liberty?
    It is the banner of the free,
    The starry Flower of Liberty.

In savage Nature's far abode
Its tender seed our fathers sowed;
The storm-winds rocked its swelling bud,
Its opening leaves were streaked with blood,
Till lo! earth's tyrants shook to see
The full-blown Flower of Liberty!
    Then hail the banner of the free,
    The starry Flower of Liberty.

Behold its streaming rays unite,
One mingling flood of braided light,—
30

The red that fires the Southern rose,
With spotless white from Northern snows,
And, spangled o'er its azure, see
The sister Stars of Liberty!
    Then hail the banner of the free,
    The starry Flower of Liberty!

The blades of heroes fence it round,
Where'er it springs is holy ground;
From tower and dome its glories spread;
It waves where lonely sentries tread;
It makes the land as ocean free,
And plants an empire on the sea!
    Then hail the banner of the free,
    The starry Flower of Liberty.

Thy sacred leaves, fair Freedom's flower,
Shall ever float on dome and tower,
To all their heavenly colors true,
In blackening frost or crimson dew,—
And God love us as we love thee,
Thrice holy Flower of Liberty!
    Then hail the banner of the free,
    The starry FLOWER OF LIBERTY.

THE SWEET LITTLE MAN.

DEDICATED TO THE STAY-AT-HOME RANGERS.

Now, while our soldiers are fighting our battles,
    Each at his post to do all that he can,
Down among rebels and contraband chattels,
    What are you doing, my sweet little man?

All the brave boys under canvas are sleeping,
 All of them pressing to march with the van,
Far from the home where their sweethearts are
  weeping;
 What are you waiting for, sweet little man?

You with the terrible warlike moustaches,
 Fit for a colonel or chief of a clan,
You with the waist made for sword-belts and sashes,
 Where are your shoulder-straps, sweet little man?

Bring him the buttonless garment of woman!
 Cover his face lest it freckle and tan;
Muster the Apron-string Guards on the Common,
 That is the corps for the sweet little man!

Give him for escort a file of young misses,
 Each of them armed with a deadly rattan;
They shall defend him from laughter and hisses,
 Aimed by low boys at the sweet little man.

All the fair maidens about him shall cluster,
 Pluck the white feathers from bonnet and fan,
Make him a plume like a turkey-wing duster,—
 That is the crest for the sweet little man!

O, but the Apron-string Guards are the fellows!
 Drilling each day since our troubles began,—
"Handle your Walking-sticks!" "Shoulder um-
  brellas!"
 That is the style for the sweet little man.

Have we a nation to save? In the first place
  Saving ourselves is the sensible plan,—
Surely the spot where there's shooting's the worst
    place
  Where I can stand, says the sweet little man.

Catch me confiding my person with strangers!
  Think how the cowardly Bull-Runners ran!
In the brigade of the Stay-at-home Rangers
  Marches my corps, says the sweet little man.

Such was the stuff of the Malakoff-takers,
  Such were the soldiers that scaled the Redan;
Truculent housemaids and bloodthirsty Quakers,
  Brave not the wrath of the sweet little man!

Yield him the sidewalk, ye nursery maidens!
  Sauve qui peut! Bridget, and right about!
    Ann;—
Fierce as a shark in a school of menhadens,
  See him advancing, the sweet little man!

When the red flails of the battle-field's threshers
  Beat out the continent's wheat from its bran,
While the wind scatters the chaffy seceshers,
  What will become of our sweet little man?

When the brown soldiers come back from the borders,
  How will he look while his features they scan?
How will he feel when he gets marching orders,
  Signed by his lady love? sweet little man!

Fear not for him, though the rebels expect him,—
    Life is too precious to shorten its span;
Woman her broomstick shall raise to protect him,
    Will she not fight for the sweet little man!

Now then, nine cheers for the Stay-at-home Ranger!
    Blow the great fish-horn and beat the big pan!
First in the field that is farthest from danger,
    Take your white-feather plume, sweet little man!

VIVE LA FRANCE!

A SENTIMENT OFFERED AT THE DINNER TO H. I. H.
THE PRINCE NAPOLEON, AT THE REVERE HOUSE,
SEPT. 25, 1861.

THE land of sunshine and of song!
    Her name your hearts divine;
To her the banquet's vows belong
    Whose breasts have poured its wine;
Our trusty friend, our true ally
    Through varied change and chance:
So, fill your flashing goblets high,—
    I give you, VIVE LA FRANCE!

Above our hosts in triple folds
    The self-same colors spread,
Where Valor's faithful arm upholds
    The blue, the white, the red;

Alike each nation's glittering crest
    Reflects the morning's glance,—
Twin eagles, soaring east and west:
    Once more, then, VIVE LA FRANCE!

Sister in trial! who shall count
    Thy generous friendship's claim,
Whose blood ran mingling in the fount
    That gave our land its name,
Till Yorktown saw in blended line
    Our conquering arms advance,
And victory's double garlands twine
    Our banners? VIVE LA FRANCE!

O land of heroes! in our need
    One gift from Heaven we crave
To stanch these wounds that vainly bleed,—
    The wise to lead the brave!
Call back one Captain of thy past
    From glory's marble trance,
Whose name shall be a bugle-blast
    To rouse us! VIVE LA FRANCE!

Pluck Condé's baton from the trench,
    Wake up stout Charles Martel,
Or find some woman's hand to clench
    The sword of La Pucelle!
Give us one hour of old Turenne,—
    One lift of Bayard's lance,—
Nay, call Marengo's Chief again
    To lead us! VIVE LA FRANCE!

Ah, hush! our welcome Guest shall **hear**
    But sounds of peace and joy;
No angry echo vex thine ear,
    Fair Daughter of Savoy!
Once more! the land of arms and **arts,**
    Of glory, grace, romance;
Her love lies warm in all our **hearts:**
    God bless her! VIVE LA FRANCE!

UNION AND LIBERTY.

FLAG of the heroes who left us their glory,
    Borne through their battle-fields' thunder **and**
    flame,
Blazoned in song and illumined in story,
    Wave o'er us all who inherit their fame!
        Up with our banner bright,
        Sprinkled with starry light,
Spread its fair emblems from mountain **to shore,**
        While through the sounding sky
        Loud rings the Nation's cry,—
UNION AND LIBERTY! ONE EVERMORE!

Light of our firmament, guide of our Nation,
    Pride of her children, and honored **afar,**
Let the wide beams of thy full constellation
    Scatter each cloud that would darken **a star!**
        Up with our banner bright, etc.

Empire unsceptred! what foe shall assail **thee,**
    Bearing the standard of Liberty's van?

Think not the God of thy fathers shall fail thee,
　　Striving with men for the birthright of man!
　　　　Up with our banner bright, etc.

Yet if, by madness and treachery blighted,
　　Dawns the dark hour when the sword thou must
　　　draw,
Then with the arms of thy millions united,
　　Smite the bold traitors to Freedom and Law!
　　　　Up with our banner bright, etc.

Lord of the Universe! shield us and guide us,
　　Trusting thee always, though shadow and sun!
Thou hast united us, who shall divide us?
　　Keep us, O keep us the MANY IN ONE!
　　　　Up with our banner bright,
　　　　Sprinkled with starry light,
　　Spread its fair emblems from mountain to shore,
　　　　While through the sounding sky
　　　　Loud rings the Nation's cry,—
UNION AND LIBERTY! ONE EVERMORE!

THE END.